JOHN PA

FROM CHOLERA
TO EBOLA

CONFESSIONS OF A HUMANITARIAN
DOCTOR

To Rel & Sue

Many thanks for a wonderful
dinner.

Best Wishes

John.

AUSTIN MACAULEY PUBLISHERS™
LONDON • CAMBRIDGE • NEW YORK • SHARJAH

A CIP catalogue record for this title is available from the British Library.

ISBN 9781528912488 (Paperback)
ISBN 9781528912495 (Hardback)
ISBN 9781528960144 (ePub e-book)

www.austinmacauley.com

First Published (2020)
Austin Macauley Publishers Ltd
25 Canada Square
Canary Wharf
London
E14 5LQ

Dedicated to

Ben, Lara and Jake,

my anchors in stormy seas

FOREWORD

There are a few books that take me right back to some raw experiences I have shelved away. In *From Cholera to Ebola, confessions of a humanitarian doctor*, I was reading about an adventurer, a committed professional, a man living with passion 'off the edge of his comfort zone' and inevitably also about a 'burnt out activist'. It was all very familiar territory. I read John Parker's book, knowing it could trigger some memories of my own travels with World Vision between 2004-16. And it did.

This is not a book for the faint-hearted. It tells of the medical missions John took as a humanitarian doctor – firstly with Red Cross and then with Médecins Sans Frontières between 1994 and 2014 – in places as distant as Zaire, Afghanistan, Nigeria, Uganda, Iraq and Sudan. He talks about these places as 'going beyond-the-lonely-planet' sort of travel. All of them facing their own brand of humanitarian crises. So, there are some common threads but the conditions, the threats, the staff challenges, the health crises, the tragic deaths, and the communities all differ in their own unique ways. John chronicles each trip – and cleverly weaves his reflections on the amalgam of trips he undertook by using the ongoing conversation he had with his psychologist – with whom he finally unpacked his story well after the PTSD his work caused him had become manifest. So, there is psychological honesty in this book.

My own experiences pale beside John's as I, for the most part, flew in to disasters and was able to leave once the work of encouraging local staff and telling the story through the media had been done. It would often leave me riddled with guilt that I could walk away and jump on a plane so easily. When I returned from my first harrowing trip in 2004 to Darfur, Sudan I found myself in tears as I spoke to the media back here in the safety of Australia. I couldn't forget the images of raped women and destitute children. Even now, sometimes images pop up when I least expect it. I can be giving a speech about all manner of subjects and I will suddenly feel my emotions are close to the surface. Something I have said has triggered a memory or the feeling of being overwhelmed that accompanied me on some of those trips. So, for my own reasons, I found John's conversations with his psychologist insightful and helpful. It's the sort of conversations I have had myself with a professional – and have been so glad I did.

Some of John's reflections on poverty also resonated so much with what I have seen and felt. He wrote of poverty as being the 'edge of survival' and how he saw resilience and faith as the only buffers, which even provided contentment and happiness in the direst of circumstances. But like me he sees poverty as a 'malignant misalignment of existence and opportunity'. And like me he felt the anger on returning to our Western consumerism at the waste and opulence – the injustice of the superficial way. We fail to see the inequity in the global share of wealth and resources.

This is a story of personal realisation. It also powerfully explains the compulsion that some feel to undertake such demanding and yet life-changing work. It is a testimony to the brave work of organisations out there in godforsaken places, working tirelessly with the extremes of human suffering. So, I think this is a book that needs to be read by everyone looking at impacting the world through humanitarian enterprise and service. PTSD for humanitarians is a very real experience and needs to be taken seriously. There is truth and insight to be found here that is invaluable.

Rev Tim Costello AO

CEO of World Vision Australia (2004-2016)

Has working as a doctor on humanitarian missions changed you, John?
Of course. I am a totally different person because of them. No one who repeatedly sees the best and the worst of humanity can stay the same.

I've worked amid war zones, refugee camps and epidemics, in remote places well beyond the *Lonely Planet*. I've suffered extreme hardship, challenge and danger and witnessed death and dying, disease and dispossession en masse. I've grappled with despair, depression and grief.

But amid all this chaos and confusion, far away from the tinsel and trappings of First World self-indulgence, I've been blessed with the opportunity to learn many vital lessons of what's really important in life and living.

I've experienced the joys and ecstasies of survival, resilience and recovery. I've learned to appreciate the essentials of what I truly need and to be grateful for anything extra. I've come to realise how those living in poverty and dispossession have few choices and we with First World privilege should not judge. I've been inspired to live my life with purpose, passion and presence. It has been an emotional roller coaster experience. My heart has constantly switched between sadness and ecstasy.

Has it taken its toll?
Very much so. The road has been rocky. It has cost me a couple of marriages, a fragmented medical career and at times has threatened my sanity. But it was not the missions that undermined me. They were uplifting, fulfilling and even fun. It was my homecomings that rocked and wrecked me. My ignorance, denial and ineptitude all contributed to years of conflict and confusion, anger and angst. They now call it post-traumatic stress disorder or PTSD.

Is that why you're here?
Yes. For years I have resisted seeing a psychologist. First it was my early bias that you had to be mad to see one. Later it was the fear that I was mad and didn't want to be found out. I've been self-treating for over twenty years, at times self-medicating with alcohol and denying anything was really wrong. Over twenty years and seven missions my symptoms have waxed and waned, from deep despair and drunkenness to irritability, isolation and guilt. I feel pretty good now but I am fed up of dancing with my demons. Are they still lurking deep in my psyche? I was hoping if I confessed all my experiences and emotions to a professional, I might cleanse my soul, so to speak; release the demons and be exorcised. Do you think it can work?

It's impossible to say. We can only try. Let us start at the beginning? Tell me of your missions.

ZAIRE
NOW THE DEMOCRATIC REPUBLIC OF CONGO
FEDERATION OF RED CROSS AND RED CRESCENT
1994–1995

KIBUMBA REFUGEE CAMP, near GOMA, ZAIRE
(now the DEMOCRATIC REPUBLIC OF CONGO), July 1994
Doctor, Federation of Red Cross and Red Crescent

The line of bedraggled refugees stretched like a snake far into the distance. Our white Toyota four-wheel drive utility, a red cross emblazoned on its bonnet, edged its way through their mass as they struggled and limped along the tortuous potholed bitumen road. Swags of possessions hung on their backs or balanced on their heads; they pushed or pulled barrows laden with pots and pans, water containers, bundles of clothes and boxes of food. One man even balanced a mattress on his head. Standing in the tray behind the car's cab I surveyed the swarming scene with dismay and disbelief.

'We don't know exactly how many refugees have crossed the border from Rwanda into Goma in the past three weeks but estimates exceed a million,' Henry, the head national nurse, confided in my ear. 'The town became a gridlock of humanity, its infrastructure overwhelmed. People were dying everywhere. Bodies littered the streets, flowed in the river and floated on the lake where water was collected for drinking. It was the perfect recipe for cholera.

'The Zairian military forced people out of town at gunpoint. Many headed north along this road and stopped just over the ridge ahead of us. A huge makeshift refugee camp has now grown. That's where we have our medical clinic.'

An eerie silence hung in the air amid a palpable cloud of despair from a people too exhausted, too scared, too debilitated to waste energy on needless talk. Many had succumbed to the rising sun's heat and lay on the grassy roadside, head resting on bony arms, eyes sunken and lips crusted with dehydration.

I was a rookie. This was my first humanitarian mission. I had never seen or even imagined such human misery. I had never smelled the pungent, clinging odour of unkempt, unwashed humanity. I began to notice that the bodies on the left of the roadside were all immobile. Some stared at me with a grotesque grin gnarled into their face. It became obvious they were all dead. Some were rolled up in bamboo mats and laid out in lines but most lay like road kill, limbs askew, staring unblinkingly into the sky.

'Anyone dead is deposited on one side of the road. The nearer to the camp, the more bodies will be roadside. "Body trucks" patrol the road between sunrise and sunset to collect and transport them to mass graves,' Henry explained. 'Anyone resting will stay on the opposite side. If they die, they will be carried across the road.'

I shook my head to wipe away these upsetting images but they remained ingrained on my retinas. The growing stench of death and decomposition floated on the still air and became overwhelming. I gagged to stop the upwelling of vomit.

'Take deep breaths and loosen your shoulders,' Henry sympathetically advised. 'You'll get used to it.' He patted me on the shoulder. I was surprised by his sensitivity and kindness. His burly shoulders, wide neck, broad nose and deep-set eyes seemed intimidating, but now his sharp jaw line was softened by a wry grin. I grinned back with a nod of my head to say *Thanks*.

The car crested the rise and a huge mosaic arena of green, blue and white tarpaulin-walled shacks extending to the hazy horizon 'It's not organised; it's not orderly. We didn't choose this site for a refugee camp,' Henry explained. 'People were forced out of Goma, and this is where they stopped from sheer exhaustion. Once a few stopped, others stayed. They just had no more energy to move on.'

To give me some idea of the enormity of the crisis, he told me the camp now covered an area of six square kilometres and housed an estimated three hundred thousand people. As I stared, my eyes watered and stung.

'Is the smog in the air from all the wood fires?' I asked.

'Partly it's the acrid smoke of the fires but that,' he pointed to the mountain by the camp, 'is an active volcano. It spews out sulphurous ash and it mixes with the smoke. The molten lava in its crater glows at night.'

I stared to the west and easily identified the volcano's smouldering peak. I could believe anything by now. My norms of reality had been shattered.

We rounded a bend and the white tents of the medical clinic jumped into view. A Red Cross and Crescent flag fluttered from a makeshift flagpole alongside. The car pulled up beside the nearest tent. As I jumped down, I wondered how I was going to work in such a remote and harsh environment. It seemed a hell on earth. My impression was fortified when I turned back towards the road. A neat row of dead bodies, forty on a quick count, lay on the roadside.

'It will get bigger as the day goes on,' Henry leaned over my shoulder and commented in a low voice, 'Many will have died in our ward overnight. Come with me and I'll show you.'

I followed him, accompanied by Mary, an expatriate nurse from the Netherlands, who had just arrived with me from Nairobi. Her eyes were opened as wide as mine.

The national nurses spread out amongst the tents, opening up flaps, unlocking boxes, arranging chairs and tables.

'Two of the small tents are used for triage and consultations. Another is for dressings and the fourth is a store tent.' Henry stood beside me pointing to the facilities. 'The large lean-to shack, made from poles and tarpaulins, is our medical "ward". We have no beds or furniture. The patients lie on a blanket over a tarpaulin on the ground. The shaded area beside the ward is for patients to stay during the day and drink rehydration fluid. Nearly all our patients are dehydrated from diarrhoea caused by either cholera or dysentery. We just do not have the facilities to isolate anyone.'

He pointed to a large yellow rubber bladder beside the tents. 'That is our only source of water. It holds ten thousand litres but we have no regular supply. The water trucks come from Goma. There are so many bladders around the camp and so few delivery trucks. They try to give us priority but be aware of saving water.'

I hated to think what would happen if the clinic ran out.

I had heard most of this in my briefings but seeing it in its harsh, raw reality was numbing.

'We'll clear out all the dead bodies and get started,' Henry kindly suggested to kick-start me into action. Assisted by two clinic guards, who also acted as porters, the four of us methodically lifted six dead bodies onto stretchers and carried them from the ward to the roadside, adding to the existing pile. My heart began hammering, I felt nauseated and confused. I'd come here to be a doctor not a mortician. The acts of lifting the bodies on to the stretchers by their arms and legs were not very dignified yet necessary to minimise contact and contamination. At the roadside we rolled the bodies off the stretchers on to the body pile for the same reason. Refugees walking on the road paused and silently watched, curious but not critical. This was their harsh reality. Ironically, although revolted by the

11

experience, I was grateful to be involved. It allowed me to show that I was willing to join in this unsavoury work and not expect to be exempt. Luckily the body pile was downwind of the clinic and the gentle morning breeze blew the stench of death away to the adjoining forest.

A cleaner came with a bucket and mop to clean the tarpaulin on the ground as best she could but the creases in the tarpaulin held dirt and god knows what else. I did not want to know. The strong smell of bleach assaulted my nose but was a welcome change.

I could see long queues of patients waiting beyond the consultation tents, extending a hundred metres or more.

'Anyone who is very sick will be brought forward to wait beside the ward. Doctor John, can you treat them? Mary, can you supervise the nurses in the ward? They are connecting and adjusting the intravenous infusions and helping the families to keep the patients clean. We have no infusion pumps and it's important to watch the flow rates, especially with the children.'

Before he had finished, a distraught mother was led to a trestle table in front of the ward, my emergency area, carrying a small child whom she laid down. The child was unconscious, her eyes rolling upwards, chest gasping, arms and legs limp like a rag doll. As I approached, she began to convulse, her small wasted body shuddering and twitching. Before I had any chance to insert an intravenous line or draw up medication she died.

I felt for a pulse and shook my head. Her mother wailed and collapsed to the ground. The nurses came and supported her to walk back to her family. The guards picked up the little body and carried it to the roadside. My first patient had died. I had not yet been working ten minutes.

And that was how it started... and continued... day after day...

You obviously found it very confronting.
I was way out of my comfort zone, medically and emotionally. The problem was so immense and overwhelming, the patients so many and so sick, the facilities so basic and primitive I wondered how useful I could be.

So, what did you do?
Luckily there was no time to think. I just did what I was told and started treating patients as well as I could.

I remembered being told by a veteran aid worker in an earlier briefing to expect to be overwhelmed and all we could do was our best. From this snippet of wisdom, I created a mantra that I kept repeating to myself, *Do what you can, ignore the rest. Do what you can, ignore the rest. Do what you can, ignore the rest.*

Repeating this mantra channelled my focus into the moment and calmed my fears and uncertainties. It was a technique that I adopted many times in this and future missions. The mantra evolved over time but it still worked.

Kɪʙᴜᴍʙᴀ Rᴇғᴜɢᴇᴇ Cᴀᴍᴘ, near Gᴏᴍᴀ, Zᴀɪʀᴇ
(now the Dᴇᴍᴏᴄʀᴀᴛɪᴄ Rᴇᴘᴜʙʟɪᴄ ᴏғ Cᴏɴɢᴏ), July 1994
Doctor, Federation of Red Cross and Red Crescent

The sun was rising over the mountain backdrop. Rhonda, tall, slim, hair braided to her shoulders and smooth jet-black skin highlighted by her ironed white nurse's dress, carried the little girl across her arms from the white-peaked triage tent. The girl's mother, wrapped in a blanket against the morning chill, followed.

'Quickly, Doctor John; she is very sick. Her name is Betsy. They have been waiting all night. She started with diarrhoea early yesterday.'

She placed the limp body on the 'emergency table' in front of me. Betsy was unconscious and I immediately recognised the signs of severe dehydration: the sunken eyes, the dry mouth, and the flaccid skin. I checked for fever and neck stiffness and listened to her lungs. We had no pathology facilities, no access to blood tests. All decisions were clinical and had to be instant.

The equipment for inserting intravenous cannulas, neatly laid out in a cardboard box, was at hand and Rhonda set up for an infusion. Enclosed in a sling I weighed her on a scale suspended from a beam and calculated the amount of fluid to be infused. Despite a tourniquet around her upper arm, there was no sign of a distended vein for her dehydration was so severe. I stabbed a cannula into her skinny arm at a common site and hit lucky. A return of blood up the needle allowed me to slide the cannula forwards into the vein. Opening the infusion, I was relieved to see the drops flowing easily. At least she now had a chance. I double-checked my calculations for her fluid load before Rhonda lifted her off the table to find an open space on the floor of the ward. The bottle of intravenous fluid would hang from the crudely fashioned beams that held the roof.

Even before she was out of sight a man, raggedly dressed in a torn and dirty blue shirt and frayed shorts, thongs on his feet, emerged from between the tents, pushing an ancient wheelbarrow, its tyre-less iron wheel wobbling unsteadily. A wizened woman, her face wrinkled and mouth toothless, a frilly blouse tucked into striped wrap-around skirt, lay curled within the barrow.

'She's my mother, Doctor. Her breathing bad.' His English was stilted but understandable. 'She got sick two days ago, her cough bad, bad, all day, all night. This morning, it real bad.'

I felt her brow. She was burning hot. Her bony chest was gasping and gurgling. Her skin was tinged blue around her lips. I listened to her lungs and heard the pneumonia. We had no X-rays to confirm the diagnosis. Giselle, slim, shorthaired and a little surly, had replaced Rhonda to help me. Although she continually wore an expression of disdain and detachment, she was super-efficient and competent. She had already set up an intravenous infusion and I easily cannulated the woman's arm for her veins were dilated and engorged by her fever.

'We'll start intravenous antibiotics,' I told the son. I did not tell him we had no oxygen to help relieve her breathlessness. I wrote the drug order in her notes and handed it to Giselle to dispense.

'Thanks, Giselle. Good work.' Did I see a slight smile pass her lips? The son and guard carried the woman on the blanket into the ward.

Patrick, another male national nurse, hurriedly carried a child out of the consultation tent to my side. He was tall and portly, his face pockmarked from acne. Stylish black jeans highlighted his white shirt. I had been told he was very experienced in bush medicine.

'Doc John, good morning. I think this boy has meningitis. He is very drowsy, has a headache and has been vomiting overnight. His neck is very stiff. He has a high fever but no diarrhoea. He's not dehydrated.'

I quickly examined the boy and confirmed Patrick's findings.

13

'Thanks, Patrick. I agree. What do you suggest?' I was learning to appreciate the competence and experience of the local staff.

'We have chloramphenicol to give as an antibiotic.'

'Good idea. You start an intravenous infusion and I'll prepare the antibiotic. I'll give the first dose straight away.'

It was a satisfying start to the day. Three serious cases all getting effective treatment. I looked out past the triage tents at the long queues of patients waiting for our treatment and then turned around to scan the line of dead bodies at the roadside. The clinic was the circuit breaker. Maybe we were having a beneficial effect?

Did you have many good days?

Looking back over that first month... no. Nearly every day was devastating: so many patients to see, so many patients dying, such primitive conditions and minimal equipment limiting our capabilities. It was these fleeting positive moments, when our treatments were slick and efficient, that helped keep a flicker of hope and optimism alive. All three patients from that day lived despite our primitive medical clinic. The joy of watching the mothers carrying their now-well children out of the clinic, the son helping his elderly mother walk home was uplifting, not only for me but for all the medical staff who were working tirelessly every day.

But it was an ongoing and draining emotional roller coaster, one moment lifted to euphoric heights with the delight of a life saved then plummeting into the depths of despair as a patient needlessly died. These swings of emotions were interspersed with unexpected sparks of joy and despair. A small girl responded to rehydration fluid being trickled into her mouth, opened her eyes and stared thankfully into mine, only for her eyes to then roll upwards as her tiny body is racked with an epileptic convulsion and she died. Then I watched an unconscious boy who I was convinced would die, but whose mother continued to syringe rehydration fluid into his mouth, drop by drop, make a miraculous recovery. It was exhausting yet invigorating, depressing yet uplifting. I was living on adrenaline.

It must have been difficult. How did you cope?

I buried my feelings and focused on the moment, repeating my mantra, *Do what you can, ignore the rest.*

What do you think happened to all those buried feelings?

I never had time to process them. It was like jumping on a pogo stick, each time struggling to regain my balance and avoiding falling off, fearful of completely collapsing in a heap. I just kept on burying them. They sank deeper and deeper into my psyche becoming more and more entangled.

It was not until after I had finished the mission that they began to surface and unravel me.

Let's go back to the mission; take me through what happened.

KIBUMBA REFUGEE CAMP, near GOMA, ZAIRE
(now the DEMOCRATIC REPUBLIC OF CONGO), August 1994
Doctor, Federation of Red Cross and Red Crescent

The cramps in my abdomen were getting worse, I felt nauseated, my belly was bloated and I had the dreadful realisation that *I HAD TO EMPTY MY BOWEL... NOW!*

Oh shit, summed up my mental and physical condition.

I was busy working in the medical clinic examining and treating the never-ending line of severely dehydrated patients. I knew that I had to relieve myself but the clinic only had one latrine. The whole refugee camp, including the medical clinic, was sited on a bed of hard, jagged volcanic rock, the old lava flows from the adjacent volcano. It was impossible to dig with a spade and difficult to crack even with a crowbar. Unable to construct normal pit latrines, a simple cubicle with tarpaulin walls had been built around a natural crack in the ground to act as a makeshift toilet but I could see a long queue already waiting beside... and my bowels were not going to wait.

Pushing aside the fears that I had contracted cholera, my mind was focused on but one thing... *I'll have to do what all the locals do... go into the forest.*

With a growing sense of urgency, I dashed out of the clinic, weaved my way through the river of refugees streaming along the road and into the adjoining forest. Ironically the refugees were banned from living on this side of the road for it was a national park. Although no shelters had been erected, two hundred metres of the roadside forest had been cleared of vegetation to build shelters and fuel fires.

My bowels were not going to wait two hundred metres. I spied a slight depression in the ground a hundred metres from the road. Practically running to the spot, I pulled my pants down, squatted and relieved myself in one fluid movement.

As my bowels were exploding, I realised that my head was visible to the crowds walking on the road but my lower extremities were shielded by the depression. Not that the sight of anyone shitting in the open would be in any way interesting. Everyone did it.

But I miscalculated.

'Muzungo! Muzungo!' Three small boys stood behind me on the edge of the depression pointing down and screaming out. Translated this means 'White man! White man!' Within seconds the whole rim was thronged with curious bystanders. It was a mass of black faces slashed with white smiling teeth. They had probably never ever seen such white buttocks before.

Caught in the limelight, I desperately tried to clench my anal sphincter muscles but they had not yet fully relieved themselves. The three boys, oblivious to my discomfort or embarrassment, approached, hands outreached, inviting a handshake.

I am proud to say that I rose to the occasion, gaining control once more of my anal sphincter, I was able to stand up, pull up my trousers, shake three grimy hands and start slowly walking back to the clinic waving my free hand to the audience whilst holding up my pants with the other.

Word travels faster than sound in a refugee camp. I had only just returned to the clinic when Daniel, one of the national nursing staff smirked: 'Hey Doctor John, I hear you gave a moving performance.'

That's pretty funny. Apart from the humorous aspect, was this a significant event for you John?
Funnily enough yes. It was as if I had revealed my vulnerability and my humanity as well as my backside. I've been told that if ever any person or group of people are felt to be intimidating, imagining them naked will counter the effect. Well, this incident worked for me... in reverse. The national staff became more friendly and approachable.

KIBUMBA REFUGEE CAMP, near GOMA, ZAIRE
(now the DEMOCRATIC REPUBLIC OF CONGO), August 1994
Doctor, Federation of Red Cross and Red Crescent

'This is the most terrible experience I have ever seen. It's unbelievable. How many people are dying? How are you coping?' Andre, with shaggy red hair and unkempt beard dangling on a gaunt face, was a young Canadian reporter visiting our Red Cross clinic. He had arrived unannounced and with our lax security had been able to wander in and around the clinic and start asking questions. He had found me beside the ward where we squatted and silently scanned the scene:

Fifty patients classified as 'very-sick' lay on the ward's tarpaulined floor with a plethora of plastic tubes dangling from suspended bottles of intravenous fluid, like the tentacles of a giant jellyfish.

Beside the ward, in an open shaded area, the 'sick-but-not-too-sick' patients sipped or were slowly spoon-fed oral rehydration fluid.

Beyond and outside the clinic a pile of the 'too-sick-too-late-now-dead' were neatly laid by the roadside, waiting for the body truck to pick them up and transport them to the mass grave.

I shrugged at Andre. 'We are doing everything we can to help but people are dying by the hundreds every day. Until there is clean water, adequate food and safe sanitation the diarrhoea and dehydration will continue to kill. We are but a band-aid on an oozing abscess.'

I thought my analogy would make a good quote. He did not seem to hear.

'What can I do to help?'

'There's nothing you can do except accurately report what's happening and let the world know.' I shrugged again.

He reached into his shirt pocket and pulled out a packet of pills. 'Will these help you?' He was holding a packet of ciprofloxacin antibiotic pills.

I nearly laughed but bit it back. He meant well but what difference would one packet of pills make in a humanitarian crisis of this magnitude. But ciprofloxacin was not in our regular drug list.

'Thanks very much. I'll keep them for a special case.' I put them in my pocket. Little did I know that, indirectly, they would later save my life.

After roaming around the clinic for a few more minutes, taking photographs and talking with the nursing staff he jumped into the back of a rusting, battered blue hire car that his driver had been guarding and headed back to Goma to write his story.

I thought no more about his visit until that afternoon as I walked through the ward. A young man, tall and skinny as a snake, lay on the floor amid a pool of bloody diarrhoea that soaked his shirt and pants. His sunken eyes, parched mouth and shrivelled skin reflected his severe condition. He rolled on the floor, clutching his abdomen, groaning with severe abdominal pain. I looked at his medical notes. The triage nurse had admitted him earlier that morning. Intravenous fluid rapidly dripped into his arm from a bag hanging above his head. I felt and stroked his burning brow, smiled reassuringly, increased the flow rate of his drip and told him he would be fine. He smiled then gasped again in pain. For no conscious reason I decided to give him the antibiotics in my pocket. His fever and bloody stool were reason enough but several patients had similar symptoms. I had him swallow a tablet supplemented with painkillers. I put the rest of the course of antibiotics in his shirt pocket. I called a national nurse over to my side to translate. 'Tell him to take one tablet twice a day until they are all finished.' He listened to the instruction, his eyes fixing my gaze, nodded, smiled then, grimacing in pain as another spasm gripped his bowel, he rolled on to his side.

The rest of the day became another frenetic blur whilst I treated patient after patient.

Later that evening, back in Goma, I was lying on my camp bed in my tent that I shared with three other expatriates. The others were still in the dining room in the compound's house that accommodated the kitchen, dining and administration offices. I reflected on the day and wondered how the young man was faring and why I had given him the donated course of ciprofloxacin. It had been an intuitive action, probably because I wanted to use the tablets before they were lost and he was in the right place at the right time.

The following morning, I searched the ward to check his condition but he was gone. Had he died? I looked over the body pile at the gateway but could not identify him. Had his family taken him? Our medical records were haphazard. I could find no entry. The guards knew nothing. They had probably slept all night.

We still had no overnight nursing staff in the camp that I could ask. The Red Cross considered it too dangerous for national and international staff to remain. The camp had no internal policing and after dark incidents of violence, robbery and rape multiplied. The clinic did not even have a surrounding security fence. I only realised this was happening at four o'clock on my first day when the national nurses removed all the intravenous infusions from the patients in the ward, giving each patient a litre bottle of rehydration fluid. Even the disposable plastic bottles were in short supply and were being reused multiple times. I was horrified that we abandoned patient treatment and care so blatantly. But my emotions were so overwhelmed and swamped by the ongoing tsunami of disaster I passively accepted the decision.

'We have no choice, Doctor John. It is too dangerous for us to stay. It is the best we can do for the moment,' Henry explained.

My search for the man was quickly diverted by the first patient being carried in to kick off the day's match of microbe versus medicine.

Two days later I was surprised to arrive at the clinic and find the young man squatting in front of the ward tent. He looked fit and healthy, dressed in newly washed, pressed black trousers and a light blue caftan. I assumed he had returned to thank us. He approached me as I jumped from the back of the utility and, eyes sparkling and mouth smiling, asked, 'Can you give me two blankets doctor, for my family?' Not even a 'Thank you for saving my life doc.'

17

'Sorry my friend, I cannot. They are only for use in the clinic and if I give you one then I must give one to everyone and then we would have none for the patients.' This was my stock reply to the barrage of requests I received every day.

'But doctor I will tell no one. My children are cold at night.' It was the stock response.

'Sorry my friend, I cannot,' I insisted.

Sensing my resolve, he shrugged, smiled and strolled off. Reassured he was well and the ciprofloxacin had worked its miracle I forgot all about him. It was several weeks before I met him again, in very different circumstances.

In what way, John?
I was as surprised as you will be.

KIBUMBA REFUGEE CAMP, near GOMA, ZAIRE
(now the DEMOCRATIC REPUBLIC OF CONGO), August 1994
Doctor, Federation of Red Cross and Red Crescent

The stammer in Rachel's voice told me it was urgent. 'Doctor JJJJohn, come quick, in the dressing tent.' Her brow was furrowed, her hands trembled and her double chin quivered. She was one of the few overweight people I had seen in Zaire. She had admitted to me during a rare tea break that her father was a successful businessman in Goma but despite his wealth and expectation that she would marry and bear him grandchildren, she had become a nurse 'to help my people'. Her heart was bigger than her body.

I was inserting an intravenous infusion into the arm of an old man who had been rolled into the clinic on the back of a handcart on which he still lay, too weak to move and surrounded by family members who, with awe and anxiety, watched my every move. They related how he had contracted profuse bloody diarrhoea the previous evening and, by early morning, had become semiconscious. His dehydration was severe. Hopefully the infusion would save his life. I handed him over to Natalie, another competent national nurse who would help the family wheel him into our ward and hurried after Rachel to the dressing tent.

A small girl lay whimpering on the trestle table with a towel over her right foot.

'What happened?'

'She was crossing the road and a truck ran over her foot. It didn't see her or stop,' replied Rachel.

'Where is the family?'

'There isn't any. She's an orphan. Some passers-by brought her in.'

I immediately recognised her face. She was one of the kids who hung around the medical clinic, begged for food and slept under the eaves of the medical tents.

I lifted the sheet and winced. The foot was mangled and deformed with fragments of bone and torn tendons exposed in the wound. At least it was not dislocated.

'We'll clean the wound as best we can, dress it and give her some antibiotics. I haven't got any tetanus immunoglobulin. Tonight, we can take her to the Israeli military hospital in Goma. We have no access to transport until then. Let's give her some paracetamol.' She needed a stronger painkiller for such an injury but it was all I had.

Taking a deep breath, I tried to relax and control the irritation that had been building up within me.

Firstly, I'd been asking for more supplies and more equipment for days. We had been running out of essential supplies; not only pain killers for severe pain but also bleach and mops for disinfecting the floors, beds for patients to lie off the ground, tables to set out dressings and chairs for staff and patients to sit upon. Henry the head nurse had been nagging me for days to fill the shortages. The answer from the medical coordinator was always the same, 'They're coming'... but they never came and Henry blamed me for the delay.

Secondly, we had been stranded at the clinic without a car. It rarely happened but today the staff had no means of emergency evacuation should a security situation occur nearby; gunfights or angry demonstrations were not infrequent and could quickly become dangerous. In preparation for a speedy exit our car was always parked facing the exit and escape route. Today, with no car we were alone and vulnerable. And now the absence of a car delayed this girl's transfer to the Israeli military hospital. It was the only emergency surgical facility in the region and situated far across the other side of the city. The Red Cross had started to build a hospital in the Kibumba camp but it was still weeks from opening. I had no direct contact with the hospital. The local phone network had collapsed. I could only hope that the Israelis could accept her.

For all this time she had lain soundless, her eyes following my every move. When I doused the wound with antiseptic and inserted a needle into her vein to give an infusion, she screwed up her face but did not cry out. After injecting the intravenous penicillin, I gave her a big smile, stroked her forehead and lifted her onto a bale of blankets that would act as a bed.

'You are very brave,' I asked Rachel to interpret. She smiled back and burrowed her face in the sheet with innocent shyness.

'Can you keep an eye on her as much as possible and I'll watch her too. It's frantic out there, so she'll just have to stay in here alone. We'll make her nil-by-mouth in case she needs surgery tonight. She can have sips of water only.' I was hoping the military hospital would be able to deal with her quickly.

During the day I kept popping in and out of the dressing tent, checking her temperature and pulse, adjusting the intravenous fluids. Sometimes she was asleep, at others, lying motionless, staring at the ceiling. Not once did I hear her cry. I gave her more painkillers.

As our day's departure from the clinic approached, we went through our heart-wrenching routine of removing all the intravenous drips from all the patients in our ward and giving them bottles of oral rehydration fluid to sip overnight. The nightly abandonment haunted me every evening. Some patients died but most survived and the following morning we could continue their intravenous regimes.

After four o'clock I bundled the little girl in a blanket and nursed her on my knees on the front seat of the Red Cross Toyota Land cruiser that arrived to pick us up. She nestled into my lap, grabbed tight hold of my left middle finger and stared trustingly into my eyes. I could not imagine what was going on in her mind.

It took an hour and a half to drive the twenty-five kilometres back to Goma. A water truck had broken down, blocking half the road. A policeman with a whistle blasting between his lips was running up and down the road frantically directing traffic with his arms. Everyone ignored him, barging their way round the obstruction, only to create gridlock congestion.

19

Nearing Goma, she raised her head and looked out of the window. I doubted she had ever been in a car before. Her eyes sparkled with a tinge of wonder but she quickly tired and fell back. I held her more firmly.

After dropping off the staff at the pick-up point we drove to the tented hospital that the Israeli army had erected on the far side of Goma. The complex of khaki tents was surrounded with a barbed wire fence. At the gate two soldiers, smart in their fiercely creased field uniforms, stood sentry, automatic weapons ready at their hips. They glanced in the window and waved us in.

I cradled the girl into the Emergency Room, brightly illuminated against the outer growing gloom and a nurse in surgical scrubs approached to welcome us.

'Here let me take her,' she offered but the little girl would not let go. Whilst comforting her in my arms I recounted the medical history.

'Lie her down on the couch.' It was a command although softly spoken. Again, the little girl did not want to let go. She screamed and screamed. The nurse gently but firmly prised her hand off my finger. Her eyes stared into mine pleading, accusing, terrified and tortured.

I had to go. It was nearly sunset, the time when the curfew, forbidding car travel in the town came into force. I murmured pointless reassurances and slowly withdrew. My heart was torn. To leave a young child who had been totally abandoned by family, community and culture alone in a strange hospital was cruel. She had suffered deprivation, starvation, and major injury and I was deserting her. I had no choice. I did not even know her name.

As we drove away in the car, I could hear her scream. I still can, especially when I watch a setting sun.

What happened to her?
I have no idea. I was unable to get back to the hospital because of lack of transport and four weeks later the Israeli military closed the hospital and left Goma. I did not even have her name or the resources to follow up her case.

I can't imagine how that would feel for you. How did you feel?
I was emotionally overwhelmed. Having to leave her at the hospital was only an exacerbation, an extension of the trauma of leaving our patients unattended overnight in our clinic. Some were critically ill but we walked out on them too. That she was so young, so vulnerable, so alone cut through my struggling defences.

I just repeated my mantra, *Do what you can, ignore the rest.*

It was life saving for me. I was so far out of my comfort zone, so far from the norms of medical practice, so far from the decencies of humanity that without a simple focus, a quiet command, a single direction I would have collapsed in turmoil. I stopped trying to make sense or rationalise what was happening because I finally realised there was no sense or rationality to it.

Did you discuss this with your colleagues?
Outwardly I showed little concern or confusion to my colleagues. I did not want any analysis or deep-and-meaningful discussion. It would have cracked my shell and shattered my defences. The national staff was brilliant. They seemed to accept the bedlam, the confusion and disarray. Zaire had been suffering conflict and civil wars for decades. As we travelled to and fro between Goma and the medical clinic, standing in the back of our Toyota utility, they joked, flirted, gossiped and laughed.

It was wonderful therapy for me. It normalised the day and distanced and distracted me from my emotional chaos. But this normality had an adverse effect. Later in the day when I again began to feel distressed, I felt I had no right to be so. If the local staff could cope with the conditions, what right did I have to feel sorry for myself? I could leave the crisis any time I chose. I was able to return to the safety of Australia. This was their home. They had no choice.

Ironically not showing any outward emotion or despair seemed to increase my credibility as a leader with both the national and international staff. They wanted a figurehead that was not intimidated or distracted and could be relied upon. This only stiffened my resolve to hide my feeling and emotions, even to myself.

KIBUMBA REFUGEE CAMP, near GOMA, ZAIRE
(now the DEMOCRATIC REPUBLIC OF CONGO), August 1994
Doctor, Federation of Red Cross and Red Crescent

'Doctor John, we need chairs to sit on; the bales of blankets we are using are falling to bits. We need more tables to keep the dressings clean.'

'Doctor John, we need a bigger tent to triage the patients. There is not enough room to examine anyone.'

'Doctor John, we need a perimeter fence to stop people walking freely through our clinic.'

'Doctor John, why do you not get these things for us?'

I was standing, crammed in the open tray of the utility 4WD with ten of the national staff being driven from Kibumba back to Goma where the national staff lived and the Red Cross and Crescent expatriates had their base. A large house and compound had been transformed into administration offices and a kitchen/dining area. All the expatriates slept four-to-a-tent in the garden. It resembled a small military camp. The 4WD utilities were the only transport available and completely inadequate for fifteen people.

I steadied myself, and listened to their complaints.

Every day I was hearing similar requests. Every day I was asking the medical coordinator for action. Every day I became more and more frustrated that nothing eventuated. We had small poky tents for consultations and a shack made of poles and tarpaulins that acted as a medical ward. There was no surrounding fence, one inadequate, stinking latrine and a continual shortage of medical equipment. With the sun warming my face and the wind stirring my resolve I decided to be proactive and take matters into my own hands.

After dropping off the rest of the staff in Goma I detoured to the Red Cross warehouse beside the airport where all the incoming stores and equipment were unloaded and stockpiled. As I roamed the rows of equipment, I discovered much of what we needed. I uncovered a cache of tables and chairs, rolls of plastic for fencing and bottles of bleach.

'But it is for the new hospital,' rattled Alfred, the store man. The Red Cross had begun to build its own emergency surgical hospital and supplies had begun to arrive and be stockpiled. I was shocked and angry that the medical clinics in the camp were being ignored and starved of supply.

'Yes, but that will not be open for another month and we need it now.'

'I cannot release it without authority, without requisition forms. You must give me the papers.'

An idea sparked in my head.

The next day I returned with the requisition forms and loaded the goods into my 4WD. I did not tell Alfred that I had acquired the blank forms from the administration office the previous evening, forged the signatures and stamped them multiple times with the most official stamp I could find using a red ink pad. They oozed officialdom and 'red tape' and were very convincing, even to me. They satisfied him. I figured the goods would not be missed for a couple of weeks. I rationalised that replacements could be flown in from Nairobi if deemed essential.

My action elevated me to become the leader of the clinic. Even Henry, the national head nurse, and normally a little standoffish and formal, was impressed. His smile joined both his ears as I drove into the clinic with all the new equipment.

'Doctor John, this is like Christmas,' he grinned and laughed. From that moment he became a powerful ally.

Now everyone came to me with their requests and problems. I was delighted. My enlarged ego was being polished and I thrived on the attention and problem solving. I became bolder in acquiring new equipment. Henry was able to barter our bales of blankets, of which we had an ample supply, for a supply of fence poles. Numerous refugees were hired, paid with extra food rations donated by World Food Program, to dig holes and build the fence around the clinic. I was able to commandeer two larger tents that I had found inadvertently stored in the wrong warehouse and inaccurately documented. I realised I had a flair to scrounge and use the urgency, confusion and disorganisation of the emergency phase to overcome the overbearing bureaucracy and officialdom, albeit underhandedly. I self-justified my deceit, rightly or wrongly, by watching the clinic transform from a group of sparse, cramped, straggly tents open to weather and intruders into a coordinated, efficient, protected, secure clinic.

It was over a week before Stephan, the medical coordinator, visited and realised what was happening, by which time the newly provisioned clinic was a fait accompli and the high staff morale and greater efficiency was apparent. He arrived, looked around with horror, talked with Henry and totally ignored me. He hurriedly departed. He was not happy. The rest of the staff smiled at me and gave 'thumbs up' like co-conspirators. It gave me some confidence but I wondered if I had overstepped the mark.

Did you become the leader of the clinic?
Yes. I was the one everyone came to for help. I was proving I was able to make decisions in difficult situations, both clinically and administratively and get things done. The staff was happy with the results.

It sounds like you were very effective. Why do you think you were so?
I've thought about this at length. In an emergency a leader, I think, needs three qualities, which I seemed to have.

And they are?
In short, single-mindedness, open-mindedness and bloody-mindedness.

Go on.
Being single-minded is to be totally focused on specific outcomes and not be distracted by all the action, drama and emotion exploding around you. My focus became treating the patients whilst improving the clinic. I could observe the death and devastation, the mounds of dead bodies, the water shortage, the starvation,

the unaccompanied children, but still remain focused on treating patients and building the capacity and capability of the clinic, allowing the surrounding suffering and mass misery to wash over me. It was challenging. My mantra helped. *Do what you can, ignore the rest.*

Being open-minded is to be open to any initiative, to think laterally, out-of-the-box and around obstacles that appear. The national nursing staff had numerous ideas on improving patient flow and treatments and I learnt to let them have their way and not impose my preconceived prejudices. They suggested using some of our food supplies to pay refugee volunteers to supervise the waiting lines of patients, protect our stores and even to roam around the camp and carry those 'too-sick-to-walk' to our clinic.

Being bloody-minded is to be able to bulldoze through obstacles if there is no reasonable way around them. In this case, I needed to ignore the inactivity of the medical coordinator and the rigid restrictions of ordering requisitions and 'acquire' the much-needed equipment. In the confusion of an emergency scenario it was not difficult to bend the rules. It worked in this situation and the clinic blossomed.

Kɪʙᴜᴍʙᴀ Rᴇғᴜɢᴇᴇ Cᴀᴍᴘ, near Gᴏᴍᴀ, Zᴀɪʀᴇ
(now the Dᴇᴍᴏᴄʀᴀᴛɪᴄ Rᴇᴘᴜʙʟɪᴄ ᴏғ Cᴏɴɢᴏ), August 1994
Doctor, Federation of Red Cross and Red Crescent

'Hey Phillipe, Claudette and I want to walk up the hill and take a photograph of the camp. The food distribution is nearly over and all is quiet. Is that OK?' I asked the head of food distribution, a tall Frenchman, straggly, thinning hair falling over his podgy face, a cigarette hanging from his lower lip.

It had been a massive day, distributing a week's supply of rice, oil and sugar to over two hundred thousand people. The Federation of the Red Cross and Crescent was responsible not only for running medical clinics in the camp but also for food distribution to the refugees. Phillipe, the man in charge, had wanted as many expatriates as possible at the food distribution site to help control the flow of people along the distribution lines and had asked some of the medical expatriates to help out for the day.

'There is always a danger of looting and it can become dangerous. Expatriates are less likely to be intimidated, bullied or threatened. If you identify any threat, radio in immediately and I'll come with assistance.' I was not reassured by his briefing but Phillipe was highly experienced and I judged he would not endanger our lives.

'Look out for the crowd getting too close to the fences or any individual becoming demanding and aggressive. The prefecture leaders have been briefed to keep control of their people but all it takes is a few hotheads or a gun to emerge and all control is lost. If it gets riotous, RUN.'

Maybe he would endanger our lives?

The site for the food distribution was at the foot of a steep-sided grassy hill, at the opposite end of the camp to our clinic. An area the size of several football pitches had been specifically kept clear for this reason. Laneways and corridors for the food trucks and queues of waiting refugee had been marked out with fences made from stakes and coloured tape.

We arrived before dawn. A fleet of six World Food Program (WFP) trucks arrived and parked in front of the command centre, a cluster of Red Cross and Crescent cars housing the communications and administration staff. The food was unloaded and placed in large stacks of sacks and tins. Red Cross and Crescent workers, recognisable by their white waistcoats immediately surrounded the supplies and secured the fences. The tension of the waiting crowd became palpable.

Over two thousand refugees had already gathered. They lazed in small groups, long trousers, open shirts, scarves, beanies and jackets insulating against the chill of the morning air. The groups coalesced and soon overflowed the allocated waiting area, spreading up the hillside like an amphitheatre. Nearly all were men.

'The women are too busy performing the child-minding and household tasks. They consider this man's work,' explained Annette, another experienced Red Cross worker, checking her sheet of allocations before the distribution began.

For the next few hours, each prefecture leader came forward, was identified and confirmed their allocation. Behind each leader, a line of silent men followed, each to pick up a sack of grain or packet of sugar or a tin of oil as they were counted and carried off.

'It's not a satisfactory arrangement,' Phillipe had disclosed. 'We should have every refugee registered and then the food can be distributed to each separate family but this disaster unfolded too quickly and haphazardly for this to happen. Now we are reliant on community leaders to distribute the food. Much will go missing in favouritism, family loyalties and pay-offs,' he shrugged with resignation. 'Hopefully the UNHCR will now organise an individual registration program. It is on their agenda.'

I watched in admiration from my allocated position as the drama unfolded. It had the tension of a movie set, but this was real. The distribution followed the set script. It was mostly peaceful and pleasant. Occasionally voices were raised. Everything then stopped whilst the commotion was calmed before the process restarted. Everyone seemed happy that the food had arrived.

'Sure John. You can go and get your photographs but stay together and both of you carry your personal radios.' I signalled to Claudette and we headed around the mass of the crowd before we climbed.

Behind the waiting crowds, the prefecture leaders who had already collected their rations were standing by their store of food and dividing it between their villages. The sacks of grain, tins of oil and packets of sugar stood in neat piles. Around each stash were more men, many brandishing machetes, waiting to carry off their village's allocation. Voices were raised, bodies were jostled and lines were pushed as everyone bid for a greater amount. Nobody here seemed happy. Sensing a pent-up tension, we widely skirted the group before we started on our climb.

There was a shout, then a scream. Claudette and I both turned around and saw a man, a sack of grain balanced on his head, be attacked by four men. With his hands steadying the sack he kicked out at them. In slow motion I watched one of the attackers raise his machete and slash into the neck of the victim. Blood spurted from his neck as he fell, partially beheaded, his sack spilling to the ground. His body had hardly hit the ground before his assailants grabbed the sack and ran off.

24

I heard Claudette gasp and she ran towards the fallen man. I grabbed the back of her T-shirt and pulled her back. 'No, Claudette, there's nothing you can do for him. Let's get out of here. It's dangerous. Anything can happen.'

I dragged her across the hillside away from the body. Already a crowd was gathering, shouting and screaming.

I radioed Phillipe. 'Head Honcho, Head Honcho this is Juliet Papa. There's been a refugee robbed and murdered beside the hill. We are heading back. There might be trouble.'

'Get back now John. We'll pack up and leave ASAP.'

Claudette had tears streaming down her face. It was her first mission too.

It sounds terrible. Were you scared John?
I wasn't scared, I was terrified. I had never seen such raw violence first-hand and so close. I knew we had to get away from the scene quickly. An angry crowd will readily transfer their anger and aggression and seek revenge on any alien person nearby. And we were aliens and nearby.

How did this trauma affect you?
Over the following days I had horrific nightmares of heads falling off bodies gushing with arterial blood... but the experience soon became diminished and distant amid the ongoing chain of horrors that I was daily witnessing. But I was more traumatised that I first realised. It was not until several years later when a soldier was hacked to death with a cleaver on the streets of London and in Syria 'Jihadi John' of the Islamic State posted a video on social media of an aid worker being beheaded and that my nightmares recurred. The simplicity, speed and savagery of such a death devoid of reason or remorse was frightening. It alarmed me that after so many years the terror could resurface and haunt me again.

It was my first exposure to the lawlessness of refugee camps. There is no police or judicial system. It is a melting pot of power plays, corruption, intimidation and both metered and senseless violence. Rape is widespread, robbery common and intimidation routine. Internal power structures and protection rackets thrive. It is a true jungle. Kibumba was probably the worst I have ever seen.

I laugh when I hear refugees being condemned for wanting to escape refugee camps to get to a country like Australia, Canada or the USA. The critic, safe and secure in their nest in the west would have no concept of the constant danger, intimidation, despair, boredom and hopelessness of life in a camp.

I'm glad you got to safety John.

KIBUMBA REFUGEE CAMP, near GOMA, ZAIRE
(now the DEMOCRATIC REPUBLIC OF CONGO), August 1994
Doctor, Federation of Red Cross and Red Crescent

'You're not to go to the camp tomorrow, John. Take the day off,' Robert, the Head of Mission, advised me.

'I can't,' I replied, 'it's frantic out there. There's far too much to do.'

'No matter, you're not to go to the clinic.' He spoke slowly and firmly. 'You've worked ten straight days, you're irritable, you're withdrawing and you're burning out. They'll manage as well they can without you. Do you understand?' His tone implied my understanding was irrelevant and there was no place for dissent.

'OK, if you insist.'

'I do.'

At six o'clock the following morning, with a heavy, guilty heart, I watched the rest of the team head out of the compound to drive to the refugee camp.

I was letting the team down. I was a failure. I was weak and inadequate sped through my mind.

Resigned to my enforced rest I sat outside my tent in a canvas director's chair, too proud, too stubborn, too angry to go back to sleep, and read a book... but the words blurred, the pages blanked and the story flagged. I was feigning interest. Giving up, I reached for my Walkman that I had carried diligently from Australia. Unfortunately, I had forgotten to bring any tapes to play but Brenda, a Canadian Public Relations delegate, had lent me a tape the previous evening. I leaned back and closed my eyes. The rising sunlight warmed my right cheek and I listened. It began with a couple of popular hits. The third track was Chris de Burgh singing *Carry Me*. Its melody resonated with my mood and the lyrics pierced my heart... a song of loss and recovery... of sadness and hope...

> *There is an answer, someday we will know*
> *And you ask her, why she had to go.*
> *We live and die; we laugh and cry*
> *And you must take away the pain*
> *Before you can begin to live again*
> *So, let it start, my friend, let it start*
> *Let the tears come rolling from your heart.*

(Written by Chris de Burgh)

... I realised I was crying. Tears trickled down my cheeks. I tried to wipe them aside... to no avail. The trickle flowed to a stream, the stream to a torrent. I dropped my head in embarrassment... and shame.

A hand clamped my shoulder. A mug of tea was thrust into my hand. I didn't dare look up to show my face. Mumbling a 'thank you', I dropped my head deeper. As the footsteps receded, I sighed and sank into my loneliness. The tears flooded and the flashbacks started.

...the old, skinny man that I'd spied on my way to the camp, silhouetted on the crest of the road by the rising sun, leaning on a stick, looking down at a body laid at his feet bundled in reed matting, two thin feet sticking out of one end; an old man fare-welling his deceased wife?

...the young woman crawling on her hip beside the road, her bloody bowels hanging, prolapsed from her rectum until, as I pass in the car, she suddenly lies prone, unmoving, eyes fixed; the flies move in

....the mother screaming in my face as I place her dead son's body back into her arms. He had arrived at the clinic severely dehydrated and died within the hour; too little, too late

....the patient lying in their watery diarrhoea unable to be cleaned for lack of water or cloth to mop it up

....the queues of outpatients waiting for hours outside the clinic in the glaring sun for treatment of their diarrhoea, fevers and infections

....the hungry children running beside the car begging for *Biskit, Biskit.*

As the recent horrors flashed like a stroboscope through my head, tears streamed down my face to saturate my neck collar, my shirtfront, even to the crotch of my jeans. I gave up caring, letting them flow and overflow, overwhelmed by the moment.

Without warning the tears abruptly stopped. I felt I had cried a gallon from a pint-sized head and I had run dry. A sense of finality, of dread, of intense fear seized me. *I've lost it... my mind, my sanity, my reason.* My whole body tensed and began to tremble. My breathing quickened; my heart raced. I could sense rising panic.

Out of the ground a sensation of calm gripped my feet, slowly spreading and rising up, a thousand gentle hands caressing my body and soul, releasing tension, relieving dread. It was as though my tears had bathed and baptised my being, awakening awareness and acceptance of my emotive body. All my angst and anguish dissipated. I slowly relaxed, suffuse with tranquillity and ease. As if post orgasmic I felt sudden relief and satisfaction. My energy and enthusiasm were revived and renewed. I thirstily sipped my tea that by now was cold but remarkably refreshing. I jumped out of my chair and spent the rest of the day hand washing a backlog of sweat-stained clothes, tidying my luggage stored under my camp bed, writing newsy letters home to my wife and three children, reading my book and listening to the rest of my tape. By the time the team returned from the clinic I was eager to engage and learn of the day's events. I could feel them stare at me and wonder, *What's he on? I'll have some of it.*

I would have struggled to explain what 'it' was. I was only aware that I was ready to continue.

Why was this so significant for you John?
I'd never cried before.

Never?
No, never. Well, not for a long, long time. Whilst holidaying at my uncle's dairy farm aged five or six, I had adopted and befriended a puppy. We had never had a dog for a pet at home, only guinea pigs and rabbits. I played with it for hours. The puppy jumped out of my arms and ran on to the driveway as my uncle was reversing his car. It was crushed and instantly killed. I ran out and picked it up. My uncle admonished me for letting it run out. I was devastated, overwhelmed with guilt at my carelessness and openly bawled my eyes out. My oldest cousin started to laugh at me and told me not to be such a sissy. It was only a puppy and there were lots more. I vividly remember my feelings of belittlement and humiliation and maybe then I decided never to again show emotions and be seen as weak and vulnerable.

Why were you so scared?
My loss of self-control. My outward display of weakness and vulnerability. The intensity of the flashbacks. It was terrifying.

So why did you lose control? What brought this reaction on?
I guess it was a mixture of physical exhaustion, emotional overload and a spiritual vacuum.

That seems very insightful.

I can say it now after much reflection and contemplation. The reaction was so intense that even now, years later, every time I hear that song it brings tears to my eyes and I have the same flashbacks although less intense.

Obviously, Robert saw the symptoms of burn out and forced me to stay home that day but I'm sure he didn't realise the long-term implications for me.

What was the long-term impact?

That day, that moment, was pivotal for me. It was a true awakening. My emotional armour was cracked. I'm embarrassed to say it took a catastrophe of biblical proportion to do it but I was brought to my knees and I glimpsed my true emotional self for the first time. My emotions had nowhere to hide anymore. I could no longer live in blissful denial of my true feelings. The crack was irreparable. It could never close. I cried many times during the mission but never so overtly. It became a safety valve for pent up frustrations, anger and feelings of impotence, injustice and despair. I am sure it saved my sanity and allowed me to remain functional. I suspect it was those delegates who did not cry who broke down and needed repatriation.

You also mentioned a spiritual vacuum?

I was brought up a Catholic but it had lost any meaning for me in my late teens. I wasn't just a 'lapsed' Catholic. I rejected its dogma and archaic institutionalised beliefs but had not replaced it with any alternate philosophy of life. It's not that I was immoral, more amoral, bouncing about, making decisions ad hoc without any moral compass to guide me.

That's interesting John but you're beginning to get a bit ahead of yourself again. This all unfolded years later. Let's go back to what happened to you in Zaire.

KIBUMBA REFUGEE CAMP, near GOMA, ZAIRE
(now the DEMOCRATIC REPUBLIC OF CONGO), August 1994
Doctor, Federation of Red Cross and Red Crescent

'Look at the women at the fence,' Clare spoke in a low voice hinting that we should be subtle.

Swinging my eyes but not my head, 'Yes, I see them.' A group of young women dressed in plain blouses and colourful, wrap-around skirts tied high under their breasts were standing or squatting outside the plastic netted fence on the far side of the compound. They chatted to each other but kept their eyes down.

'Some of them are the mothers of the children in here.'

'But this is an orphanage?' I questioned.

'No, it's an Unaccompanied Child's Centre or UCC,' she corrected. 'Get your terminology right.'

'Well, yes, so if their mothers are here, surely they aren't "unaccompanied" as you call it.'

'I don't call it that. It's the politically correct jargon that we have to use in our reports.' Despite its charming Irish lilt, her voice was getting irritated at the imposition of the bureaucratic demands. She shook her head to rid herself of the thought, her black hair shimmering in the sunlight.

'Even so, why are you looking after the kids if their mothers are outside?'

'I don't know for sure they are the mothers but my local helpers tell me so. They apparently "abandoned" their children early in the crisis knowing we will take care and feed them so they can use their ration allowance to give more food to the rest of the family.' Clare was the expatriate nurse in charge of the UCC, run by an Irish NGO. She had seventy-five children in her care.

'Is the food ration that critical?' I asked but already knew the food allowance was well under basic daily needs, especially when the food rations are allocated en masse to the prefecture leaders for them to distribute. The amount of food that filtered down to the vulnerable, the women, children and elderly, was greatly reduced from the ration given.

'The mothers hang around here to see their child from a distance and check they are still alive. Hopefully, as the rations improve and the camp becomes safer, they will be able to come and collect them.'

'How do they choose which child to abandon?'

'It's usually the second youngest child. The youngest will still be breastfed. The second youngest is the bottom of the food chain in the home purely because they are the smallest. The older children are stronger and will take more food. They are all hungry.'

'So are your children in the UCC mainly two to three-years-old?'

'No, many are but there are still many truly unaccompanied children, many of them orphans, ranging from two to twelve years old. Thank god we have the older children because they help us with the smaller ones. I think you brought us ten children who had been living around your medical clinic when we first arrived.'

'I did. It was a huge relief...' I was interrupted...

'Hi Doctor John.' I turned around and immediately recognised one of the 'orphans' whom I had brought to the UCC.

She smiled and put out her hand begging 'Biskit, biskit?' Old habits die hard.

I smiled back and gave her a high five. 'Hi Rascal,' I called her by the nickname we had given her. She was a confident and charming child, about six years old, with a gleam in her eye. Tall for her age, lithe in stature, she held a cheeky grin between her dimpled cheeks. She was the leader despite being so young. During the morning she and her friends would scamper off to scavenge for food and water and return at lunchtime.

From the very first day in the camp I was unable to eat my lunch. We were all supplied with an army ration pack crammed with a tinned meal, biscuits and chocolate. Despite the national staff closing the tent flaps for privacy I could never overcome the feelings of guilt at eating whilst surrounded by thousands of starving refugees. Instead I would take the food outside and share it with the children. This arrangement persisted for two weeks until the UCC home had opened and I could transfer them to their care.

I was delighted she was still safe.

'Natasha is a great help. That's her real name. She only told us last week. Her parents and siblings were killed in the genocide. She prefers the name Rascal!'

I had been asked to visit the home to treat some of the children and advise on their hygiene. Another UCC home had recently suffered an outbreak of diarrhoea, causing several deaths. They did not want a repeat here.

Clare explained, 'All the UCC homes suffered overcrowded conditions when first opened because they were swamped with children. Now more homes have opened and we are less crowded and better equipped and staffed. Our kitchen is kept spotless.'

I stayed silent for I knew that the kitchen cooked on wood fires, had limited bench space, cramped fridge accommodation and very primitive washing up facilities. Compared to a first world kitchen it was, at best, a camp kitchen. But I also knew that despite these restrictions the food was properly stored, hand washing procedures were strictly enforced, the food well cooked and all used pots and pans were washed quickly and thoroughly. It was as good as it would get.

'What will happen to them all?' I probed.

'Hopefully many of them will be reclaimed or found by their families as the emergency and chaos come under control. We have registered them all with the Red Cross tracing service so families in other camps will know they are here. Those whose families have been killed or died here in the cholera epidemic will be fostered out to families from the same prefecture or region. At least that way they will later return to the area from which they originate and maybe get found by extended family. We are talking with the prefecture leaders for their ideas and find what is culturally acceptable.'

Rascal had been hanging around us during this conversation. I had no idea her English was so advanced. She really was a smart kid.

'Hey Doctor John. You take me back to Australia, hey?'

How did that feel for you, John?
The street kids, for that is what I called them, initially upset me. They were starving, dressed in rags and totally alone in a hostile, dangerous and bleak environment, their only schooling hunger and hardship. I could not understand how kids as young as four and five could exist, roaming amid the throngs of refugees who were all struggling to survive. They hung around the medical clinic begging and sleeping under the eaves of the tents at night. As well as sharing my lunch, the other medical staff gave them biscuits and leftover food, but we did not want to become a feeding centre. We were working flat out with desperately sick people and had no time for childminding.

When we left at the end of the day to return to our accommodation in Goma, I would cut several blankets in half and give one half to each child. I had no idea if they kept them, sold them or had them stolen.

Each morning I collected several packets of biscuits from the Red Cross kitchen to feed them. It wasn't much but it was all I could do. I was so relieved when they were transferred to the UCC home.

Yes, but how did you feel?
I felt frustrated, impotent, angry… and guilty… very guilty that such innocence was so abandoned and exposed to such danger and hardship. Kids of that age at home in Australia are protected and pampered. The world might suck, but when it involves young children the world sucks much worse. Every child should be safe and loved, not vulnerable and alone. Every child should have access to a secure environment, health care and education. These are basic human rights. It is so wrong.

It sounds like it was very difficult seeing innocent young children in such a vulnerable situation. How do you feel these years later?
I have grandchildren now. I want them to be safe and loved but a bit of me wants them to have a touch of the resilience and resourcefulness that I saw in Rascal. A

privileged childhood that is over-parented, overprotected, and overindulged does not foster such qualities, especially in our culture of instant gratification and high expectations for minimal effort. How can a young child learn self-sufficiency, self-control and tenacity without being challenged by some loss, hardship or disappointment? There are some things that cannot be taught. You have to live them.

GOMA, ZAIRE
(now the DEMOCRATIC REPUBLIC OF CONGO), August 1994
Doctor, Federation of Red Cross and Red Crescent

'The mail's arrived,' Glen, the cook, shouted out the news from the top of the steps of the main house. 'It's on the dining room table.'

I had just returned from the medical clinic after a long day. I dragged my weary, lethargic, dehydrated body along the dusty path between the rows of tents and waved him a thank-you, only to collapse in the green and orange striped canvas director's chair outside my tent. Sixteen four-man khaki canvas tents, arranged with military precision in four rows, dotted the garden of the high-walled compound. All I wanted to do was to tease the boots off my swollen ankles, raise my legs on to a stool and drink cool water. After a day's work in the medical clinic, I was physically and emotionally exhausted and reeked of sweat, earth-dust, wood-smoke, volcanic ash and all the body fluids that had splashed over me. My next focus was to get stripped, bathed and changed.

I was vaguely aware the Red Cross Beechcraft plane had arrived that morning from Nairobi in Kenya, our supply base, and I was hoping there would be a letter from home. It was only three weeks since I had left but it seemed like months and I missed my family. No mail had yet arrived. The Internet was still a fantasy. A family photograph, my wife and I sitting on the sofa with the three kids draped around us, taken earlier in the year, was folded in my pocket wallet and in the evenings, after dinner, I often found myself looking at it with pride and love. A crease in the photo was cracking our torsos but all the grinning faces remained clear.

I tried not to hurry my ablutions. Poor water pressure reduced the shower to a mere trickle. Rather than run around trying to get wet I used a bucket of water to slosh jugfuls over my head, lathering up my body then sploshing off all the soapy suds. The water, decanted from the black plastic water storage tank beside the shower recess, was luxuriously warm, heated up by the day's fierce sunlight.

Dressed in fresh shorts and T-shirt I strolled over to the house as nonchalantly as I could, hiding my boyish excitement, and looked slowly through the pile of letters sprawled over one end of a table. Flicking through the last few envelopes my heart sank with disappointment then flooded with relief as I recognised my wife's handwriting. The postmark indicated it had been posted to our logistical base in Nairobi ten days earlier from Australia.

Gripping the thick lilac envelope firmly I sped back to my tent. Any pretence at nonchalance evaporated. I was desperate to read the news. My excitement was rewarded with a lengthy, newsy letter from my wife, how they were all missing me but wishing me well. My three children had each written shorter letters about their school and friends, swimming in the creek, a bonfire on the beach, playing the piano. It was such a relief to sense their normality and a boost to my resolve to do my best in these difficult surrounds. The last line of the last letter affected me the most. My youngest son, Jake, aged eleven ended...

'Dad, I love you, by all the stars in the sky, times all the grains of sand on the beach, times all the watermelon pips in the world. Your son, Jake.'

Even now it brings a joyful tear to my eye but that day I cried with love when I read it. I wondered if he one day would be a great poet? I reread the letters every day and they became a source of comfort for me. I began to appreciate how important the love and support of my family was to my wellbeing. I felt so lucky. I received many more letters from family and friends that boosted my morale and energy.

Jake's next letter was not quite as poetic. He concluded, 'I hope you remember how much I love you Dad, because I don't want to write all that out again.'

That night I tossed and turned in my bed, unsettled with a bout of homesickness. I had a quiet cry in my pillow, not wanting to disturb my three tent-mates.

I talked myself to sleep telling myself it was normal and repeating, *this too will pass*, another mantra that has since served me well.

The following morning dragged. My body and mind were tired after the fragmented night's sleep and the tsunami of sick and dying patients surged on. By mid-morning I became overwhelmed with anxiety. *Would this ever end? Were we having any effect on the health of the camp? Would more epidemics break out? Measles? Typhoid? Typhus?* My head began to spin and I felt faint. I walked out of the clinic on to the roadside.

Standing outside the gates I stared at the distant volcano belching its ash into the sky, took multiple deep slow breaths and calmed my mind with more mantras. *This is just the 'what-is'. This will pass. Do what you can and leave the rest. This is just the 'what-is'. This will pass. Do what you can and leave the rest.*

From the corner of my eye, I saw a youngish man trudging along the road towards me. Clad in dark blue slacks, a dirty white shirt, and a maroon beanie perched high on his head, his face was a mask of torment with tears streaming down both cheeks. In his arms, he carried the dead body of a young boy, about eight or nine years old.

He approached the pile of corpses beside me and bent over to lay down his son but suddenly stopped. He looked at me, maybe through me, and his face screwed up with indecision. He looked at me again, slowly shook his head, stood up straight and turned, crossing the road and disappeared into the trees of the forest beyond.

I could sense his dilemma. He was unable to leave his son on the body pile, to be carted off to the anonymity and indignity of a mass grave of nameless and numberless corpses. He would rather lay his son in a single shallow grave in the quiet of the forest. It was not as secure but maybe it felt more dignified.

I felt alarmed. How could I be feeling sad with homesickness? My son was healthily and happily at home. I would be home soon enough enjoying his cuddles and company. He would only remember the cold body in his arms and never watch him grow.

I felt accused and found guilty.

I shook my head. Shamed and humbled by the father's courage I hurried back to the clinic to treat more sons and daughters.

**KIBUMBA REFUGEE CAMP, near GOMA, ZAIRE
(now the DEMOCRATIC REPUBLIC OF CONGO), September 1994
Doctor, Federation of Red Cross and Red Crescent**

'Doctor John, there's an unconscious man having a convulsion outside. Can you see him now?' I was bandaging a wound in the dressing tent and instantly stopped to follow Natalie, the triage nurse. A middle-aged man, his clothes heavily bloodstained, lay on a stretcher made from numerous interwoven tree branches on the ground beside my examination table. Kneeling beside him I could see he was deeply unconscious and having a Grand Mal seizure. His limbs were shaking, his face was contorted and coloured a purplish blue. Blood was matted over the right side of his head. I could feel a depression of his skull beneath a ragged laceration.

'He was attacked and beaten on the head with a glass bottle early this morning,' one of his companions confided. 'Is he going to die?'

He obviously had a depressed skull fracture but I had no X-ray and there was no surgical hospital nearby. The Israelis had gone home and the Red Cross hospital was still being constructed. My immediate concern was to stop the fitting and quickly inserted an intravenous cannula to give diazepam, a simple antiepileptic drug. His body relaxed and the fitting stopped.

I had worked in a neurosurgical unit many years earlier and had observed several skull fractures being elevated... but had never done it... and although I had the basic instruments to suture a wound, I had no suitable surgical instrument to elevate the skull... except for the blade of my Swiss army knife.

With no access to any sterilisation equipment I scrubbed the penknife thoroughly in soapy water then boiled it in water for 20 minutes. Meantime, I cleaned the wound and cut away the ragged crushed skin. When the penknife had cooled, I slipped the blade under one of the fragments of bone and levered it up. Luck was on my side and there was an instant and audible pop as the lining of the bone attaching the fragments hoisted the other fragments. The many onlookers all stared at me, some suspicious, some impressed, some wondering what I had done.

'That's fixed,' I over-confidently declared and hastily inserted skin sutures to close the skin.

'We'll give him some intravenous antibiotics and observe him,' I told Natalie. 'Can you tell the relatives we've done all we can. He'll either regain consciousness... or he won't. It's up to the gods now. The family can nurse him here tonight and we can give more antibiotics in the morning.' She nodded and interpreted my prognosis. They looked at me and nodded.

A few minutes later whilst I was splinting a broken leg, Henry, the head nurse interrupted me again.

'Doctor John, there's a man in the triage tent with a hole in his head. Can you see him?'

'Is he unconscious? Is he fitting?'

'Oh no, he walked in and is chatting away. He's had it for three months.'

I was intrigued and followed Henry.

Sitting at the examination table, conversing and laughing with the nurses was a man in his mid-twenties wearing camouflage pants and military boots with a Jimmy Hendrix T-shirt and blue denim waistcoat... probably ex-military. He was wearing a battered straw hat.

Henry stood beside him to continue the presentation. 'Doctor John, this man was hit in the head by shrapnel three months ago. The wound was surgically dressed in a local medical clinic for several weeks and had fully healed, except for a hole. He wants to know if we can fix it.'

I was even more intrigued. 'Show me.'

The soldier bent his head towards me and removed his hat. On the very top of his head was a hole about the size of a twenty-cent piece that extended right through the skin and skull. I could see the unprotected brain pulsating inside his skull. A fly buzzed by and rested on his scalp. I waved it away.

'Tell him he needs to have an operation to close the skin over the hole but we cannot do it at the moment. Our hospital will not be ready for at least a couple of weeks. If he comes back then, I will arrange it.'

'He says the flies are always thick on his head and crawl through the holes in his hat. What can he do?'

'Wait here.' I hurried back to the dressing tent, rummaged through my backpack and returned. I handed him my bright red beanie that I wore in the mornings to warm my head whilst standing in the tray of the utility being driven to work.

'Tell him to keep wearing this beanie. It will keep the flies out.'

Henry translated my instructions and the man nodded, smiled, jumped up, grabbed and shook my hand with gusto and gratitude and left.

Interesting cases John. How did they progress?

Thankfully the patient with the depressed fracture made a full recovery. He regained consciousness that night and went back to his shack later in the day with a full course of antibiotics and his head bandaged like a football. If he had not regained consciousness, I would have had to discharge him to be tended by his family in their shack. We did not have the facilities for long-term care. I'm sure he would have died. That was the reality of the time. He returned the following week to have the sutures removed and was very thankful.

Three weeks later when the Red Cross Surgical Hospital opened in the Kibumba camp I asked the surgical staff to inform me if the second patient presented for treatment. After a month he still had not arrived and I was disappointed. Did he die of infection? Did he go elsewhere? Was he still walking around with a hole in his head?

Two months later I was shopping in a market in Goma. The security situation had eased and we were now allowed to visit specified parts of the town during daylight hours. A few restaurants and bars had even re-opened, mainly to service the ever-growing population of humanitarian workers that now numbered thousands. I was lazily chatting to friends from another NGO amid the market stalls when I spied a bright red beanie bobbing up and down the crowded heads on the far side of the stalls. I abruptly broke conversation and ran in pursuit. He was stunned when I grabbed his arm and pulled off his beanie to check if the hole persisted. The defect was as big as before, exposing his brain. I practically dragged him back to the hospital and arranged for his admission but he smiled the whole journey. He later told the staff that he had been too scared to visit the hospital. The next day we operated and fashioned a skin graft to cover the defect. When he was discharged, I presented him with a new beanie.

These sound like exceptional cases but why do they stand out for you?
Both gave me a shot of professional pride, of high outcomes in a resource-scarce environment. A simple manoeuvre with a red Swiss Army knife and a gift of a red beanie saved two lives.

KIBUMBA REFUGEE CAMP, near GOMA, ZAIRE
(now the DEMOCRATIC REPUBLIC OF CONGO), September 1994
Doctor, Federation of Red Cross and Red Crescent

'Doctor John, they are building another medical clinic down the road,' explained Roland, the head guard who seemed to gather news before it happened.
'Who are they?' I asked.
'I don't know but they're efficient. It's nearly finished already. Their tents are erected, the security fences are built, and even the pathways are gravel. From the smell they have a kitchen cooking food.'
I was delighted. It would take some of the load from our clinic.
'I'll walk down and introduce myself.'

The guard at the gate introduced me to a very slim French woman dressed in black jeans and red tank top.
'I am Nina, the head nurse, Doctor John. You are very welcome. Would you like to look around?' she offered in a heavy French accent and a sense of pride.
'Yes please,' I enthused.
She led me through the ten-metre long tents, sturdy in structure with tubular aluminium frames that interconnected, creating spacious wards and rooms for clinics. Rows of camp beds were waiting for patients. Tables, chairs and cabinets were neatly arranged for nursing stations. Boxes of pre-packed medical kits were stacked, ready for use. One tent was heavily shelved with medications. Behind the tents a lean-to kitchen was cooking hot meals. Multiple latrines had been chiselled into the ground.
I learned that nursing staff would be present day and night to tend the patients. I was impressed... and envious. How could they be so efficient when we were so laborious and slow?
'How do you create all this so quickly?'
'Everything is pre-packed and we have a large team of logisticians to build it for us,' she explained. They had achieved in two days what I still could not provide after four weeks.
As I walked back to the Red Cross clinic, my head was spinning with plans for improvements and expansions of our clinic. We can keep on improving... and we will... but a thought sparked distantly at the back of my mind... *Next time I come away on a humanitarian mission I'm coming with them.*
Who was it? It was Médecins Sans Frontières.

And you did return with Médecins Sans Frontières did you not?
Yes, my next mission was with them.

How did you feel about the Red Cross? Did you feel let down by them?
No. There was nothing wrong with the Red Cross. It was not established to build and run primary health care clinics in emergencies whilst that is the core business of MSF. I was naïve.

The Red Cross is actually two organizations, the International Committee of the Red Cross, or ICRC, and the International Federation of the Red Cross and Red Crescent, or IFRC. The first is a Swiss organization that specialises in humanitarian diplomacy, helping detainees and prisoners, tracing and connecting people in disasters, providing surgical support in disasters and war zones amongst many other roles.

The second is a Federation supporting all the national Red Cross and Red Crescent societies around the world – about 190 of them. They are quite distinct and independent of each other.

In a national disaster, it is the local national Red Cross society who is responsible to organise and coordinate the response, asking help from the Federation if required. In Zaire, in Goma, the disaster was so huge and the local society so dysfunctional that the Federation took the leading role. It was a rare and unusual step and exposed its poor infrastructure and expertise to manage emergency primary health care.

I was to learn that MSF is a unique emergency medical humanitarian organisation and was designed to react quickly and effectively in any humanitarian disaster. It has five operational centres, France, Belgium, Spain, Netherlands and Switzerland facilitating rapid response. Their logistics are legendary with equipment and medications organised into air-transportable kits stored in various locations around the world ready for immediate dispatch to any emergency where their highly trained logistic staff can rapidly and efficiently create a well-equipped base from which their medics can work. I would find out how effective in later missions.

KIBUMBA REFUGEE CAMP, near GOMA, ZAIRE
(now the DEMOCRATIC REPUBLIC OF CONGO), September 1994
Doctor, Federation of Red Cross and Red Crescent

'The Head of Mission wants to see you when you return to the compound, John.'

Stephan, the medical coordinator was visiting the medical clinic in the Kibumba refugee camp. Inwardly he was furious that I had gone over his head, installing all the new equipment that I had underhandedly acquired and building a perimeter fence using refugee labour but he was saying nothing to me. I presumed the Head of Mission (HOM) would deliver the rebuke. I was expecting a reprimand but it was worth it. The clinic was so much more efficient, safer, weatherproof and comfortable. But a niggling doubt hovered. *Had I gone too far? Could I be sent home in disgrace?*

'No problem, thanks Stephan. I'll see him this evening.'

In our pre-departure briefing, it had been emphasised again and again how important it is to remain civil and respectful in all things, to all people, no matter what aggravation may occur. Living and working so intimately under so much tension can quickly lead to petty dispute, accusation and misunderstanding. Once something is said it cannot be taken back and in the tented compound where we lived there was no place to hide. I did not dislike Stephan, I just found him ineffectual. I was relieved his attention mainly focussed on organising the construction and fitting out of the new surgical hospital and he was out of my hair. That evening I called in to the office where the HOM was working late.

'John, I've been told that you have upgraded the clinic without the permission of the medical coordinator. He is not happy.'

36

'Yes, I'm sorry about that Robert but I knew he was busy constructing the new hospital and did not want to bother him on something so trivial and straightforward. The clinic staff was most helpful assisting me and it all happened so quickly and efficiently that I did not ever consider he would mind.'

'I'm told the clinic is working well now.'

'Very much so. Our patient numbers have doubled. Our tents are now weatherproof which seemed urgent considering the rainy season is about to begin and the clinic is now secure with a perimeter fence and effective crowd control.'

'I agree John and am happy it has happened. In fact, I would like you to become the Director of all four of our Primary Health Care Clinics. You can upgrade them all to function as Clinic One. What do you think?'

I was floored. This was unexpected. 'I'd be delighted.' I floated out of his office. I wasn't being sent home. I'd been promoted!

KIBUMBA REFUGEE CAMP, near GOMA, ZAIRE
(now the DEMOCRATIC REPUBLIC OF CONGO), September 1994
Director of Primary Health Care Clinics,
Federation of Red Cross and Red Crescent

'We're going to have to move Clinic Three,' I reported to Robert, the Head of Mission. 'It's been constructed in a slight depression in the rocky landscape and when it rains the site is flooded. Even the consulting tent becomes a lake.'

Since my recent promotion to Director of the Primary Health Care Clinics, I had been reviewing all our four Primary Health Care Clinics. They were spread throughout the six square kilometres of Kibumba camp to give as wide a medical service as possible. Clinics One and Two were on the main bitumen road but Clinics Three and Four were sited deep within the camp and more difficult to access. All the clinics provided similar services but Clinic One was by far the most efficient. Clinic Three needed a dramatic update.

'I'm planning to hire labourers and move it tomorrow. I have permission from UNHCR to use a higher site two hundred metres further down the road. It shouldn't take long. It's a simple operation.'

Little did I realise how wrong I could be.

Robert, with more pressing problems on his plate, waved at me absent-mindedly, seemingly content with my arrangements.

Clinic Three was positioned well off the bitumen road that skirted one border of the camp. Numerous dirt tracks penetrated the camp, weaving between the clusters of tarpaulin-clad shacks that clung together like oysters on a rock, allowing vehicular access. But once the rain began, the tracks would transform into rivers and swamp. Rain was forecast in the next few days. I needed to hurry.

Early the following morning, accompanied by ten labourers in a flatbed truck, I arrived at the clinic. The plan was to empty, dismantle and move the clinic's four tents and equipment to the new site in one day. The clinic's medical staff, having struggled with the earlier flooding, were delighted and eager to help.

The refugees watched us quietly from outside the perimeter fence of green plastic sheeting as the contents of the tents were packed on to the truck, outer guy ropes were untied and the tents collapsed and folded. They were curious. Or so I thought. As I dashed around, organising and coordinating the staff, I failed to sense the mood of the onlookers.

Raymond, one of the gatekeepers, sought me out.

'Doctor John, the people are angry. They think you are taking the clinic away. They want the clinic to stay. The other clinics are too far away.'

'It's OK,' I naively reassured him, 'Tell them we are only moving it down the road to the Y junction.'

In any refugee camp rumours and misinformation move faster than logic and reason and take on a life of their own. By the time I headed back to the gate with Raymond the crowd around the fence was thicker. I could see their scowling faces and sense their anger.

'Can you summon the village elders so I can explain?' I asked Raymond, himself a refugee living next to the clinic.

'Yes, but it's too late.'

Several young men had broken through the back fence, grabbing anything they could lay their hands on before running off. I saw one man jumping back over the broken fence with a chair on his head. Another refugee had a mattress. The nursing staff shouted at them to no effect. It had become a free-for-all. Thinking they had been abandoned, more and more refugees broke down the fence to pillage the stores and equipment. It was chaos. I shouted to all the medical staff to withdraw to the vehicles for safety.

The weather came to my rescue. A storm, charged with heavy biting torrential rain, broke from the overhead clouds adding an angry thunderous roar to scare off the marauders. The crowd around the clinic ran off to shelter. I followed Raymond to find the village elders.

I sat on a broken wooden crate in a hut with six elderly men. Rivulets of water trickled through several holes in the roof. Most ran down the walls but one dripped into an empty vegetable oil can with a regular splash that distracted my eyes like a flickering TV screen. I explained our plans and reasons to move the clinic and reassured them it was not being removed. They nodded their heads but kept their eyes downcast to the floor. I finished.

The oldest of the elders looked up. His eyes were empty and his voice terse. 'Why did you not tell and consult with us about moving the clinic? It is important to us, to our wellbeing. You think you can come and go as you wish.'

I felt embarrassed and inadequate. In my haste, I had not even exchanged full introductions and did not know his name. I humbly apologised for my oversight and offered a lame excuse that the decision was hastily made and there was little time to consult but it sounded hollow, even to me, and would have fallen flat to my audience. I then asked if we could meet regularly to discuss the clinic and their needs and help prevent a recurrence. It was an offhand suggestion, a form of 'damage control' to pacify their disappointment but it proved a huge success. I also asked if they could ask their community to return the stolen goods.

I was amazed. The majority of the stolen furniture was delivered to the new clinic. Many of the smaller goods, blankets and medicines were lost. I could not have expected more.

More significantly, the monthly meetings, which eventuated, were highly productive. A community-liaison person was established who organised education classes covering hygiene, clean water, contraception. A community health worker was hired encouraging anyone sick to attend the clinic and helping us follow up discharged patients. I was able to establish similar programs in all the other clinics.

It sounds you were on a learning curve?

I was grovelling on the bottom of it but it was a start. These lessons proved vital in later missions.

What in particular?

I began to appreciate how important it is to take time to have formal introductions and explanations. Rushing into business is both rude and counterproductive. In Western society introductions are a hurried and informal affair: a name exchange, a handshake and then straight into business.

In West Africa an introduction can take many minutes, wishing well the health and prosperity of themselves, their wives, their children, their extended family, even their livestock, all quietly murmured whilst shaking the other's hand. At every encounter it is the same process and duration. Often both parties are talking at the same time, ploughing through the formalities, shaking hands, nodding heads, and catching eyes.

It encouraged me to slow down and overcome my impatience. I began to appreciate that time is indeed relative. What I might consider important was commonly irrelevant in terms of outcome. Having a clinic operational as quickly as possible, consulting with patients and doling out medicines may be the outcome desired and expected by coordination teams, desks and donors but spending a little time to establish community involvement and approval will return an even better outcome. If there is no local ownership and input for a medical clinic, it will be mistrusted and shunned.

I also learnt that showing due respect of the elders is paramount. In western cultures elders have lost their status. They are often considered techno-dumb, out-of-touch, anti-progress or semi-demented. Their care is out-sourced to community organisations and nursing homes. In African cultures, the elders are still revered, honoured and looked after by family.

Did you find it easy to adapt to these ideas?

I found the interest and involvement of the community refreshing and humbling. They were very appreciative of our efforts and advised me of their modest needs; soap for washing the children, clothes for the frail and elderly, water containers, cooking pots and sanitary pads for the women. These were as important as, if not more important, than providing medicines for the sick.

I can proudly say that from the dregs of a washed-out disaster, emerged my introduction to the power of early and open community communication. It resulted in a simple but effective integrated community medical clinic. I now realise that many of my most compelling lessons only resulted from mistakes and mishaps. Experience is something I accumulate... ten minutes after I need it.

KIBUMBA REFUGEE CAMP, near GOMA, ZAIRE
(now the DEMOCRATIC REPUBLIC OF CONGO), September 1994
Director of Primary Health Care Clinics,
Federation of Red Cross and Red Crescent

A crowd of young men shouting slogans and defiantly thrusting their arms above their heads blocked our road. They walked with a combative and threatening attitude towards us. It was a demonstration of sorts but what about, I had no idea? The camp was seething in discontent and angst. Irregular food rations, rape and pillage, rumour of forced repatriations to Rwanda all added to the fear and insecurity.

Yves, my driver and I were heading to Clinic Four sited even deeper in the camp, along rutted tracks that weaved between the cramped, crowded shacks and outcrops of volcanic rock. Recent rains had transformed them to rivulets, wide puddles and muddy quagmires. It was a slow arduous journey.

'This looks like trouble, Yves. Can you turn around and let's get out of here?'

'There's nowhere to turn Doctor John and too many people behind to reverse quickly.'

'Pull to the side and see if they will pass? Check all the doors are locked.' I grabbed my radio and called base to let them know what was happening and our location. I was fully aware no one could help us.

A press of young male bodies soon surrounded the car. Many wore beanies resplendent in vivid colours that contrasted with their plain dun slacks and open neck shirts. The roof resonated with the pound of angry fists. Faces, pushed against the windows, smiled menacing grins. Two men jumped on to the bonnet and stomped. The car started to rock, first gently then ferociously, the tyres bouncing in the air. I feared we might soon be overturned.

'Stay in the car,' I advised Yves. I tightened my seatbelt... 'unless there is fire,' I loosened my seat belt. My pulse was racing and a sense of dread filled me. *Were we to be the scapegoats of the mob?*

I noticed one particular face pushed on to the windscreen staring at me. Even with its squashed nose and cheekbones, I recognised the young sick man whom I had dosed with the course of ciprofloxacin weeks earlier. He smiled a squashed smile and pushed himself off the car. He began shouting out to all the men around the car and the car stilled and fell back on to its wheels.

'What's he shouting?' I asked Yves.

'He says you are the doctor who saved his life and are a good man. No one must hurt you. I think he is a leader.'

The crowd passed. His face again appeared at a side window. He grinned, gave a thumbs-up and disappeared. I never saw him again. Shaken but reassured we were safe, we continued on to the clinic.

Did you fear you or Yves might be harmed or killed?
Momentarily yes, I was very scared... but my mind was suddenly intrigued by how life can twist and turn about, for this small, unexpected incident suddenly changed my outlook.

I had been feeling despondent and frustrated at how slow my improvements to the clinics had been progressing. My blunder of moving the clinic weighed heavily. I was feeling a fraud. Life was becoming difficult and a drudge.

After this episode my mood instantly lifted. When the car settled back on its suspension and the crowd passed harmlessly by, my spirit bounced and soared, lifting as light as air with a whoosh of exhilaration. The previous problems that had been weighing on me spontaneously evaporated. I intuitively knew that everything would now work out.

Maybe this was my karma, a reward for my previous good deed to the man who saved us. I'd like to think that but admit it is fanciful. Maybe it was the relief of escaping danger?

Maybe we all need a little life-threatening moment to reinvigorate us.

KIBUMBA REFUGEE CAMP, near GOMA, ZAIRE
(now the DEMOCRATIC REPUBLIC OF CONGO), September 1994
Director of Primary Health Care Clinics,
Federation of Red Cross and Red Crescent

It was the dead of the night. I was dragged out of a deep, deep sleep by a low-pitched, thunderous rumbling that echoed all around. The ground seemed to be shaking and shuddering. The first thought that slithered from my groggy brain... *What's happening, an earthquake?* Quickly followed by *Where am I?* and finally, *Oh shit!* as I orientated to being in Goma and the warnings about the volcano flashed into my consciousness.

Goma is situated in the shadow of Nyiragongo, an active volcano that belched ash and sulphuric gases all day and radiated a fiery red glow into the blackness of the sky all night. It is constantly active and over the past hundred years had erupted thirty-four times. The UNHCR, in overall charge of this humanitarian mission, had imported Japanese volcanologists to monitor its activity. Sensors had been strategically placed around the volcano's rim for continual recording.

No warnings of imminent eruption had been announced but information leaflets had been circulated. They warned that a sudden eruption was unlikely but not impossible. They also warned that the lava from this volcano had extremely low silica content making it unusually runny and it could flow at speeds of a hundred kilometres an hour. Being less than twenty kilometres distant I had calculated that if the lava did flow, I would have twelve minutes to escape.

But escape to where? The leaflet failed to suggest action if there was an eruption. Where would the lava flow? Downwards of course, but to which side of the mountain? How wide would the rivers of lava be? Could they flow even faster? These questions were all unanswered. I had considered sprinting to Lake Kivu, a few hundred metres from our compound, diving in and swimming far out of reach of any red-hot molten lava flow... but the leaflet had also mentioned how the cooling lava would release poisonous gases that, being heavier than air, would spread unseen over the water's surface and suffocate anyone on the water. It was a conundrum. Would I be cremated in red-hot lava or drown, asphyxiated by poisonous gas?

In my sleep-doused state, still groggy and disorientated I stood unsteadily outside my tent in my pyjamas looking at the red sky, trying to make sense of the scene. No one else was moving. Should I scream out a warning? Was I the only one aware of the danger? My mind wavered between inaction and overreaction. I could not see a middle ground.

Whilst my resolve wavered, another cacophony of thunderous rumbling shuddering enveloped me, reverberating through my chest. Sound pressure waves hit like a huge bass speaker blasting out a beat. My heart was pounding, my chest was panting and sweat lingered on my brow. I stood transfixed, confused, petrified, scanning the volcano for signs of danger. But there was no molten lava belching into the air or streaming down the slopes. No rocks were being hurled high into the heavens to cascade all around me. There were no geysers of gas breaking or belching from the earth beside me. The thunderous rumblings echoed and I began to be suspicious... *Could the rumblings indeed be thunderous? Could this be... thunder?* ...but there was no rain, no wind, no lightning.

Igor, my Russian neighbour wandered past.

'Impressive thunder, hey John!' He smiled at my perplexed look and continued towards the latrine.

My world crashed down. I was immediately deflated and embarrassed by my indecision and near-panic reaction. Any self-image of being 'cool and collected' under pressure had just been publicly shattered.

'Just admiring the volcano,' I squirmed.

My fears eased, my bowels squeezed and I wandered after Igor to the latrine.

Why were you embarrassed John?
It's ironic. My friends all think I'm brave yet the thing that scared me the most during my whole mission was a thunderstorm.

Why is that so ironic?
Disease and death, pestilence and infestation, guns and machetes, robbery and rape have surrounded me yet the threat of these dangers did not greatly scare me. I fully acknowledged and respected the danger and didn't take stupid risks. To a point they can be controlled. It's all part of the adventure. If I'm not afraid, then I am not brave. I feel other people transfer their own fears on to me and tell me I'm brave. If I deny it, they think I'm being modest. If I accept their accolade, I feel a fraud. The possible volcanic eruption scared me because it was an unknown and uncontrollable force.

But isn't bravery doing things that are dangerous? And surely having guns pointed at you is dangerous?
Climbing a mountain is dangerous but if the climber isn't afraid of heights, they are not brave, just skilled. I think they are brave for I'm scared of heights and the thought of hanging off a vertical face is terrifying. The climber is just exhilarated.

Isn't part of their exhilaration the fact they are defying death?
No, I don't agree. If they thought they would die, they wouldn't be there. They know falling is a possibility... but not for them... it's a form of denial. They have assessed all the risks, minimised them with equipment, training and rigid procedures. It is clinical. There is excitement at achieving the climb, defying the odds and returning safely, but fear only happens when things go wrong. If nothing goes wrong, there's no fear, no bravery.

It sounds like you are a little defensive and analytical about being brave? Does being brave make you uncomfortable?
Maybe. I feel a fraud, undeserving of the honour. To me, bravery is deliberately undertaking an activity despite feeling a great fear. The greatest is probably an action that has a high possibility of injury or death. The soldiers in the First World War going over the top of the trenches into a hail of enemy fire and near certain death, the Anzacs storming the beaches on the Gallipoli peninsular and being shot to pieces and the pilots in the Battle of Britain flying sortie after sortie knowing they will probably be shot out of the sky were all amazingly brave.

But of course, bravery is not only a military phenomenon. In a less dramatic scale and one I encounter in my workplace is the patient who endures a medical treatment fearful of the unknown outcome, the intrinsic pain and possible complication without complaint. They are brave. Less clinical, anyone who actively takes on an activity out of their comfort zone despite their fear of failure, ridicule or isolation is also brave.

My missions are mere jaunts into remote, troubled regions for my personal adventure with little risk of death. That is not brave. It is the national staff that I leave behind who are in far greater jeopardy. They live in constant fear; of losing their jobs and having no income, of being beaten, robbed, and intimidated by militia or of being killed. I always have the luxury of returning home whenever I wish. They must remain... so yes, I do feel undeserving.

When my fear is then exposed by a mere thunderstorm, I feel even more a fraud. That's ironic!

BUKAVU, ZAIRE
(now the DEMOCRATIC REPUBLIC OF CONGO), October 1994
Director of Primary Health Care Clinics,
Federation of Red Cross and Red Crescent

From the moment I arrived, I was unwelcome.
'Why have they sent you John? We can manage the clinic,' complained Annette, a tall French nurse with a ponytail pulling her hair tightly back to accentuate a narrow face with firm thin lips. Michelle and Marie, two Belgian nurses stood beside her, eyeing me with suspicion. 'Yes, why 'ave you come?' snarled Marie with a heavy accent.

It had started the previous day. I had been summoned by Abdul, the new Egyptian Head of Mission, 'John, your clinics in Goma are running well. We have a clinic in the Nyariragamwe refugee camp near Bukavu, run by the Belgian Red Cross that is not performing well. They see very few patients and the camp management is complaining. The Belgian doctor is leaving this week and the Federation of the Red Cross and Crescent is taking over responsibility for the clinic. I would like you to go and rebuild it. Do you mind?' He looked at me over his horn-rimmed glasses with some pleading in his eyes. His wavy brown hair and thick moustache softened his chubby face. He smiled. 'Bukavu is a lovely town at the other end of Lake Kivu. The Belgian delegation is living in a lakeside hotel... with showers... a restaurant... a well-stocked bar. You are well qualified and the best person to do this.'

He knew how to massage my ego. He also knew I had been living in a tent for two months, showering outside, under a trickle of tepid water, eating plain and repetitive food and too tired to go out to the few bars emerging in the town. I needed no more convincing.

'When do I leave?'

'Tomorrow. I've arranged for the Red Cross plane from Nairobi to divert and it will take you there on its return leg.'

He had been that confident!

I stared at Annette. I was taken aback by their aggression. 'I think the Red Cross is trying to standardise the clinics. We have four similar clinics in the Kibumba refugee camp,' I stammered, struggling to be convincing and diplomatic, not my strongest talent. I could hardly say, 'Your clinic here is complete crap, inefficient and poorly run and I've been sent to put it right', but I wanted to.

And I might as well have well said it for I was immediately isolated and ignored. Abdul had forgotten to mention it was a French-speaking mission. My

French is rudimentary at best and I could not readily follow conversations, especially when rapidly spoken. Standing in the bar or sitting in the restaurant I would try to look relaxed whilst everyone talked around me in French. Michel, a short, scowl-faced mechanic in charge of the fleet of cars took great delight in embarrassing me by talking simplistic French in a heavy Marseilles accent making it impossible to understand even a word.

'Your French is no good eh John? Why did you come eh?'

Marcel, the air operations delegate, refused to even talk to me.

Abdul had also forgotten to mention that the Nyariragamwe refugee camp was twenty five kilometres from Bukavu along a pot holed, corrugated dirt road that after any rain transformed into a muddy, treacherously slippery quagmire sided by steep hills prone to landslides, precipitous edges prone to subsidence and even an ancient, wooden bridge, that threatened to collapse into the swirling waters of the river below. The hour's journey could easily double.

'We'll have to take down those four tents and replace them with two larger tents, make the compound smaller and more compact and then build a surrounding fence,' I concluded to myself. I was alone. On the first day, I had surveyed the clinic, paced it out and talked to the local national staff. It was obvious to me that the existing clinic's layout was haphazard and totally inefficient. A cholera isolation ward, built at one end of the clinic for an earlier epidemic was a useful structure to preserve. Beside it was a fully functioning pharmacy. The last job I needed was to move it. But the tents used for consultations, dressings, minor surgery and storage were too far apart, too small and in poor condition.

I expected to get resistance to my plans and was not disappointed.

Annette complained. 'Where will we see patients during the move?'

Michelle added. 'The clinic needs to be large to protect from cross-infection.'

Marie joined in. 'The smoke from the kitchen fire will make us cough.'

Rather than try to convert an unconvertible force I spent the next two days finding the equipment I needed in the local warehouses and arranging for its transport to the camp. At least I now had official authority to order and acquire whatever I needed. Michel, in charge of the vehicles, was predictably uncooperative.

'I cannot hire a truck until next week, John. Do you think this is Australia, eh?'

'I've already found a truck and have hired it for you. It will pick the material up in the morning.'

'But you cannot do that, it is my job.'

'Then do it,' I snapped.

'I can do this on my own but it will be much sturdier and quicker with your help,' I was trying to convince Martia, the logistics coordinator, to help me move the tents. Maybe my diplomatic powers were improving because, although at first reluctant, when she saw my hand-drawn plans and appreciated my determination, she agreed to help. It was the catalyst I needed. Next day she accompanied me to the camp and hired many refugee workers to help.

It was, fortunately, a warm sunny day. Giving very short notice to the French nursing staff... well... maybe... none at all... we moved the beds, tables and chairs out of the tents to beneath a row of leafy trees where outpatients could be consulted in the speckled shade and in-patients could bask in the filtered sun's rays.

The smaller existing tents were quickly dismantled and replaced by two large tents, like mini marquees, that we erected close together near the main entrance. I had acquired plastic sheeting to create partitions within the tents giving patient privacy. Around the perimeter of the clinic teams of labourers dug postholes, standing the uprights and unrolling more plastic sheeting to completely fence off the clinic. By sunset, the clinic was finished. All the furniture and patients had been transferred back into the tents. The rebuild was completed in a day.

That night at the hotel I was totally ignored. Martia smiled at me but kept her distance for I was branded and taboo. I had trodden on too many toes, bruised too many egos, offended too many staff... but I did not care. The clinic was just as I had planned and I knew it would work. I had three more weeks left in Bukavu to train and upskill the national doctors with our medical protocols and I knew they were keen and enthusiastic. I went to bed early and happy.

It sounds like it was a successful mission, John?
It was and I'm proud of what I achieved but it was a difficult time and I struggled to cope.

In what way?
I was terribly lonely. I had no idea how isolated and alone one can feel when surrounded by people who ignore and even deride you. I had no one to talk to, never mind confide in. I had no outlet of support. There was no mail, telephone or Internet. Being away from Goma I received no mail. I read and reread my letters from home but that was all the comfort I could muster. I could not even find seclusion in my own room for I was sharing with two others.

The loneliness and isolation soon began to sap my energy and resolve.

How did you cope?
I forced myself into a routine to fill my day; work, exercise, reading, meditation. In my meditations, I repeated my mantra, *This too shall pass.* It was a useful tool to reassure me that my loneliness was temporary. I could then concentrate on getting through the next day. Sometimes I cried myself to sleep, my proven pressure relief valve. I survived. It did indeed pass... but it was a bloody long month.

NYARIRAGAMWE REFUGEE CAMP, near BUKAVU, ZAIRE
(NOW THE DEMOCRATIC REPUBLIC OF CONGO), **October 1994**
Director of Primary Health Care Clinics,
Federation of Red Cross and Red Crescent

'You are looking sad, Doctor Nukunda?' We were sitting at his desk in the medical clinic in Nyariragamwe refugee camp discussing the day's patients. I was spending my days with the national doctors reviewing cases, revising medical protocols, and up-skilling procedures.

The clinic was now housed in a mini marquee tent, four metres wide and ten metres long, supported by two central poles that peaked the canvas like a circus tent. Three doctor's cubicles on one side were partitioned with a tarpaulin for privacy but, being open at the top, air could circulate. Open flaps at either end of the tent allowed the breeze to blow through and give relief against the searing heat outside. The other side of the tent acted as a dressing and emergency area.

'It is nothing Doctor John. Thank you for asking.'

'But you always seem sad. Is there something I can help with?' I usually avoided this situation. Everyone in a refugee camp has a 'sad story' and needs help but Doctor Nukunda was an exceptionally talented and dedicated doctor who worked longer hours than necessary and would be the principle doctor once I had departed back to Goma in another two weeks. I needed him.

He hesitated but sensed my genuine concern. 'It is my children Doctor John.'

'What's wrong? Are they sick?'

'I don't know where they are. I don't know if they are alive.'

'Aren't they with your wife?'

'My wife is dead. The Interahamwe murdered her. They came to our village looking for me, to kill me as a Tutsi sympathiser because I treated them in my clinic but I was away. She worked as my nurse so they killed her. My brother witnessed it. Then they went to my home but my brother had to flee and does not know what happened. I think they may all have been killed.'

I was stunned. I had been working with him for two weeks and had no idea he had such a story.

'Who was looking after them? How many children do you have?'

'My sister was our housekeeper. She cared for my three children whilst we worked.'

'How old are they?'

'The oldest is eight and the youngest is four.'

'Have you registered them with the Red Cross? They operate a tracing system in all the camps and towns.'

'No. I have been working full time in the camp and the Red Cross have not come here. Their nearest office is in Bukavu.'

'Write down all their names and birthdays and I'll call into their office tomorrow. It is near where I am staying.' It was the least I could do.

Arriving back at my accommodation, a small hotel near the lakeside, I walked back to the Red Cross office. A light was still shining in the window and I knocked on the door.

'We are closed. Come back tomorrow,' a female French accent boomed.

'I cannot. I work at Nyariragamwe camp and leave before you open.'

The door opened and a middle-aged female face, grey-streaked hair and flared black glasses, stared at me. 'Come in then. How can I help?'

Her name was Marlene and her voice softened as I explained the circumstances.

'There are thirty camps in this area. I haven't had time to get to them all yet, especially Nyariragamwe. It's one of the most distant. Fill in these forms and I'll send it tonight. I have a batch to process. If I hear anything, I'll contact you.'

I thanked her and headed back to dinner.

Next day Doctor Nukunda was delighted and all day offered continual and profuse thanks. His smile and more relaxed attitude were thanks enough.

'We'll have to wait and see.' I did not want to dash his hopes but I didn't want his expectations to be unreal. His kids could well be dead.

I was about to leave Bukavu in two days' time and return to Goma. My task of setting up the clinic and updating the doctors was complete. I phoned Marlene to tell her of my departure and to contact the Head of Mission in Bukavu if any news arrived.

'I have news for you. A message arrived last night. I was about to call you.'

I waited for his patient to leave the cubicle before I entered and sat at his desk.

'I've heard from the Red Cross,'

'What did you hear?' His body tensed as he examined my face for clues.

Unable to contain my joy I bumbled... 'All your kids and sister are safe in a refugee camp in Burundi.'

He jumped up, pulled me to my feet and hugged me. Tears were streaming down both of our faces. We held hands and danced in a circle, whooping and laughing uncontrollably.

The nurses and doctors in the other cubicles and dressing area all came and watched, wondering what had ignited this show of joy.

How did that feel for you?

Obviously, I was so happy for him. And it gave me a great emotional boost that I was instrumental in helping him. It certainly offset much of the sadness of the disease and death that surrounded me each day, at least for a moment.

But my greatest feeling was of humility. That he could so silently grieve for his wife, suffer such uncertainty for his children and sister and still work so effectively as a caring and dedicated doctor was awesome. If my wife had been murdered, my children missing and I had to flee my country, live in a refugee camp and work daily in a clinic, I wonder what mental state I would exhibit? And here I was feeling sorry for myself because no one spoke to me and I felt lonely.

When I later asked him how he coped he confided he had little choice. He was living with his brother and his family in the camp. He was the only wage earner and they depended on him for money. Working in the clinic was a distraction from the emotional pain and boredom of refugee life and he was grateful for the opportunity. He had planned to return to Rwanda at the earliest chance to search for his family but had no idea when that might be. He had not appreciated that the Red Cross Service was so effective. He thought it was just a political ploy... 'just like the UN'.

Before I left Bukavu I drove him to the Red Cross office to fill in forms to request that his family be transferred to Nyariragamwe. After I left, we lost contact. I never heard if it happened.

Nyariragamwe Refugee Camp, near Bukavu, Zaire
(now the Democratic Republic of Congo), October 1994
**Director of Primary Health Care Clinics,
Federation of Red Cross and Red Crescent**

'Eh John, the Nyariragamwe camp is having a festival on Saturday. We have been invited by the camp committee to attend as 'honoured guests'. There will be traditional food, dancing and sports. Are you interested in coming?'

Annette, the head nurse, was standing in the clinic reading from a scroll of paper that had just been hand-delivered. Her heavy French accent made the invite both appealing and amusing. I was even more amused that she was being friendly to me. I had to control my cynicism and wonder what was behind it. I had been unwelcomed ever since I had arrived in Bukavu to reconstruct the medical clinic three weeks earlier. She rarely made conversation. Now she was being effusively friendly. Maybe the tide was turning?

'Too right. I would love to see some local culture. What's the festival about? Are you attending?'

'The camp committee wants to bring normality and identity back into their lives, a symbol of recovery from the turmoil. The UNHCR has given funding. It will be fun. Yes, I am going too. We can come out in a car together.'

Now I was really suspicious.

We arrived early. Unlike the refugee camps around Goma, the Nyariragamwe camp was planned and organised for it had been built before the refugees arrived. Orderly rows of white tents were set across a slight incline with ample banks of pit latrines and water points sited at the ends of alternate rows. At the bottom of the hill, a large open field had been transformed into the festival site.

Our white skins and grimy-white MSF T-shirts announced our arrival and we were eagerly met by one of the camp committee members, Beatrice, who looked over eighty years old with her greying, thinning hair, wrinkled face and toothless mouth but I knew her to be only fifty. Her brightly patterned dress of green, yellow and blue waves and her effusive gummy smile brought a sparkle to our welcome. She gave me a hug. I had excised a skin tumour from her leg two weeks earlier and she thought I was her saviour.

Annette looked at me with surprise and smiled, then sidled up next to me, linking her arm through mine. I was startled by her closeness. After weeks of adversity I was confused but made no protest. Beatrice led us to the elevated VIP platform shaded from the sun with a large tarpaulin. The poles had green-leaved creepers and multi-coloured streamers wound around. Posies of flowers adorned the tables. It overlooked a wide grassy open area that was already surrounded by a throng of refugees sitting on the grass. Many of the medical clinic's staff was among the crowd. Annette waved happily to them, smiling and laughing. I wondered if she was high on drugs but her pupils were normal and there was no smell of alcohol.

About ten men were cutting the grass, walking slowly in a line, slightly bent at the waist, their double-edged curved machetes swinging in unison, side to side, slicing the grass low to the ground. It looked to be an accident waiting to happen but somehow everyone kept his exact distance and no one was decapitated. I wondered if this is why I was invited.

'We are very happy to see you, Doctor John. Come and sit.' Manuel, the camp leader welcomed us. I had met with him several times asking advice about the clinic. He had been helpful and supportive. Annette was not directly addressed. It was assumed she was my partner and would follow. 'This is Annette, our head nurse,' I added. I did not want to be rude but thought it important for her to be recognised. I would be leaving soon. Annette was here for a few more months.

Manuel was a little taken aback but recovered, 'we are happy you could attend too Annette.' He showed us to our seats at one end of the front row. Annette smiled at me, squeezed my arm and whispered, 'Thanks, John.' It was a good time to mend fences.

A solid high-backed seat, each arm carved like a lion's paw, sat in the centre of the row. 'Who's the honoured guest?' I asked Marcel, indicating the chair.

'That is the throne for the Mwami or King of South Kivu. The camp committee has invited him so our people can thank him for his people's generosity and hospitality to allow our camp to be sited here. I was intrigued by the politics. Was this whole festival in his honour?

We were offered a drink, a choice of water, fruit juice, Cola or Fanta. I sipped my water and watched as the field and platform quickly filled with people. The decibels rose with excitement, chatter and laughter, shrieking children and crying babies. Everyone was here.

A shiny white saloon car, complete with a small flag flying from a wing mirror, pulled on to the grass and sped to the front of the platform. The king had arrived. He was younger than I had imagined a king should be, about mid-thirties, with neatly trimmed short brown hair, simply dressed in casual slacks, buttoned white shirt and patent leather black shoes. His wife was elegantly dressed in a brightly patterned mushanana, a wrapped skirt, bunched at the hips with a sash draped over the shoulders, all worn over a tank top. His secretary, a short bespectacled man clutching a briefcase, trailed them.

After prolonged handshakes with the camp committee members, everyone was seated and the music and dancing began. The initial dances were performed by the schoolchildren, the boys in loincloths with creepers draped around their necks, the girls in plain mushanana, headbands and necklaces. A group of drummers, great swathes of straw-coloured hair sprouting from their heads, emerged from the crowd to accompany them. The rhythm and beat of the drums and dancing entranced me and time flew. The crowd, now all standing and swaying with the music, were enthralled; all clapped and many danced on the side-lines.

After an hour an intermission allowed refreshments to emerge. The sun was high, the sky was clear except for one cumulus cloud about five kilometres distant. I did not notice it... till later.

'The adults are going to dance the amarabe dance,' Annette whispered in my ear. 'It is the most famous traditional dance.' A troupe of adult dancers resplendent in blue and white costume ran out to the centre of the field amid great cheers from the audience. Nine men beat the drums and the dancing commenced. It still is a bit of a blur for I was again totally immersed in the music when a loud thunderous roar splintered the air and a bolt of lightning crashed down striking three men standing on the perimeter of the field, about fifty metres to the side of the platform. Their bodies were hurled into the air and thrown far apart. An eerie silence turned into screams as panic spread and people ran in all directions.

'Let's go and see,' I suggested to Annette. She nodded.

We ran over to the men. The first was unmoving, staring into the sky, his face a rigid contorted mask. Twenty metres past him the second man was lying unconscious but breathing. Nearby the third man was moaning and writhing in pain.

'I'll look after the unconscious one. Can you check the first case? He looks dead. The 'moaner' can wait.' I checked the man's airway, breathing and pulse and felt his neck and back for signs of injury. All seemed clear so I rolled him into a coma position. Annette gave me a 'thumbs down' for the first case and moved over to assess the third man who was still moaning. I needed to transfer them all to the emergency area of the medical clinic. There was no local referral hospital. They would recover or die with our limited medical service.

Three makeshift stretchers were fashioned from trestle tables and the patients were quickly carried to the clinic. I formally declared one dead and his body was moved to one of the cubicles until the family could claim it for a quick burial. I could see Annette talking to the family outside the entrance of the tent.

I handed the other two patients over to Doctor Nadir, the national doctor on call for the clinic. He was competent and we discussed ongoing treatment. The unconscious patient was rapidly developing heart failure and despite oxygen and intravenous medications was deteriorating. The third man was complaining of deafness but looked as if he would live. When I had done all I could, I returned to the festival. The dancing had not restarted but the feasting was in full swing.

The king approached me and enquired about the patients. I gave a short account. He was very shaken. 'How could lightning strike from a clear sky?' I did not know and could give no explanation.

'It is good you were here, Doctor John. The victims were moved quickly and the festival could continue. It could have been a disaster.'

'It was a disaster,' I undiplomatically reminded him. 'One man dead and probably two.'

'Oh, I am sorry Doctor John, you are right. Please forgive my insensitivity. I meant that it was good the festival continued, even if subdued. The people need some fun, not more despair.'

Annette returned by my side and slipped her arm through mine. 'The second man died. He fitted just after you left and arrested. There was nothing more to do. The third man is getting better. That was well handled, John. You are a good doctor.'

I was astounded by her compliment and certainly did not feel competent. I had done nothing to deserve praise. 'Thanks. I saw you with the dead man's family. How are they?'

'Devastated. They are worried it was God punishing him. I don't know what he might have done.'

'It was certainly an "Act of God" by insurance definitions. Let's eat. I'm famished.' She squeezed my arm again and followed.

The king sought us out in the crowd with two cans of beer. 'Have a drink. You deserve it.' We opened the cans and he raised his can for a toast, 'To peace and prosperity,' he royally commanded, the first of many.

Later that evening Annette and I were being driven back to Bukavu. 'What a bizarre day,' she commented. 'Lightning strikes and royal toasts,' she slurred. We had both had a few beers.

'Indeed,' I replied, 'I hope the lightning wasn't aimed at me and they missed.'

'Probably they were pissed too,' she giggled... and snuggled up to me.

'Thanks for a good day Doctor John. I am sorry your stay has not been a happy one but you have changed the clinic so well. It is lovely to work there now and the staff is so happy. I am sorry we made it difficult for you,' she snuggled closer.

I was stunned by her apology and wondered if it was the beer talking.

'But before you get too cocky Doctor John, just know I am gay. Today I needed to be publicly seen with you to avert suspicion and let the locals know I am not available. You are a powerful figure so they will not dare touch me now. I hope you don't mind.'

I just tilted my head, pouted my lips and shrugged; as she had said, 'a bizarre day'.

BUKAVU, ZAIRE
(NOW THE DEMOCRATIC REPUBLIC OF CONGO), November 1994
Director of Primary Health Care Clinics,
Federation of Red Cross and Red Crescent

'Doctor John, there is a meeting before dinner at the hotel. You need to be there.' Annette informed me as we arrived back from the clinic.

'But I'm leaving tomorrow. My job is finished. I don't have anything to meet about.'

Annette shrugged, 'Maybe but I think you should be there. You may be surprised.'

I was intrigued. I had planned to spend my last evening alone, to sit by the lakeside with some sandwiches and a beer and read my book, soothed by the gentle lapping of the waves on the rocks and watch the sun settle beneath the watery horizon. I had come to enjoy my own company and socialised very little with the rest of the team. It was the most peaceful strategy I had found to minimise the animosity of the other expatriates.

I arrived in the dining room just before dinner to find everyone present. To my amazement, Pablo, the Head of Mission in Bukavu met me, shook my hand, handed me a glass of white wine and tapped a glass to command everyone's attention.

'Today is Doctor John's final day with us. He is flying back to Goma tomorrow. I wish to thank him for his excellent work in renovating the clinic in Nyariragamwe camp which is now working most efficiently.'

Everyone clapped and even a half-hearted cheer broke out. He proposed a toast to my safe journey and success for the rest of my mission.

I was floored. For four weeks he had practically ignored me and had remained aloof and distant to all the conflict I had encountered. I suspected this was Belgian diplomacy at its best. Rather than allow me to leave disgruntled, I could be sweetened and appeased with some compliments, to report well of the mission back in Goma.

Everyone raised their glasses and drank deeply. Maybe they were just glad to see the back of me?

What did you report back to the Federation on your return to Goma?
I decided to leave all the conflict and discontent behind me. I kept my reports factual with no mention of my treatment. It was over. I had completed all that I had intended. I would not return. I just wanted to look forward. I was reminded of the mantra, *This too will pass*. Well, it had passed.

Do you ever resent how you were treated?
No... it was the past and a bit of me is proud to have achieved what I did despite the hostile environment. It was a useful lesson for me... *when the going is tough... the not-so-tough can still forge on, head down, eyes focused and do what has to be done.*

Moreover, holding resentments and animosities is a bit like taking poison and expecting someone else to die. Those who ignored and isolated me will probably have forgotten all about me or crack the odd joke about that 'stuck-up' English doctor who intruded and invaded their territory. Only I will suffer. It is a lesson that has often helped me move forward without bitterness and discontent jaundicing the future.

If only I could rid myself of some of the other traumas so easily.

KIBUMBA REFUGEE CAMP, near GOMA, ZAIRE
(now the DEMOCRATIC REPUBLIC OF CONGO), November 1994
Director of Primary Health Care Clinics,
Federation of Red Cross and Red Crescent

'You're a pain in the arse John. Why not piss off and leave us alone.'

Sally, the head nurse of Clinic Four challenged me head on. Her eyes were narrowed and face determined. 'We can manage the clinic quite happily without you. In fact, it was better when you were away. Your interfering and unsolicited advice is unwanted. Go back to Bukavu.'

Sally was a Kiwi and did not mince her words. She was newly arrived and had recently taken over charge of the clinic.

'I am changing and improving the clinic's layout. If I need your help, I'll ask for it. Please go away,' she persisted.

I had arrived at the clinic to observe the new arrangement and had made some suggestions. They obviously were unwelcomed and taken critically. It had not been my intent.

I was confused. I was obviously no longer welcome. I had just returned from Bukavu. Before I had left Goma, I had been happily accepted as the director of the medical clinics. Or so I thought?

I left and drove back to Goma.

'John, the emergency is over. There is no urgency anymore. There's no need for drastic and decisive decisions. There is no rush to do everything straight away. The expatriate staff, especially the nurses want to be part of the decision-making. They need to feel consulted and empowered. They are professionals and very capable. You're being dominant, bossy and overbearing. Back off and let them come to you if they need help... which they don't seem to. Look at it that you have done such a good job that you are no longer needed.'

No one was being diplomatic to me, especially the new medical coordinator, Julius, a straight-talking Swiss with mousey flaky hair and bushy eyebrows, a piercing gaze and firm mouth.

'John, you're tired and threatening burn out. You've been working non-stop under immense pressure for three months. You did a magnificent job in Bukavu, which needed a shake-up, but the clinics here are working well. There is no cause to interfere. The nurses need some autonomy. You're due for five days R&R leave in Nairobi. Go and rest. We can talk about your role next week.'

It felt like a dismissal and it probably was. I left and headed back to my house. I had at long last moved out of a tent into a comfortable spacious house in the town that I shared with two other expatriates. I had my own room, a shower that flooded hot water and a veranda shaded by lush vegetation. It was luxury... but I was unable to settle, like a tiger pacing a cage... feeling abandoned and alone.

It sounds like that wasn't easy for you John to feel abandoned and alone. So, what did you do?

I flew out the following day and took my R&R in Kenya. But despite all the luxury of a tourist hotel and a game park, I could not relax or rest. I was irritable, slept poorly and felt impotent.

I feared I had lost my relevance and had become supernumerary. I was worried I was not needed and my contract would be terminated. I had been living on adrenaline for so long the thought of heading home to my more mundane general practice was frightening.

Were you tired and burnt out like Julius suggested?
Well... yes and no... I was certainly exhausted and had lost weight with the constant activity and nervous energy but I still felt exhilarated and enthusiastic to take on new challenges. I had gained amazing experience. It was as if I had already completed two missions and I was raring to go again. There were just no new challenges.

And?
And I needed them... and if I stopped, I might have to reflect on what I had been through... which was enormous... and process some of the emotion I had repressed and... god, I sound like a psychology textbook...

John, our psyche has many layers... like an onion... you're just peeling away the first layer.
Onions make you cry.

Precisely. Tell me more of the mission.

NAIROBI, KENYA
November 1994
Director of Primary Health Care Clinics,
Federation of Red Cross and Red Crescent

'Hey John, are you flying back to Goma today?'
   'Too right Bernard. I'm on the Red Cross plane at eleven o'clock. Why do you ask?'
   'Could you carry a package for me?'
   'Sure thing. What's in it?'
   'You don't want to know.'
   Bernard was the financial controller for the mission in Goma. He was based in Nairobi, Kenya, the logistical base for the mission in Zaire. I could guess what was in the package but wanted confirmation. I was returning to Goma after my R&R leave in Kenya, well-earned after three months in the field. I had just spent two days at Treetops, a luxury hotel beside a game park where the animals could be viewed from the lounge. I had soaked in the bath, slept in crisp cotton sheets and eaten gourmet food. After suffering a lumpy mattress and stringy goat stews for weeks on end it had been sheer luxury.
   'I do want to know what I'm carrying, especially across an international border.'
   He pointed to a package on his desk, a twenty centimetre-sided cube, wrapped in brown paper and heavily bound with white tape emblazoned with Red Crosses and Crescents.
   'It's money.'
   'How much?'
   'Quarter of a million American dollars.'
   I gasped.

Bernard explained. 'There is no banking system operational in Goma. It is a complete cash economy. We need cash... lots of it. How do you think we've been paying the bills?'

'OK,' I agreed.

Bernard drew out a paper from a file and slipped it on to the desk in front of me.

'Can you sign this?'

'What is it?'

'A form to take responsibility for the money.'

'So, what happens if I lose it?'

'Then you have to refund it.'

'No way Bernard, find some other sucker.'

'Well I suppose we can bypass the formalities,' he conceded. 'Come and pick it up when the airport bus arrives.'

'Do you have a bag for it? I can't fit it into my rucksack.'

'I'll find one.'

I returned an hour later. The money was now contained in a bright pink paper bag with string handles and emblazoned with the name and logo of a local fashion store.

'Couldn't you have found me something more conspicuous?' I teased.

'It will look as if you have just bought a last-minute present.'

Departure procedure from Nairobi airport on the Red Cross plane involved a mere cursory glance at our passports, all the paperwork having been completed by the Red Cross air operation's staff. I sauntered on to the plane carrying the package as hand luggage and stowed it at my feet. I did not want to lose sight of it.

Goma airport usually had relaxed arrival procedures. The airport had become one of the busiest in Africa with planes of equipment and food arriving 24/7 importing supplies for all the one hundred and twenty agencies that were now operating in the region. Airport fees, warehouse rentals and transport costs had escalated to extortionate levels but immigration, custom and security were normally slack. Today something had changed and there was a queue for a customs baggage inspection. I looked at my fellow travellers for answers but they had no idea what I was carrying. My heart was racing. I could feel panic start to rise in my throat. What would happen if they found the money? Confiscation? Imprisonment? What would the Head of Mission say?

As I neared my turn for inspection an idea welled up. Inspiration? Desperation? I didn't care. When I was asked if I had anything to declare I looked very sheepish, put my hand luggage between my feet and opened my rucksack pulling everything I could on to the bench under the pretext of finding my first aid kit. Fortunately, my worn, unwashed underwear and socks were on top. I flamboyantly found my first aid kit, opened it spilling out its contents to find an ampoule of morphine. I made a fuss saying I knew it was a dangerous drug but that I was a doctor and I always carried it on overseas trips and did I have to declare it. Everyone behind me was staring at me, mouths agape, wondering what was affecting me. Happily, the customs officer was irritated by my antics, wasting his time with my clumsy declaration and waved me through. I stuffed everything back into the rucksack, bent down, retrieved the paper bag from between my feet and walked as slowly as I dare into the arrivals lounge. It was full of nondescript drivers, tipsters, hawkers and soldiers, all looking disinterested in my person. I wondered how they would react if they knew what I was carrying in my pink paper bag, enough cash to fund their dreams many times over.

Outside the lounge, I double checked for potential muggers and strolled across the car park to the waiting Red Cross car and a direct lift to the office where I could offload the package and end my introduction into international smuggling!

GOMA, ZAIRE
(now the DEMOCRATIC REPUBLIC OF CONGO), November 1994
Director of Primary Health Care Clinics,
Federation of Red Cross and Red Crescent

'John, the primary health care clinics in the camp no longer need a director. As you can see the nurses are running them well and I can oversee them with little effort.' Julius, the medical coordinator and I were sitting in the dining area in the house of the Red Cross and Crescent compound. It was otherwise empty. All the accommodation tents in the garden had been removed as houses became available to rent. Only the administration staff now lived in the compound and they were busy in the office. I had only returned from R&R the previous day and had been hanging around helping in the kitchen all morning to keep busy.

I knew it. These were my marching orders. My heart sank and I braced myself for the dismissal.

'However...'

My ears pricked up... my heart missed a beat...

'However...' he lingered sensing my fearful anticipation... 'However, Doctor Patrick has to leave early. His wife is sick and his position of Medical Director at the hospital needs filling. Are you interested?'

Is the pope a Catholic? Does it snow in Antarctica? Is Liverpool the greatest soccer team?

I paused, took a deep breath and quietly answered. 'Yes, that would be great, thanks.'

'He's leaving this evening. If you head out to the hospital this afternoon, he can give you a handover. He knows you will be coming. Are you able to commit to a three-month position? It would be a great relief.'

Yippee, yippee Yeh! Lordy, Lordy Bee! Ha-aa-aa-al-la – luu-uu-uu-uu-uu-uu-ujah! My inner being continued to sing and dance in circles. Outwardly I continued calm and cool.

'No problems Julius. Thanks very much.' I stood up and wandered out.

You were relieved?
I was ecstatic. If I had had to return home at that time, I would have been devastated. I was feeling a complete failure and useless. This was a second chance.

Why did you feel a failure? You admit the clinics in Goma were running well. The clinic in Bukavu was functioning fine. Everything you had managed so far was a success.
I felt I had embarrassed and shamed myself with my arrogance. My early success in leadership had blinded me. In my few days of inactivity, I had reflected on my actions and realised I had been completely caught up in a narcissistic self-indulgence. Sally had taught me a harsh lesson. I am still grateful to her. In the first month of the mission in Goma and again in Bukavu I had been selected to lead.

55

The situation was dire and I was decisive and direct in getting things done. Some people didn't like it but the results justified the methods. I was used to shooting from the hip and getting my way. But now the situation was completely different. There was no emergency. The initial horrendous death rate in the camps had fallen to near the local normal rate. Life was returning to routine. The urgency for action had gone and the requirements for a leader had changed. Team members wanted consultation, consensus and empowerment. Many of the team members were new and had arrived whilst I was in Bukavu. I had returned and had been giving unwanted advice and direction without consultation. No wonder I had annoyed Sally and some of the other nurses.

Now I had a new opportunity to manage the Red Cross and Crescent Hospital, to be more communicative and consultative and hopefully vindicate myself.

KIBUMBA REFUGEE CAMP, near GOMA, ZAIRE
(now the DEMOCRATIC REPUBLIC OF CONGO), November1994
Medical Director of Red Cross and Red Crescent Surgical Hospital

'Welcome, Doctor John and congratulations on becoming hospital director.' Doctor Patrick gave me a smile... or was a smirk? He shook my hand so profusely I worried it would dislocate. We stood in the doctors' office, a tent six by four metres that housed four desks and several chairs. The director had a dedicated desk. Everyone else shared the rest.

I had driven out to the hospital immediately after my meeting with Julius. It was sited on the Goma side of the Kibumba refugee camp and avoided the main congestion of cars and trucks navigating their way through crowds of refugees walking on the road in their daily quest of foraging in the forest for firewood, building materials and food. The hospital was a collection of multipurpose ridge tents, from grand marquees to more modest offices. An imposing fence of plastic sheeting topped by razor wire surrounded it. A large vehicular gate besides a smaller pedestrian gate was the only access. A large sign stood beside. The guards opened the gate and Mabele, my driver, was able to park in space provided.

'I did not plan to leave so early but I'm glad you are available to take over. As you know this is a fully tented surgical hospital, a bit like *MASH*... but we don't have a Klinger. We have ninety beds and only provide emergency adult, paediatric and obstetric surgery. There are no elective surgeries or normal birth deliveries here. There is actually no elective surgery in the entire region. Normal births routinely occur within the camp, usually supervised by traditional birth attendants.

'The surgical staff consists of four Rwandan and one expatriate surgeon. The standard of nursing in the wards and operating room is poor and one of my priorities was to start in-house training. I hope you will continue that. A small portable X-ray machine is our only imaging and a small laboratory provides simple blood tests. Alas no blood transfusion facility is yet available and our oxygen supply is limited to several large oxygen cylinders that are for anaesthesia use only. Importing oxygen cylinders is proving a nightmare.

'I have to go now. I'm sorry this is so brief but my plane leaves in two hours and I still have to pack. Good luck.'

He had barely left before a nurse came crashing into the tent.

'Doctor John, a woman has just arrived bleeding very heavily after a difficult delivery. We cannot find Doctor Rancid. You must come quick.' She turned and ran out. Luckily, I ran after her, for I had no idea where the obstetric ward was located.

The delivery tent had two delivery beds. A woman lay limply on one, staring vacantly at the ceiling and groaning feebly. A middle-aged nurse, her hair in disarray, a strand hanging over her face, stood beside her with one hand pushing up the patient's vagina, her other hand pushing down on the lower abdominal wall to compress the uterus. The floor was awash with blood.

'She delivered her tenth child in a shack near the hospital and began bleeding immediately the baby was born. Her husband carried her in. I've slowed the blood loss but it is still flowing. Her pulse is a hundred and forty and we couldn't get a blood pressure. She's bleeding out.'

'Keep rubbing the uterus through the abdominal wall. You're slowing the blood loss,' I encouraged.

I turned to the other nurse.

'Give her ergometrine 0.25 mg intramuscularly into her outer thigh whilst I cannulate a vein.'

I hastily lowered the head of the bed, put on latex gloves and grabbed the emergency trolley containing the necessary equipment. The woman's skin was cold and clammy, a sure sign of haemorrhagic shock. Although she was underweight, her veins, empty of blood, were difficult to identify but luckily one did stand out. As I slipped the cannula into the vein my glove tore and blood from the cannula ran into the gap. I did not have time to stop and mop it up but hurriedly secured the cannula with tape and connected a bag of intravenous fluid. The nurse applied a blood pressure cuff around the bag and inflated it to squeeze the fluid to flow faster.

'Now give her another ampoule of ergometrine intravenously and slowly.'

Meantime I pushed the trolley to the other side of the bed and fumbled to get another cannula out of the drawer. I needed a second infusion set up to hasten her resuscitation.

A sharp pain stabbed my left hand. The needle from the first ergometrine injection was sticking in the back of my left hand. The nurse must have left it lying on the trolley. I looked around for a sharps' disposal container. There was none to be seen.

I pulled the needle out and cannulated another vein, connecting a second bag of fluid.

'How's the blood loss now?'

'It's slowed dramatically.'

'Keep the pressure on for a while longer. You're doing a great job.'

Doctor Rancid ran in, red in the face and puffing.

'I'm sorry. I've just heard of the emergency. I was seeing a patient in the paediatric ward.'

'That's OK. I know how busy you are. The patient is stabilising. Can you take some observations and then I'll hand over the case? I want to wash my hands.'

I went to a sink, took off my gloves and washed the blood off my hand. The puncture wound from the needle stung but I was more concerned about the possible long-term complications from the needle stick injury, especially as my hands had been flooded with the patient's blood.

Having a needle-stick injury must have been a worry. How did you feel?

I knew there was a danger of catching AIDS, hepatitis and syphilis but at the time I was too focussed on resuscitating the mother to give it attention. Later I had the woman's blood tested for the infections. The four days waiting for the results were nerve wracking. Luckily, she was negative to all three. Nowadays there is a prophylactic course of antiviral medication to protect against HIV infection but at this time it was not available. The incident did highlight to me the urgency to start in-house nursing training to ensure that all sharps are safely disposed of at point of use. I also imported pressurised foghorns that could be sounded whenever an emergency occurred allowing staff to respond promptly. It proved a sound strategy and was effectively used on many occasions.

I'm glad to say that the woman survived despite her haemoglobin falling to a quarter of normal.

I also made it a priority to request a cross-matching service in our laboratory so at least we could get blood donated from relatives and transfuse it in these severe cases. Unfortunately, it did not happen during my tenure.

It sounds like your first day at the hospital was stressful?

More eventful than stressful. This is the type of work I love. I had not even formally started the position yet. It was a much better start for me at the hospital than my very first day at the outpatient clinic where my first patient died before I even had time to treat her.

GOMA, ZAIRE
(now the DEMOCRATIC REPUBLIC OF CONGO), November1994
Medical Director of Red Cross and Red Crescent Surgical Hospital

'Juliet Papa, Juliet Papa this is Head Boy, Head Boy; over,' the radio on my hip echoed. The radio call was from Abdul, the Head of Mission. I felt slightly irritated. It was my day off. I had just started eating my lunch on the back veranda overlooking a small garden of flowering shrubs, enjoying the space and solitude.

'Come in Head Boy.' His sense of humour for his call sign was pathetic.

'John, one of our cars has been in an accident. Sonya, Louise and the driver are in the car. I'm heading out to get them. A local woman has been injured, and she's on the roadside. It sounds like there are some angry people gathering. I'll pick you up en route; over.'

'Will-do; standing by.'

Car accidents in many countries are scenarios that can quickly escalate and turn nasty. The car driver is often dragged out and beaten. If an expatriate is involved, even as a passenger, money may be demanded or even worse. Sonya and Louise were nurses returning to base from a coordination meeting. They would be very scared. Hopefully, they would have locked the car doors before radioing in for assistance.

Abdul and I had managed two previous accidents. We had an unwritten process. I would tend to any injured person and distract the crowd whilst he would extract the passengers and driver, transfer them into another car and then negotiate a settlement with the family of the injured person. We always wanted to ensure any injured party would be fully treated but would not meet exorbitant demands.

Two cars skidded to a stop in a cloud of dust outside my house and a back door thrown open of the lead car. Abdul, in the front passenger seat, as always, was immaculately dressed in a handmade suit, pressed shirt and tie. Although overweight he looked trim. He oozed an expensive aftershave and an air of authority and his natural charm was engaging and relaxing. I jumped into the back with my emergency medical pack. He scanned my creased jeans, sandals and T-shirt with a sardonic smile. I had not even closed the door before we sped off, wheels spinning, flying even more dust into the air.

'Hey, slow down Bruno, I don't want another accident,' I whimpered. It was water off a duck's back. Bruno was a young frustrated rally driver who only had one speed, 'faster'.

My heart sank as we approached the accident scene. A crowd of at least a hundred surrounded the car. All I could see of our car was the white roof and the Red Cross flag fluttering from its VHF aerial. All else was a throng of pushing, surging bodies, faces pressed to the windows, arms raised, banging the roof. Other cars were locked into the gridlock of bodies. Shouting, screams and honking horns bellowed. Even worse, four soldiers were waiting in the shade of the trees beside the road, rifles slung under their arms, smoking cigarettes.

'The Zairian army has the reputation for poor discipline and poor pay. They may be looking for a payoff too,' Abdul added.

I took a big breath.

'The usual John?' Abdul suggested.

'Let's do it.'

I jumped out the car, my medical bag slung over my shoulder, my stethoscope around my neck. It was a powerful status symbol and as I headed to a woman lying in front of the car in the middle of the road, a passageway opened up before me and closed ranks behind. All around, a sea of wide-eyed faces stared. Some were curious, some smiling and some not.

I walked around the injured woman a couple of times to press the crowd backwards and create space then pointed to a couple of older men in the front row, indicating I wanted them to keep everyone back. It always worked. They had been given a status and with a sparkle in their eyes, they would act as my crowd controllers shouting at any onlooker who sneaked too close. One had a cane that he waved flamboyantly in the air.

Luckily, I could see the woman was not critically injured. She was wailing loudly indicating a healthy airway. Her skin colour showed an adequate blood flow and she was moving her arms and head. Her right leg lay still and looked swollen and deformed.

I squatted beside her and smiled. My chore was to entertain and distract the crowd whilst I stabilised her. I had learnt that mime is a powerful medium and that I had a modicum of talent. My first challenge was to engage the crowd. Once laughing they normally attracted all the other bystanders to come and watch, removing the focus of attention away from the Red Cross car and staff. Abdul could then open the doors and extract the passengers.

I am told I have a 'flexible face' and my facial expressions can be extreme. Whilst examining the patient I used widened eyes, raised eyebrows, and gasps of surprise, often directed to small children in the front of the crowd. Although initially nervous they will giggle, laugh spontaneously and infect the crowd.

The woman had an obvious closed fracture of her right lower leg and multiple abrasions on the other. I gave a painkilling injection and was beginning to immobilise the leg with triangular bandages, amusing the crowd with flamboyant bandage folding and knot tying, when a gun barrel prodded me on the shoulder.

I used the barrel as a prop to further amuse the crowd by looking super scared and putting my eye near the barrel as if to look up it. The crowd thought it hilarious and so did I.

I could not have been more wrong.

Assuming I would see a smiling face, I peered up the barrel to its owner… and heard a loud click… the safety being switched off. A slim muscular arm held the gun, one hand gripping the stock tightly, and the other hand was at the trigger, a finger poised. He wore the smatterings of a military uniform, torn and tattered and supplemented by a khaki waistcoat, bandana and dirty beanie. But it was the face that terrified me; staring, glazed, unfocused eyes with pinpoint pupils, a frown of annoyance and a pointed jaw, teeth tightly clenched. I was looking into the eyes of a drugged-up psychopath.

I thought I was dead.

The crowd sensed my dread. An eerie hush descended like a fallen falcon. I could sense all eyes fixed on me. I immediately dropped my gaze and turned to continue bandaging the leg with slow deliberate actions. If I was going to be shot in the head, I did not want to see it happen.

The soldier shouted something at me and I pointed towards Abdul saying quietly he's the boss. He kept prodding my back and neck with the gun but I avoided looking up and continued to point and talk in a quiet voice. A boot kicked my side and I fell over. Footsteps walked away from me.

I inwardly sighed relief and kept my head down. My patient had quietened in a drug-induced ecstasy. Her legs were trussed together for splintage and support. She was ready for transport. Some of the locals had scavenged an old door to act as a make-do stretcher. I directed her lift on to the door and onward to the back of a beaten-up utility commandeered to transport her to the now-functioning Goma hospital.

When I looked back to Abdul, I could see that the two nurses and driver of their car had been moved to the getaway car, which was driving off. Abdul was talking to a small group of men including the soldier. Throwing my bag over my shoulder I hurried back to our second getaway car now parked up the road in the shade of a tree, pointing back towards town. I raised an arm with 'thumbs-up' hoping Abdul would see me from the corner of his eye. Bruno was at the wheel, engine running, alert and ready to leave in a hurry if necessary.

It took Abdul another fifteen minutes to extricate himself from the scene. He sat back in the passenger seat, as always calm and unflustered.

'What did you organise Abdul?'

'The family will bring the medical bills to the office tomorrow. I told them we would pay the usual hospital charges. The soldier accepted five dollars for his "crowd supervision". Our mechanics are coming from base to retrieve the damaged car.' I laughed but inside I was shaking and my bowels churned.

How did this incident affect you?
When I got back to the office Abdul and I sat together and talked it through. He could see me kneeling with the gun at my head and decided his interference would only aggravate the situation. He knew I would stay calm, and not antagonise the soldier so he kept visual contact hoping my pointing towards him would lead to eye contact and bring the soldier over, which is what happened.

That night I had a few whiskeys to help me sleep. I was a bit... a lot of an emotional mess. My eyes would well with tears for no reason, I had shivering fits despite a comfortable air temperature, and I avoided everyone, not wanting to retell or revisit the scene for the umpteenth time.

I had naively misread the danger and had toyed with the gun barrel, thinking that being in a crowd I was safe. What a stupid reaction. My confidence evaporated when I saw his face and realised he was in his own world. At that moment I expected to die. As time passed, I knew I would survive but it was a struggle to stay calm and focused.

What unsettled you? The fear of death?
No, not the fear of death. I'm not religious but I do believe I am a form of spiritual being in a temporary earth suit. What happens after this life, I have no idea. I like the concept that I am presently in a spiritual adventure theme park and presently on 'Ride Earth'. Once the ride ends, I regain my spiritual awareness and join another queue for another ride. It might be flippant but reckon it's better than the heaven/hell theory.

So no, I am not fearful of death. I think I was upset because I'm not yet ready to die and I feel unfulfilled in this life. The ride isn't over yet and my brush with my mortality pushed it into my face. I still have more to accomplish.

Did you go to any more accidents?
There was another incident a few days later that Abdul and I attended. I was a bit hesitant but the proverb about quickly getting back on the horse after a fall proved true. I did exactly the same routine and it worked perfectly. In fact, it was a great theatrical success and I had the crowd, and even the patient, belly laughing. It was probably the most effective remedy for my anxiety. I felt rejuvenated and had no more meltdowns.

KIBUMBA REFUGEE CAMP, near GOMA, ZAIRE
(now the DEMOCRATIC REPUBLIC OF CONGO), December 1994
Medical Director of Red Cross and Red Crescent Surgical Hospital

'Doctor John, what the hell are we doing here?' Curtis, one of the air operations team, had seen me having a beer in the La Pa bar, one of the few bars that had reopened since the influx of refugees had shut down the town six months previously. He sat down, posing his question before I'd even had time to say hello. He obviously needed a listener for his problem He was a serious character, very politically aware and astute. He stared at me through his horn-rimmed glasses with an expectation of deep analysis. The rhythm of the Congolese rumba pulsed in the background as Wendo Kolosoy's music played from the antiquated jukebox. I was feeling relaxed and not in the mood for philosophy.

'I'm having a beer, Curtis. What are you drinking?'

'No, no Doctor John. Why is the Red Cross in Goma?'

'First let me buy you a beer.' I waved at the barman and ordered two more beers. 'We're giving humanitarian aid to these refugees. Surely you've seen the hundreds and thousands of them in the surrounding camps?'

'Yes, I know, but these people... the Hutus... they committed a genocide earlier this year. For god's sake Doctor John... the Interahamwe, the Hutu Militia, murdered over eight hundred thousand Tutsis and their sympathisers in only a hundred days.'

I interrupted, 'I know this, Curtis.'

'Maybe, but did you also know that when the RPF (Rwandan Patriotic Front) army invaded Rwanda in defence of the Tutsis and the Interahamwe began to lose ground, they practically herded the Hutu tribe out of Rwanda into Goma as camouflage for their retreat.'

'No, I thought it was all voluntary, that they all fled in fear.'

Now it was Curtis who interrupted. 'Something else you wouldn't know is that the Kibumba refugee camp was not formed by accident. The Hutu refugees did not just stop there because of exhaustion as we were told. The Interahamwe chose the site because the Rwandan border is only five kilometres to the east. They have set it up as camouflage for their military headquarters from which they can regroup and reinvade.'

'I didn't realise that. As you said, we were told it was exhaustion that made them stop. I must admit at the time I thought it was a weak excuse. Why would three hundred thousand people choose a bleak, rocky, barren, waterless site to camp?'

Curtis was in full flight. 'And we are inadvertently supporting the Interahamwe to maintain that base. Much of our food and medical aid is being siphoned off for their use. The Interahamwe don't want their Hutus to return to Rwanda. They've spread misinformation that the Tutsi's will slaughter anyone returning to Rwanda. I've also been told the Interahamwe are threatening their own people who want to return. The UNHCR is just being manipulated.' By now he was literally gasping with indignation.

'How do you know all this Curtis?'

'It is being widely discussed in the press and in humanitarian circles. I get papers flown in. MSF France is threatening to pull out of the camp because of it.'

'I'm just a rookie Curtis but the people I treat are normal men, women and children who are sick and dying. They may be being manipulated by their militia but that's not my problem and I can only deal with what I see.'

'Maybe Doctor John, but you need to be more aware. Is all this aid justified or is it just a knee-jerk guilt response; the West feeling guilty for not sending UN and US protection before the genocide?'

'I've no idea, Curtis. I can only do what I can and ignore the rest.'

Why bring this up, John? Did it upset you?
No, I wasn't upset but I was unsettled. I had observed men in military uniform and a few military vehicles around the Kibumba refugee camp but had not noted any specific military establishment.

I now wondered if the man I had seen being robbed and partially beheaded was a victim of a military-led operation. Maybe he would not contribute any rice to the military so they killed and robbed him as a warning to others.

If the refugees were acting as a screen for the Interahamwe and we were supporting them, what was to be done? Was it ethical? Were we part of the problem?

So, what did you do?
I put it into the too-hard basket and continued what I was doing. I became more attentive to what I saw around the camp but I was now based in the hospital on

the edge of the camp and did not travel around the camp as before. We were also so busy I had little time to ponder.

It did open my awareness to the politics of humanitarian aid. I realised how naïve I was and made an effort to learn the political context of future missions. It added to the fascination of the work.

But Curtis was right. What were we doing there? Were we propping up a corrupt regime that caused the crisis in the first place? Was the tail wagging the dog?

This individual dilemma was solved two years later when I was long gone. The Tutsis, now in control of Rwanda and fed up with the incursions into Rwanda by the Interahamwe, attacked Zaire and dismantled the refugee camps near the Rwandan border, including Kibumba. Inside of two days one hundred thousand Hutu refugees were forcibly repatriated into Rwanda, another fifty thousand fled deeper into Zaire, many of whom were slaughtered in the ensuing First Congo War. The hospital was totally destroyed.

It started me wondering if humanitarian interventions actually had had any real long-term benefit.

KIBUMBA REFUGEE CAMP, near GOMA, ZAIRE
(now the DEMOCRATIC REPUBLIC OF CONGO), December 1994
Medical Director of Red Cross and Red Crescent
Surgical Hospital

'Doctor John, Doctor John, there has been a truck rollover eight kilometres down the road. Injured people are arriving.' Joshua, the head gateman, had run into the doctor's tent with the news.
'Thanks Joshua, I'll put out a 'Red Alert'. You need to be ready to open the gate for any vehicles with injured people... but please let no one else come in. Is that clear?'
'Sure, Doctor John.'
Luckily it was eight thirty in the morning and the operating list for the previous days and overnight emergencies had not started but the theatre staff had arrived.

A truck rollover in this region would always involve multiple casualties. All trucks on the roads were not only grossly overloaded, they were also covered with passengers, like fleas on a dog, clinging to the ropes securing the cargo, nestled in the niches, hanging from the back gate or sitting on the cab. In a land with no public transport or safety guidelines, it was a common means of transport.

I hurried to the casualty area by the main gate. Already the staff was activating our mass-casualty-plan. Collapsible camp beds were being erected, intravenous infusions were being hung, and boxes of dressings and bandages were being unpacked.

'Hey, Doctor Naviro, can you start a triage inside the main gates.' He was standing at the emergency tent nurse's desk writing some notes. A young Zairian surgeon with wiry hair and a huge grin, he was very capable and personable. Nothing was ever too much effort for him. He smiled a wide beam, 'Sure Doctor John. This first patient has only a broken humerus with a few abrasions. He was thrown clear of the truck as it began to roll. Amazingly, he then jumped on to the back of a passing lorry and was the first to arrive here. He said the overturned truck was loaded with passengers so we'll be busy, eh?'

'We'll soon see.' There was loud honking of horns outside the main gate as several cars were demanding entrance. The flood had begun.

I strolled around the area to ensure all the plans were underway. The store tent would be the 'black' area where anyone who was hopelessly injured would be laid gently on a bed, given strong analgesia and allowed to die in peace accompanied by their family and a watchful nurse. The 'green' area in the dining tent accommodated the 'walking-wounded' who had minor injuries and could wait for a while. A nurse would keep observing and assessing them, provide simple pain relief and clean minor wounds. A 'yellow' area for serious but non-life-threatening injuries was positioned at the far end of the emergency tent. Immediate life-threatening injuries were treated in the 'red' area beside the nurses' desk.

Our facilities and equipment were basic: the limited supply of oxygen and one cardiac monitor were in the operating theatre for surgical use only. We had no respiratory ventilators or blood transfusion service. But we could clear airways, infuse intravenous fluids, vent ruptured lungs, stop external bleeding, take X rays, set bones and operate on obvious internal injuries. Anything more complex would be a problem. My concern was not to devote large amounts of our limited resources, personnel, equipment and operating time to hopeless cases that would probably die. I was relieved to see Doctor Visser, a Dutch expatriate surgeon, arrive. He was a veteran war surgeon, vastly more experienced than me and I knew he would oversee the more complex treatments. I needed to keep an overview.

The deluge continued as more injured patients arrived and were unloaded in the entryway for triage. Shouts, screams and groans filled the air as staff and relatives scurried around the injured moving them to their triage area. The expatriate and national staff worked effectively. Most injuries were non-life threatening although three patients were lying with catastrophic injuries in the store tent, the black area.

'Doctor John, I need a hand,' Doctor Naviro called. He was kneeling on the ground in the parking area huddled over a bundle and surrounded by three adults. Hurrying over I knelt beside him and looked into a folded blanket. A little girl lay with her head in a bed of congealed blood. A huge head wound gaped with fragmented skull exposing the brain. An eye hung from its socket. Her head had been crushed. I was amazed she was still alive. She was unconscious and fitting but breathing.

'What should we do with her?' All the three adults stared at me. I assumed them to be her mother, father and maybe aunt. I could see their eyes pleading, their bodies begging.

If she had been an adult, I would have had no hesitation and sent her to the store tent to die... but I couldn't.

'I'll carry her into the casualty area and cover the wound. Tell her parents she is dangerously ill and we will do what we can,' I lied. I carefully picked her up and carried her to the 'red' area where I covered the head wound with a bandage, and gave her a drug rectally stop her convulsions and a painkilling injection. I whispered my intentions to Olive, the nearest nurse, to let her rest there. She stared at me with questioning eyes until I indicated the grieving family. She nodded in understanding and I left to continue my supervision.

I was sad but relieved when the little girl died half an hour later and I watched the family carry her body, wrapped in a blanket, out through the gates. I could not imagine their grief but felt comfortable that the parents felt she had had full attention.

The next two days were frantic whilst the casualties were slowly cleared. Six people had died. Ten patients were admitted for ongoing treatment, six requiring surgery, and twenty-eight were treated for fractures and wounds but sent home. I stayed at the hospital for two days snatching sleep and morsels of food as the opportunity arose. It was a great team effort.

How did you handle all this trauma?
Like always, I repressed all the horror and heartbreak whilst it was happening. After returning back to Goma, exhausted and emotionally depleted, I had a private cry, especially for the little girl. It was the small children dying who rattled me the most. Crying surrendered my resistance to hold in the grief and allow some of the frustration and sadness to escape.

I later ran a meeting to debrief all the staff, to not only learn how we could improve the disaster plan, but also allow staff to offload their feelings and express how it affected them. I thought it would be constructive.

Was it useful?
It was a disaster.
The national staff did not engage in the process at all. They sat, blank-faced and said nothing. Most of the expatriate staff was also hesitant to publicly show any emotion, except for one English nurse who poured out her anguish whilst crying profusely. Her fellow English nurse consoled her but it seemed to strike horror among many of the other international expatriates where being so publicly emotional was not acceptable. I never tried the same process again.

'It is part of normal life, accidents and death occurs every day,' Doctor Naviro rationalised to me. 'If you cannot accept it, maybe you should not be working here, eh Doctor John?'

So, you and your staff had no outlet for your feelings?
No, times might have changed but in 1994 the unspoken pressures were to either *not have feelings* or *keep them to yourself.*

Unfortunately, the English nurse continued being distraught and dysfunctional. She was evacuated back to the UK the following week. A French nurse also showed signs of distress. She began taking days off work, first for diarrhoea, then a migraine, then sore throat. She became withdrawn, missing meals and meetings and lost weight. These are classical signs of what then we called 'burn-out' and impending psychological breakdown. It would now be classified Acute Stress Disorder. She too was urgently repatriated for treatment.

KIBUMBA REFUGEE CAMP, near GOMA, ZAIRE
(now the DEMOCRATIC REPUBLIC OF CONGO), December 1994
Medical Director of Red Cross and Red Crescent Surgical Hospital

'Doctor John, Christmas is coming. We must buy some presents for the children, otherwise, they will have nothing and it will be a sad day,' Helena, the national nurse in charge of the paediatric ward, suggested not-so-subtly as she leaned over my shoulder whilst I was updating my medical notes at the desk in the paediatric tent. Although only whispered, her proximity seemed to amplify the command. She was a tall, lithe woman with finely sculptured facial features and moved with grace and poise. As I turned to face her, she swung towards me and our eyes met, only inches apart. She smiled.

'It is important. Do you not think so Doctor John?' Her use of the rhetorical question at the end of her statements fascinated me.

'I think you're suggesting that the Red Cross should buy them, do you not mean?' I countered.

'What a good idea you have Doctor John. I knew I could depend on you,' she squealed, locking in the idea as if it was mine and already decided. She gave me a peck on the cheek and walked off, mission accomplished. I was shocked by her intimacy and my temerity but inwardly laughed at how she had cleverly manipulated me, but aware I must maintain healthier boundaries with her.

That evening I discussed Helena's suggestion with the expatriate medical staff and it was unanimously agreed for everyone to donate towards presents for the children and the national staff.

'We'll buy the presents. We're off to Nairobi for R&R,' offered Margaret and Trish, two nurses caught up with the enthusiasm. I was most grateful for there were no retail outlets in Goma.

When they returned carrying mountains of bags they were amused. 'You'll never believe it but the only dolls we could find in Nairobi were white. We searched high and low for coloured dolls but they did not exist. We bought them anyway for the girls and a selection of trucks for the boys.' Margaret looked exhausted. They had spent two of their five days leave shopping for the presents as well as an assortment of games, balloons and lollies to supplement the Christmas stockings that had been made from discarded World Food Program food sacks by one of the national nurses with seamstress skills.

The ward was decorated with a selection of colourful streamers that were draped over large banana leaves suspended from the tent's roof beams. A few fairies and baubles dangled amongst them.

Christmas Day arrived. All the staff on duty, plus a few more who had driven out from Goma especially for the present giving waited patiently until Dr Visser, adorned in a cotton wool beard and red shirt, arrived 'Ho-Ho-Hoing' with a sack over his shoulder. The children and their mothers giggled in amazement and delight. They had never seen the like. Every face was beaming. Most small girls cuddled their dolls and tucked them into their bed with no awareness of skin colour. Those boys able to get out of bed were soon racing their trucks around the floor in a frenzy of high-pitched whines and screeches. The staff mingled amongst the children to play and share the joy.

I was especially attached to a five-year-old girl, Nancy, an orphan with no family. I had admitted her a month earlier after she had fallen into a fire and severely burned both hands. Several fingers had been amputated and her burns were dressed daily. She had endured these painful ordeals with little complaint. The burns were slowly healing. I tried to give her special attention and care. Nancy reminded me of my patient whom I had abandoned at the Israeli hospital four months earlier and it both eased my guilt and gave great joy. I watched her unwrap her doll whom she immediately tucked into bed beside her for her attention quickly turned to a boiled lolly wrapped in a clear cellophane wrapper, twisted at either end. She picked it up and tried to untwist the wrapper but with fingers missing and bulky bandages, was unable to grip it firmly. I held out my hand to help but she hissed at me to stop. I was startled by her ferocity and watched in fascination. I was not alone. Like a spreading epidemic, the whole ward had increasingly become silent as we mentally joined her struggle with the wrapper. It fell on to the bed. Everybody silently groaned in dismay. She picked it up again, using her teeth to stabilise it and slowly, ever so slowly, over several pain-staking minutes she untwisted the ends. The lolly was adherent to the paper. I could sense everyone willing it to fall but it remained stuck. With the wrapper unfurled she, at last, was able to grip it with a hand and push the sweet off into her mouth.

It might have been the winning goal at a Grand Final or Super Bowl for the whole tent erupted with a whoop of joy, tears streaming down cheeks, hands clapping and laughter gushing. She looked around the adoring faces and her face erupted in an enormous smile, initially in surprise but then enjoying the adulation and attention. With such determination, I had no doubt that she would make a full recovery and have functional hands. It was the best Christmas present I could have.

It was a special moment for you John?
Yes, it was a moment of pure pleasure and joy that helped counter many of the moments of despair and despondency that I had recently experienced... but it was more than that... it was also a communal moment of compassion and care. I could sense everyone's empathy and excitement as we all watched Nancy manipulate the lolly wrapper. It was palpable. I had never felt such intensity of spirit, of support, a wanting of a will for her to succeed. I do not know if we were supporting Nancy in her determination or she was supporting us, giving us faith in the power of healing, of overcoming adversity, of teaching us patience and tenacity. It was such a small and short effort but it was an immense and meaningful message.

KIBUMBA REFUGEE CAMP, near GOMA, ZAIRE
(now the DEMOCRATIC REPUBLIC OF CONGO), January 1995
Medical Director of Red Cross and Red Crescent Surgical Hospital

'John, the ICRC delegation is visiting and inspecting the local male prison tomorrow. Their team is short of a doctor. Are you interested in helping them out?' Abdul had intercepted me as I returned from the camp. 'They have been supportive of us in Goma and I'd like to help them out if possible.'

'Sure thing. I'd like to see what an African prison looks like,' I naively replied.
The following morning, I jumped into the International Committee of the Red Cross and Crescent car that pulled up outside my house. 'Thanks, John, for helping us out at a critical time. Our doctor contracted pneumonia and has been flown back to Europe.' Claude, the Head of Mission, a tall, broad-shouldered and bearded Englishman who reminded me of Little John of Robin Hood fame, welcomed me. 'We've been negotiating this visit for over three months and if we postpone it might never happen. Have you assessed any prisons before?'

'Never.'

'Narelle beside you is a psychologist.' A slim woman in her early thirties gave me a smile and small wave. Her fiery red hair streamed backwards into a long plait that fell forward over her left shoulder, stark against her white Red Cross T-shirt.

'She will interview each prisoner, hopefully without guards present so they can talk freely. Meantime you can examine each prisoner in another room. Hamid, also beside you, will be your interpreter.' Hamid smiled, offering his hand that I duly shook.

'Ask about any complaints and symptoms. Malnutrition and poor hygiene are the norm here so infestations, dental caries and skin and chest infections are common. Examine particularly for signs of neglect, abuse and torture such as burns, bruising and scars. I have a template for you to note and draw your findings. A checklist of common problems is included.'

'How many prisoners will we see?'

'I don't know. We'll work that out when we are there. Sometimes these occasions are very opportunistic. But the guards can be very intimidating, especially to the prisoners. I will negotiate the conditions and ask that you hold back any personal comment no matter how terrible it might seem. Is that clear?' He looked directly at me, eye to eye.

'Understood,' I replied, somewhat intrigued but with a twinge of anxiety tugging at my intestines.

The prison was a thirty-minute drive out of Goma set in an open bush-land area. Its four-metre-high, windowless concrete and brick walls, capped by rolls of rusting barbed wire, were imposing and forbidding. We parked in the shade of a solitary tree and walked to the tall double-gated entrance. A smaller pedestrian door, set beside the vehicular entrance, opened before we were able to knock. A guard wearing a ragged dark blue uniform supplemented with a Nike baseball cap called us through into an open courtyard buzzing with prisoners and flies, heavily littered and smelling a mixture of mildew, sweat and faeces. Drying clothes were draped over the inner low roofs and doors. The inner walls were painted a dirty jade green and cream.

A silence passed over the prisoners as everyone stopped, frozen in the moment, and stared at us. Their faces were thin and gaunt, their eyes scanning and suspicious. I waved and looked around but all eyes immediately dropped to the ground, too wary to connect. Everyone began to shuffle around again. We had been assessed and dismissed as non-threatening.

Wood smoke belched from the far end of the yard. I guessed it was from a cooking fire and could discern the semblance of a queue along the adjacent wall. I assumed they were waiting for food. The odour of unwashed bodies and stale urine engulfed me as we were led through the crowd.

'Come this way please.' The guard forged a pathway through the prisoners towards the shadows of an administration building. I trailed behind Claude, Narelle and Hamid, clutching my medical bag, nodding to individual prisoners. A few silently scrutinised me but most looked away.

We entered the cool of the building and a spacious office. The prison director stood up behind his chair to greet us. 'Welcome, we are happy to see you. We hope you can help us.' He motioned us to sit on a collection of rickety chairs around his desk as he settled his heavy frame back into his chair, puffing from the effort. He picked a cigarette from a pack on the desktop and lit it up, stroking his nicotine-stained moustache in thought.

Claude introduced Narelle, Hamid and myself and organised for our boxes of supplies to be brought in from the car. It was probably why we were so welcome.

'The prisoners are housed in the pavilions you see within the walls. Each cell was originally built for two prisoners but now each cell can accommodate up to six. We are very overcrowded. We have little money for food. We rarely get paid. Can you help us?'

'Can we talk with and examine some of the prisoners. I would like to choose them. Is that permissible?' Claude was using the director's request to his advantage.

'Of course. First I can show you around.'

The stench of urine and shit overpowered me as we entered the first pavilion and my stomach heaved and I wanted to vomit. Swallowing madly to quash the reflex, I noticed Claude and Narelle suffering too.

'We have no latrines here. There is a bucket in each cell.'

The cell, about four by two metres, had two bunks against one wall. A small barred window high up on the far wall provided dim diffuse light. Old paint peeled off the walls exposing damp plaster beneath. I could not imagine how six men could live here. The bucket obviously overflowed for the floor was urine sodden and spotted with faeces. The director said nothing but led us further down the corridor allowing us to peer into the various cells. They were all as terrible.

'We cook in the courtyard.'

'What do you cook?' I asked.

'Mainly rice and vegetables. We have no meat except for the occasional goat. Hopefully, we provide one meal a day. Some prisoners have families who bring in food or pay guards to buy it for them.'

'How long are prisoners kept here?'

'Most are awaiting trial. Many have been here over a year.'

We entered a smaller building where two offices had been cleared for our use except for a desk and two chairs. Narelle took one room and me the other. I would use the desk as a couch, a bit short but better than the filthy floor.

Over the next three hours, I saw twenty prisoners assisted by Hamid. All were underweight, lice-infested, covered in skin sores, many with bruises and abrasions. A couple had burns from cigarette ends. They refused to say how they acquired them despite the guards being shunted out of the room. All were grateful for our visit and quickly pocketed the soap and medications I handed them.

'We will complete our report and send you a copy,' Claude briefed the director as we departed. 'Thank you for your cooperation. We will contact you about any further supplies we may provide. I can make no commitment at this time.'

I strolled back through the courtyard. It was as crowded as ever. I could not imagine anyone wanting to spend time in his cell. The crowd again opened and closed around us as we left but a few faces smiled at us. We had obviously made some prisoners happier.

'Well John, what did you think?'

'It's terrible, inhuman, degrading. What can you do?'

'Believe it or not, that is one of the better prisons I have visited in Zaïre. We will provide a report to outline the conditions and continue diplomatic pressure for more prison funding and improved human rights. Nothing changes quickly here.'

'Do not forget that what you have seen is confidential and you must not discuss it with anyone. Our credibility depends on it. Do you understand?'

'Yes, Claude.'

How did this visit affect you?

I was appalled and disgusted. It was sobering and a wake-up-call to me of the importance of human rights. The acceptance of inhuman conditions, the misery and social injustice were frightening. But I think it was the atmosphere of hopelessness that appalled me. The prisoners were all downcast, unknowing if and when they would be brought to trial, many not knowing their charges or if any defence was even available. If that was a moderate prison, I can only wonder what a bad one looks like.

I was grateful to get back to the refugee camp where conditions were slowly improving, everyone was free to roam, food and water were now sufficient if not plentiful and hopefully, the refugees would soon be able to return home. Even a small semblance of hope can lift the human spirit and make difficult circumstance bearable.

KIBUMBA REFUGEE CAMP, near GOMA, ZAIRE
(Now the DEMOCRATIC REPUBLIC OF CONGO), January 1995
Medical Director of Red Cross and Red Crescent Surgical Hospital

'Juliet Papa, Juliet Papa this is control,' my personal radio attached to my belt blared. I was sitting at my desk in the doctors' office at the hospital in Kibumba refugee camp sorting through the week's operating lists.

'Go ahead control. This is Juliet Papa; over.'

'Doctor John, UNHCR has requested we attend Katale Airstrip where a plane has to make an emergency landing. Can you assist? Over.'

'Where is this airstrip?' I had no idea there was any such facility in the near region. He gave me the coordinates and I pinpointed it on the map taped to the wall of the tent. 'I can't be there for an hour. What's the problem?'

'The plane cannot lower its landing gear. It is circling to waste its fuel. Good luck.'

'Hang on. How many passengers on board?'

'They didn't say. Control standing by.'

I radioed the driver of our stand-by car, a Toyota 4WD, to meet me at the main hospital gate and ran to the emergency tent, commandeered Doctor Ashti and two national nurses to join me. We grabbed two 'major trauma boxes', a selection of emergency drugs and six stretchers and rushed to the car. In less than ten minutes we sped out the gates. Rusti, our driver, delighted in using the 'emergency' excuse to recklessly speed, hand on horn, blasting any pedestrian to jump backwards or wayward driver to swerve sidewards. I tightened my seat belt and took deep breaths. It was pointless to tell him to slow down. We used the travel time to plan for our arrival.

Fifty minutes later we spied the grassy airstrip running parallel to the road. There was no sign of any plane but in the airstrip's car park I was amazed to find six other 4WDs haphazardly parked. Every medical agency in the area must have heard the radio call and had sent teams.

'Hi, I'm Doctor John, the director of the surgical Red Cross Hospital. Who's in charge here?' I asked all. No one answered. An overweight local man, his ragged blue shorts, checked shirt, Nike baseball cap all grease-stained stepped up. 'I'm Jason. We have the airstrip's firefighting equipment,' pointing to an ancient rusting white utility with several fire extinguishers tied to the back tray. 'But I just work here. I'm not in charge.'

'Thanks Jason. I'll coordinate this if no one has any objection,' I suggested. No one objected. 'Does anyone know any details?'

Jason spoke up. 'It's a Beechcraft Musketeer with pilot and three passengers on board. They still have about twenty minutes fuel to burn.' We all listened and the plane could be heard circling high above.

'Are any doctors here experienced in emergency medicine?' I asked. Four of the assembled crowd raised hands.

'OK, here's the plan.' I outlined the rudimentary sequence Doctor Ashti and I had discussed en route. 'Your four cars and the fire truck will park well off the strip, about halfway down. Have your resuscitation equipment ready. When the plane lands... or crashes... no one is to approach it except for the fire truck. Jason, you and your partner will check for fire and douse any flame or escaped fuel with the extinguishers. When you're happy the fire risk is low, signal the 'all clear' by raising your arms. The four medical vehicles can drive towards the plane but stop twenty to thirty metres short and walk in. Assess and assist all four passengers and call us in for any more assistance and equipment. We may have trouble removing injured bodies from the fuselage but we can work that out at the time. Everyone else stays back at the end of the runway until the doctors call for back up.

'Is that clear? Does anyone have a question?' There was no question, comment, dissent or discussion.

'Let's do it then.' Everyone wandered over to their cars and sped off.

I was about to get back into our car when a shiny grey ambulance, blue light flashing proudly on its roof pulled off the main road and parked beside me. The engine died as a slim, tall pale man with a gaunt face wearing rimless glasses, a receding hairline and dressed in surgical scrubs jumped out the passenger door.

'Hello, I am Dr Schroeder. I am here to treat any casualty. We have all the emergency equipment,' his strong German staccato commanded.

I was aware that a German NGO was flying in rotations of doctors and nurses every two weeks to work in the crisis. The only problem was there was nowhere in the camps for them to work. It was a misplaced form of 'humanitourism', bringing in medical personnel for the 'feel-good' experience but lacking substance, logistic or commitment. Having no medical work for their clients in the camp the agency had imported ambulances in which the frustrated medics could drive around and transport sick patients from the camp to the various medical clinics and hospital. Ironically, they were only insured to travel on bitumen roads.

He opened the side door of the ambulance that glistened with monitors, a ventilator and oxygen bottles. 'I can coordinate the emergency. It is what I do in Germany.'

'That's all very well doctor but you're too late. Everyone is in place and the plane is about to descend. If you park to the side of the runway, we can summon you if anyone is critically injured,' I tried to soften my tone for his intentions were kind if somewhat unrealistic.

I turned and jumped into the car before he could argue. We parked well off the runway and watched the plane fly a low-level circuit before making its final approach. As it descended, my nerves tensed, judging, with my inexperienced eye, that the pilot was far too high. At the last minute, he dropped the plane, flared its wings and made a perfect belly flop landing skidding along the grass, finishing with a soft thud.

Even before the plane had come to a stop every car on the airfield was accelerating like the start of a Grand Prix Race fighting for poll position, all wanting to be first on the scene and screeching to a stop only metres from the plane. The cloud of dust churned up by multiple skidding tyres completely obliterated the view for a full minute. The fire truck, blocked by the traffic jam, could not even approach the plane.

As the dust settled, I watched all four passengers climb out the plane and start pumping the hands of the medical crews and fire staff, grinning ear to ear and laughing with relief. One of them even lit a cigarette and threw away the match.

So much for your grand plan, eh Doctor John. Don't apply for any disaster coordination job. It not your forte,' chuckled Doctor Ashti. 'I hope there isn't a fuel leak or we might be exceedingly busy.'

We watched for a further five minutes as the crowd dispersed, jumped back in the car and turned to the road. The German ambulance was parked where we had left it, its blue light still flashing, bonnet up and the driver leaning over the engine. Doctor Schroeder, red-faced and fuming, was screaming. 'Hurry up, get the engine repaired. We must go to the plane...'

I waved and smiled as we passed.

Doctor Ashti whispered, 'So much for high tech equipment. Maybe there is a god?

KIBUMBA REFUGEE CAMP, near GOMA, ZAIRE
(now the DEMOCRATIC REPUBLIC OF CONGO), January 1995
Medical Director of Red Cross and Red Crescent Surgical Hospital

'John, the hospital is using too much water.' Abdul, the Head of Mission, had called me to his office in the Goma compound before I headed out to the hospital in the camp. 'It is very expensive and increasingly unreliable to cart it all from Goma. The road is too unstable for heavy traffic. It is beginning to deteriorate and the water trucks keep getting bogged or breaking down. I've just arranged for a specialised team from the Swedish Red Cross Society to come out and sink boreholes near the hospital. Hopefully they will find water for us. It will be so much easier with our own bore. They are arriving next week. Can you look after them?'

'No problems. What equipment will they use? Surely, they're not flying in a drilling machine. They weigh twenty tons or more.'

'They are hiring equipment in Goma. Apparently, they are well experienced in working in third world countries.'

I met the team at the airport armed with a cool box of chilled drinks ready to welcome and refresh them. Anders, a mechanic and Franz, a logistician, accompanied the project leader Bjorn, an engineer.

As we sipped cool lemonade, I asked Bjorn about his work. He was in his forties, fair balding hair and a short goatee beard. 'We travel to many countries to set up water projects. This will be a simple job, John. We will soon have a water bore for your hospital. Who is looking after your water at the hospital at the moment?'

I explained. 'There is a delegation from the German Red Cross. They maintain the water tanks, pumps and chlorination of all the water. They are very efficient.'

'I am sure they are able to do that.' A tone of aloofness tainted Bjorn's remark. I could sense an international rivalry.

They spent the rest of the day organising their equipment and arranging for the drill to be collected and transported out to the hospital site.

We met at the hospital the following morning. It had been built on the flattest area of the region. Bulldozers and blasting had levelled rocky outcrops but jagged volcanic mounds and pinnacles still surrounded the site. It was a merciless moonscape.

'How are we going to drive over this?' Franz complained. 'We cannot drill here.' He was slightly overweight and sweating profusely in the harsh sunlight.

I could sense their defeat. I could not see how they could drill there either.

'We knew it would be difficult. That's why we asked for your help. If it was easy, we would have asked the Germans.'

There was a pregnant pause.

'Yes, it will be difficult but we will find a way,' Bjorn declared.

You'll make a diplomat yet, John.

It was a rare moment of inspiration… and it worked. They toiled for three weeks. With a team of labourers, they hauled their equipment over the jagged rocks, at times dismantling the drill and carrying and dragging the components over and around obstacles. They drilled several bores… but did not find any water. They were so disappointed and despondent.

I held a small 'thank you' party for them the night before they departed.

'Thank you, John, for your help. I am sorry we did not find you water. Get the Germans to cart more water for you. They are good at that.'

ZAIRE TO TANZANIA, SWITZERLAND AND AUSTRALIA
February 1995

How was it coming home from the mission?

It was a disaster, a total unmitigated disaster.

I flew from Goma in Zaire to Zanzibar in Tanzania for a five-day holiday; to lie on a beach under a palm tree, go fishing on a coral reef in a dugout canoe and eat local fresh seafood. But before I even began to unwind, I was again flying back to Geneva in Switzerland for debrief.

Geneva was a fiasco. Nobody at Red Cross HQ seemed remotely interested in what I had experienced. After two pointless meetings with indifferent medics I was committed to a consultation with a psychologist. She was a middle-aged lady with heavy make-up, wearing a tight clingy dress and knee length boots. She too seemed totally disinterested in my experiences and kept glancing out of the window.

When I mentioned that I had not had any early morning erections for the first month of the mission she stopped. Her eyes narrowed and she transformed from a disinterested dullard to an investigative detective, firing into life to interrogate me, wanting all details of my erectile history. When I tried to reassure her, it had only been a temporary lull and I was now functioning normally she would not change the subject. I was initially flabbergasted, then exasperated. I eventually walked out. She was obviously more disturbed than me. I was never going to see another psychologist.

The following day, I flew long haul, Geneva to Melbourne, Australia for a further half day's debrief with the Australian Red Cross before enduring another long flight back to Queensland in northern Australia. I arrived home on a Friday, physically exhausted, emotionally depleted and jet-lagged... and returned to work in my general practice on Monday.

It was a harsh transition. One week I was working in a third world emergency hospital dealing with death and disaster, the following week in a first world general medical clinic dealing with coughs and colds. I was totally disorientated, disillusioned, irritable, indecisive and resentful.

To add to my misery my medical partners were unsupportive and ignored me for several days. Although they knew and had agreed for me to join the Red Cross and go on a humanitarian mission, the emergency nature of this mission had given only two days' notice for my departure and I had left the practice precipitously. They had been stressed by my sudden absence and had endured a higher workload. I felt unwelcomed, unwanted and isolated.

Did they not diagnose you with PTSD?
No. I think they considered me to be selfish, self-centred and ungrateful. PTSD was not a diagnosis commonly considered in civilian populations. And I did not diagnose it either.

How was it at home?
Home was supportive. My wife was warm and welcoming and gave me space to adjust. She had taken the children to the UK to stay with her parents for several weeks during my mission and had had an adventure of her own. She did not complain about my irritability and I was too self-absorbed to be sympathetic. My kids swamped me with love and cuddles, unfazed by my irritability and vagueness.

How did this progress?
I receded into an automated, zombie-type state, blindly following old routines and medical protocols, reproducing the motions of normal life but in a detached, remote, impersonal way. I felt alone, isolated and different. I was there... but I wasn't. I withdrew into a hole and peered out nervously and suspiciously... I knew that nothing at home had changed... but me... and that changed everything.
I was living in a parallel universe; someone was acting my part in life but it wasn't me. It was a bad dream and if I ignored it, I would wake up and everything would be normal again.

And did you wake up?
Not really. The isolation and bewilderment seemed to subside over time but never disappeared. Amazingly it was my patients who were my best therapy.

Some would come in and say, 'I know this is trivial compared to what you've seen doc but'... and then tell me their symptoms. I always reassured them, 'Suffering is not a competition. Just because others suffer more does not invalidate yours.' That became a powerful jolt to jerk me back to some form of normality, give back some perspective and allow some empathy to return to my work.

Other patients would wander in and comment, 'Have a good holiday doc?' I smiled to myself and thought, *If only you knew,* bemused at their lack of insight or interest.

One patient was special. He was dying of pancreatic cancer. I visited him at his home for many weeks and we became friends. We talked about life and death, living and dying. He confided many of his life's regrets and mistakes and I confessed to him many of my experiences, feelings and anxieties. I had never revealed my feelings to anyone before.

So, why do it now?

Probably because I knew he would die soon and my secrets would be safe. It would be much easier for me to recount all my thoughts to you if you were dying too... but that's a big ask.

When he died, I was very upset. I had lost my emotional safety valve.

Then something very strange happened to me. I wrote a poem about him. It just emerged... from where I have no idea... then other poems emerged... reflecting ideas bouncing in my head... poems about gratitude, courage, generosity, friendship; concepts that were becoming more meaningful and substantial to me.

I discovered poetry suited my way of thinking... and writing... short, concise, crystallised, metaphorical... it just flowed and helped me confess and consolidate my thoughts.

Why were you so surprised by this?

I was amazed for I hated poetry. I had memories of being forced to recite poetry in English Literature classes at school. Commonly it was an obscure Elizabethan soliloquy or an Edwardian love sonnet that I could barely comprehend. I suffered a mild stutter that was accentuated when nervous, so of course, it became more pronounced when forced to recite. As I walked back to my seat my classmates sniggered and ridiculed me. 'Sssssssssissssssssy JJJJoohn.' I was embarrassed and humiliated and I lived in fear of poetry. 'John the Poet' was an oxymoron.

Are you surprised that you became more philosophical about life?

My mission in Zaire changed me. A part of me was damaged and dysfunctional but another part of me had been awakened, enlivened, even enriched. Maybe that first cry was the catalyst. Maybe with the post-traumatic stress, there is a post-traumatic growth... but at the time I had no insight. I knew I was emotionally more self-aware but paradoxically this created more confusion rather than clarity. I might have been more in tune with my emotions but I still did not know how to play them. They were all in minor key and discord. I was certainly more appreciative of my life, my health and my wealth. I was more curious about my spirituality... but I was not happy. Yet I was not unhappy. I had nothing to complain of... it was more a deep discontent, a feeling of being a fraud, of being inauthentic and unfulfilled. I did not know whom I was or what to do.

So, what happened?

I tossed and turned in life, losing direction, dissatisfied with general practice, feeling a failure as a husband, unable, maybe unwilling, to confide with anyone. I avoided conflict both without and within. I might have been more aware of my feelings but I did not know how to corral them. Over the following years my life disintegrated. My marriage broke up, my medical practice fragmented and my sanity struggled.

What did you do?
I ran away...to Afghanistan...with MSF!

Northern Afghanistan
Médecins Sans Frontières
2000–2001

Walls of sandbags surrounded the doors and windows of the house to protect against bomb and blast injuries. A three-metre high mud wall trimmed with rusting coils of barbed wire surrounded the compound. The scene was softened with numerous colourful, fragrant flowerbeds fruit trees and a heavily laden grapevine that crowned a pagoda. I sat in its shade, in the garden of the compound enclosing our accommodation, offices and warehouse in Mazar-I-Sharif. It is the largest town in northern Afghanistan, famous for its fifteenth century Blue Mosque, a shrine to Hazrat-e Ali, the cousin and son-in-law of Muhammad.

'Our medical clinics are strictly segregated into male and female sections.' Ewald, the Head of Mission, was briefing me shortly after my arrival. 'The female section has only female staff and patients and vice versa. It is a strict demand of the Taliban. They even have a 'Department of Vice and Virtue' who make spot checks on our clinics and arrive unannounced to confirm and enforce the segregation. We call them the "V and V". On one occasion they jumped in through the windows of the female section to catch any male breaking the rules.'

'No way,' I uttered unbelievingly.

'It's true. And it's ironic that the Taliban insists on female doctors and nurses yet they have closed all schools and universities to females. It is all very illogical but we work with what we have.

'The Taliban now control ninety per cent of the country. Their enemy in this civil war, the Northern Alliance, are presently penned into the north-eastern corner of the country, but this may change as the war progresses. We have fortified the house in case the war front moves this way.

'The Taliban tolerates our presence. We maintain the only medical service for the civilian population in the north of the country. They say they have no interest in running a medical service. They are too busy fighting the war against the Northern Alliance.'

'How many clinics are we running?'

'At the moment we have sixteen across the north. Hopefully we will open more. You are responsible for eight clinics and their surrounds, four in Mazar and four to the south and west. The most distant is in Maymana, two hundred kilometres west. The most remote is Charkint, in the mountains, thirty kilometres south. All the roads, even the main highway, are in poor repair having had no maintenance for over twenty years. Travel is slow... very slow. The journey to Maymana is ten hours, to Charkint four hours... and that's a good day. Every journey out of the city must have a written travel permit from the Taliban. I will arrange that. Is that clear?'

'Sure thing.'

'Maybe you can start visiting the city clinics tomorrow.'

'*As-salamu Alaykum,*' Doctor Shamir greeted Doctor Basir and myself as we entered the male section of the first of the four city clinics I was to visit. Built with mud walls and corrugated iron roof, the long rectangular single-story building was divided into two. One end for males, the other for females. The male clinic was gloomy, two dim globes battling the darkness of the waiting room. A tiny window high in the wall was curtained in cobwebs. The walls were bare and grimy. Elderly men and one adolescent boy sat huddled in small groups, chatting in lowered tones. They shuffled uncomfortably as we entered.

'Wa'alaykum as-salam,' I replied in unison with Doctor Basir. Doctor Shamir smiled and shook my hand profusely. He wore a white coat two sizes too big, a stethoscope hanging loosely from a pocket. Jet-black hair fell over his forehead highlighting dark brown eyes that sparkled with glee.

My companion, Doctor Basir, was the senior national doctor and my assistant, advisor and interpreter. Short and stocky, square shoulders, a round face with a black wispy beard, his appearance reflected his stoicism and dependability. He became a valued adviser and friend. We were escorted into Doctor Shamir's room carefully scrutinised by every eye in the waiting room.

'You are very welcome Doctor John. Would you like some tea?' I would soon learn that the Afghan hospitality is legendary and they are a generous and congenial people.

'Thank you but no, we will not delay you. How is the clinic?' I immediately wondered if it was an insult to refuse. Doctor Shamir did not react. Doctor Basir later reassured me that in this professional setting it was appropriate.

'The clinic is running very well. We have plentiful supplies and medications. MSF is well-organised,' his compliments flowed. He seemed happy and content. 'But I would like to show you a case, for your opinion, if you don't mind?' His formality was humbling.

'Of course, I'd be delighted.'

He stood, poked his head out of the doorway and called a name. A youth and his father entered and sat next to Doctor Shamir's desk. I had the feeling that this had been specially organised and I was being tested.

'This is Abdul. He is fifteen years old and complains of weakness and lassitude for many months. Would you like to examine him?'

I decided to take the challenge and rather than prolong the process with further questioning, I quickly examined Abdul from head to toe.

'He is underweight, slightly anaemic and has enlarged lymph glands in the back of his neck. Does he have a cough? Is there any TB in the family?'

Doctor Shamir smiled. 'Yes, his grandfather was recently diagnosed. He does not have any cough but I agree with you, Doctor John. I also think he has TB but we cannot test so we will commence treatment and watch him. Thank you for your opinion.'

'Come this way Doctor John,' Doctor Basir hurriedly beckoned me to follow him as he disappeared behind a carpet hanging on the wall and through a discrete doorway that led into a storage cupboard within the female clinic. It seemed very covert. 'We have built secret doors in the Mazar clinics for us to safely access the female clinics. The staff are happy for us to enter but we set sentries at the outer door to check the "V and V" spies aren't around.'

The female waiting room was the complete opposite of the male side. The room was brightly illuminated and crammed with women and young children. Infants were shuffling around the floor and climbing over their mothers. The walls were lined with health promotion posters, advertising vaccinations, antenatal clinic, and hand hygiene. Many women still wore their burqas but had thrown the front panel over their head to expose their faces and normal everyday dress and jewellery. I was surprised at their fashionable clothes and made-up faces. Natasha, the midwife, saw my astonishment.

'We are just normal women Doctor John. We like fashion and beautiful things. Just because we must wear a burqa outside does not change us.'

I felt stupid and humbled and realised how much the burqa dehumanises the wearer.

'Of course,' I apologised. 'It is all so new. Forgive me please.'

She nodded and smiled.

Doctor Asma walked from the dressing room with a mask over her face, keeping her sterile gloves in front of her face. She glimmered wearing a multi-coloured, intricately embroidered dress with a heavy gold necklace gleaming on her neck. Her straight black hair was tied back in a short ponytail.

She greeted us. 'As-salamu Alaykum.'

'Wa'alaykum s-salam,' I replied in unison with Doctor Basir. It was to become routine.

'Come in, I am removing a tumour.' She returned into the dressing room and we followed. A patient lay swaddled in drapes on the couch. A large incision on her left upper chest was packed with gauze.

'She has a lump in the breast that I have removed. It does not look malignant. I am just starting to close up. Would you like to help Doctor John?'

'I'd be delighted.' I quickly scrubbed and gloved my hands wondering if I was being tested again?

'We have run out of surgical gowns so we must be careful of our clothes. I have used a local anaesthetic as we have no facility for general anaesthetic. It has worked well.'

She removed the packs from the wound that had stopped the bleeding and sewed the deeper tissues together. I watched in fascination at her dexterity and skill.

'There is no accessible hospital care in the city so we try to do as many procedures in the clinic as possible. It is not ideal but this is war,' she shrugged acceptingly.

Doctor Basir smiled as we drove back to base. 'Are you impressed Doctor John?'

'Very much so. The clinic is well set up and staffed. You have done an amazing job.'

'Tomorrow we shall drive to Maymana. I will ask Ewald to apply for a travel permit.'

How were you accepted John? You seem to have passed their first inspection.
Yes, it was gratifying to show the staff I was a competent doctor. But all national staff is very wary of new expatriates and I wanted to take a back seat for a while and observe and listen. I was determined not to be the dominant, bossy, pushy leader, which had been my undoing in Goma. This was not an emergency humanitarian mission, more one for capacity building and development with plenty of time to improve services and up skill the staff.

Were you able to lead in a supportive fashion?
Yes and no. The clinics were efficient and I was happy for them to run with little interference, only to give staff training and logistical support. But I was soon to discover that the outreach program of this mission was unlimited. We were trying

to extend the vaccination program around each clinic, regularly visiting outlying villages to provide a full vaccination service. The epidemiological data that we collected weekly from our clinics enabled us to identify possible epidemics in the region, especially of measles and cholera and allow early intervention. We also surveyed for child malnutrition in vulnerable regions, areas destroyed by war and drought, and, where appropriate, commence feeding programs. To keep all this rolling often needed me to be more assertive than I had planned.

You mean single, open and bloody-minded?

Yes and no. The beauty of MSF is that they have developed simple methods to assess evolving medical scenarios. They were quick to respond to changing needs and moving populations, flexible to alter focus in epidemics and malnutrition and ready to provide support in expertise, logistics and finance. I rarely needed to be bloody-minded anymore. I was a pig in mud.

MAZAR-I-SHARIF, NORTHERN AFGHANISTAN
October 2000
Field Coordinator, Médecins Sans Frontières

'We have been invited by the local military commander to watch a Buzkashi match at the local football stadium next Friday. Does anyone want to go?' Ewald, the Head of Mission, announced the invitation at the weekly team meeting. Several hands shot into the air including mine. I was eager to see Buzkashi, probably made most famous in the movie Rambo III.

A headless body of a calf or goat is dumped in the centre of the field with the opposing teams on horseback lined up on either side. A rifle shot starts the game when each team tries to pick up the carcass, carry it around a turning point at one end of the field and throw it into a scoring circle at the other end. It is skilful and dangerous. The riders must lean off their horses close to the ground to pick up the carcass. They carry whips to fend off other riders. The only rule prohibits intentionally knocking other riders off their horses. A referee is appointed to determine which team has the principal remnant when it is torn apart.

'I thought Buzkashi is illegal under the Taliban regime?' I asked.

'Officially it is but local tradition seems to overrule it here,' Ewald clarified.

'The stadium is used on Fridays for executions, stonings and amputations under Sharia Law.' Caroline, a Belgian nurse with a strong sense of social justice queried, 'Surely this is not part of the proceedings?'

'No, it is a totally separate occasion but I'll double check.'

'Maybe, but should we go anyway?' she added, 'It could be interpreted that we are showing support for the Taliban regime.'

Ewald quickly interrupted. 'This is not a Taliban event. It's a local tradition and the national sport of Afghanistan. I am happy for us to attend. It will be a chance for us to meet more local people and show our appreciation of their culture.'

The following Friday six of us climbed on to the small but packed spectator stand at the football stadium wrapped warmly in fleece jackets against the autumn chill. Most of the crowd wore lambskin coats or *patoos*, long woollen shawls wrapped around them. I wore my Chitrali hat, a traditional Afghan hat, to the great amusement of the crowd. Bodies shuffled along and up and down the benches until a length of vacant bench appeared on the front row. We were obviously welcome. A mass of bearded grinning faces beamed at us. There were no women and Caroline pulled her shawl tightly around her head to try and be less conspicuous.

Ahmed, one of our national logistic team came and joined us, sitting beside me. He pulled his *patoo* tightly around his chest. 'Welcome Doctor John, I did not know you were all coming. My brother is the organiser of this game. We are honoured. Have you seen a Buzkashi game before?'

'Only in the movies.'

'It is an ancient game. Some say it was the Mongols who used their enemies instead of the calf... their live enemies!'

I had heard rumours of captured Russian soldiers being used in more recent times but did not comment.

'The horses are specially trained. It is a great honour to win a game. The prize is secondary.'

The starting shot was fired and the two teams spurred their horses to cluster around the carcass, pushing opposing horses and riders so one team member could pick it up.

'The calf is headless but it has been soaked in water all the day before to make it harder meat. Goat is not as strong as a calf.'

I hardly heard his commentary for the action was intense. Horses crashed into each other, their riders plummeting from side to side trying to grab the carcass off the ground without getting crushed. Other nearby riders used their whips to make space before holding the whip in their mouths to free their hands on the reins. The crowd stood, cheered and screamed their support. The carcass is eventually picked up by a leg and the rider gallops from the melee of horses down the field but is immediately attacked by an opposing rider who grabs another leg and tries to tug the carcass free. Meantime another team member cuts ahead to turn the horses away from the turning point.

'How long does the game last?'

'It can go on all day but this game lasts two hours. Only ten men can ride at any one time in any team. It is very tiring.'

I looked at the field and counted at least thirty horses in the skirmish but did not comment. I sat completely absorbed and wondrous of the horsemanship and sheer grit of the players who only wear a heavy coat and an optional round fur-trimmed hat with quilted earflap as protection from falls and lashes of the whip. Rugby football looked like 'pass the parcel' in comparison.

The game continued in intensity and ferocity for the full two hours. When the goat was dumped unceremoniously into the scoring circle in front of the main stand there was a huge roar of appreciation before the game resumed. I think the final score was 4-2 but still had no idea who either team represented.

At the end of the game, one rider approached our seats on his horse, bowed and shouted to Ahmed.

'That is my brother, Ghulam. He asks if you would like to ride the horses and play a game.'

I was tempted but I knew my horsemanship was infantile compared to what I had just witnessed.

'Tell Ghulam I am honoured but will decline. There is no comparison to the riding of the Afghan. I salute him.' I waved and he laughed, turned his horse and raced away.

Did your attendance help embed you in the local population?
I've no idea but I was impressed that despite all their hardships, the social disruption of being forcibly occupied by the Taliban, an ongoing civil war and being globally isolated by UN sanctions the Afghans preserved their customs and communal spirit. I felt privileged to have witnessed this game and be made so welcome. I saw it as a symbol of their resilience and hardiness that has allowed them to survive throughout the centuries. They have been invaded by Alexander the Great, Genghis Khan, the Mongol emperors, the British and most recently the Russians but no one has ever dominated them. It made me think about cultural resilience.

In what way?
The Afghan people (and I'm not meaning the Taliban) are super-resilient. They are doggedly independent with intense ethnic loyalties, strong family and community units, dogmatic beliefs, rigid protocols and an ability to accept hardship. It may not be democratic but it has stood the test of time.

Our western cultures wobble on opinion polls, twitter trends, Facebook likes, Instagram 'influencers', 24/7 media bites and selfies. It suffers fragmented families and cracked communities. It has no consistent moral compass and cries hysterical outrage when attacked or offended.

Terrorist attacks: New York, London, Paris, Boston, Nice, Manchester have produced political chest thumping, seas of flowers, a media frenzy and declarations of unity and cohesion but I only see more division and self-interest. Everyone soon disperses and returns to their narcissistic lifestyles of discontent, WIIFM and WIFI (*What's in it for me?* and *Who is fucking interested?*)

And how does this make you feel?
Disappointed and sad. But there is nothing I can do about it. It is the 'what is' and I have learnt to observe and surmise. I might be completely wrong and when in crisis, the western cultures can consolidate and find cohesion, courage and resilience. Time will tell.

In mountains south of MAZAR-I-SHARIF, NORTHERN AFGHANISTAN
November 2000
Field Coordinator, Médecins Sans Frontières

'I want to extend the vaccination program deeper into the mountains. The vaccinators are walking to the surrounding villages from the Charkint clinic but if we use horses, they can venture much further and include several more villages.' I suggested my idea to Ewald, the Head of Mission. 'These programs are essential to improve health and will prevent more disease and death than any of our other interventions,' I added to boost my argument.

'I agree John. If you write a proposal and cost it, I'll forward it to the desk in Brussels.'

'I've already done it. It's in your inbox.'

Two weeks later approval came through.

Charkint is in the foothills of rugged mountains south of Mazar-I-Sharif. The thirty-kilometre drive involved four hours of bone-crunching, jaw-jarring, body bruising motoring. The route was a four-wheel drive track that followed a wide riverbed, a carpet of rounded river stones that squeezed through a narrowed gorge, dark in shadow and protected by ancient fortification. The track left the river to scramble up steep hillsides, over rounded brown hills, crossed cols and passes to cruise along green valley floors, lush with apricot trees and drooping vines, heavy with grape. The township itself was small and sparse with no obvious commercial centre. The clinic, a squat rectangular mud-walled, flat-roofed building fronted a two-storey house at its rear where the doctor and his family resided. A forty-four-gallon drum incinerator stood proudly beside the entrance.

Haschem, my national logistics coordinator and Ali Mohammed, my driver, accompanied me. We planned to stay for three days

'Welcome Doctor John,' Doctor Aziz, the resident doctor in Charkint clinic and his wife greeted me as sincerely as a long-lost relative. He was a swarthy, heavily built man with a fine shock of black hair and bushy beard. His wife was petite, slim and fair-skinned, her face modestly shrouded by a scarf. Their young son and daughter stood shyly beside them, both images of their parents. We sat on a hand-loomed carpet in their small sitting room behind the clinic drinking green tea and I told Doctor Aziz my ideas about extending the vaccination program.

'It is an excellent plan Doctor John. Our head vaccinator, Hunji, is perfect for you. He knows every rock of the mountains and was born on the back of a horse. I'll send a message to him.'

His wife was even more enthusiastic. 'There are still many childhood deaths in our region. I often talk with the mothers who lose their children. They are desperate to have their children vaccinated. This will be very welcome.'

I was very moved by their endorsement.

We spent the night on sponge mattresses on the floor of the clinic after a meal of rice and mutton prepared by Doctor Aziz's wife. We were all weary after the rough 4WD trip.

Hunji, a local Hazari, one of the local ethnics in central Afghanistan, was short but burly. He looked like Genghis Khan, with Mongoloid features, slanted piercing eyes, thin eyebrows, and a wide droopy moustache. He was delighted with the concept of riding horses between the villages.

'Ah Doctor John, you are a prophet. I have been saying we must ride to the villages. My cousin has horses for hire. I can arrange it for tomorrow.

The horses matched the country, a wild mountain breed, short and sturdy that came fitted with a threadbare rug, weatherworn saddle and a rope across the horse's shoulders with a loop at either end for stirrups.

With Hunji leading a packhorse laden with our cold boxes and clothes the two us headed off into the mountains. Haschem had a stock-take to complete. I was high on adrenaline thinking life could not get any better. It was a magical way to travel the hills and escarpments, surrounded by open space and silence, the heat shimmering the parched ground, the browned hills aglow, an eagle soaring their up-draughts as my joy soared my spirit.

My ecstasy was short lived. I had previously ridden a horse but was inexperienced. As the terrain became more rugged, I began to feel more and more insecure, perched aloft the horse's back as we crossed deep river gorges, scrambled up and down steep rocky paths, followed narrow ledges siding precipitous falls. Luckily my horse found its own way and I kept the reins slack, shifting my weight in the saddle to balance.

Hunji taught me to wear a headscarf that fell across my face to protect from sun and sand. We passed villagers working subsistence farm practices; wooden ploughs pulled by oxen, hand-cutting and threshing the wheat and manually cleaning the corn. Women were brushing the hillside, collecting and picking up sheep dung for fuel. Children tended the goatherds or collected cow dung to splatter and dry against mud walls to create 'cow pats'.

'The cowpats are used as fuel for heat and general cooking but the sheep dung is specifically used for baking. It gives a hotter, more constant heat.' Hunji explained the intricacies of Afghan baking.

I passed a young man leading a donkey on which sat a young heavily pregnant woman. I was reminded of the biblical scene of Joseph leading Mary to Bethlehem.

As the sun started to fall behind the mountains, we arrived at our first village consisting of about fifty mud-walled buildings. Young girls peeped modestly but curiously over the surrounding walls covering their faces with their head shawl.

Hunji and I set up the cold box and vaccination equipment in the house of an elder, helped by Amir Gul, a local health worker.

I was surprised when the children arrived. None of their mothers wore a burqa, only shawls covered their head, their faces exposed or partly screened by a fold. They carried their children on their hips or backs and proudly presented their vaccination cards, eager for their children to be vaccinated. Hunji explained that burqas are enforced in the cities but in the distant villages, out of sight of the Taliban, folk were often more liberal.

He was hilarious, organising the women into line with arms waving and shouted instructions. Amid the screams of crying babies and babbling mothers the three of us vaccinated over thirty children before it was dark.

Our meal that evening was more modest, rice with vegetables. I contributed bags of rice and spices that I had carried from Mazar-I-Sharif to supplement the village's supplies. I did not want our visits to be a drain on their meagre food stocks.

As we sat and ate with the men of the village, they told me how the vaccination program had improved the health of the children. Deaths from whooping cough, diphtheria and measles were now rare. They had not seen any tetanus for over a year.

We set off shortly after sunrise having quickly eaten a breakfast of flat bread and green tea. I was ecstatic. This was the best adventure and fun. The fun ended when Hunji decided to give the horses a gallop on a flat valley floor.

'No Hunji,' I shrieked. He laughed and rode off. My horse followed for I was incapable of holding it back. I hung on to the pommel of the saddle for fear of life and limb, my legs desperately trying to grip the horse's flanks but frequently flying out to the sides like a sail flapping in the doldrums, trying to balance my body over the horse.

'Whoa, Whoa,' was all I could scream in fear. Hunji thought my antics were hilarious and roared with uncontrolled laughter. Although he nearly fell off his horse in mirth he kept on galloping.

Amid all this mayhem, as I desperately clung on to my horse, a memory of a recent medical case at another remote clinic flashed into my mind. A young man had stepped on unexploded ordnance deep in the mountains and his foot had been partially blown off. His friends had carried him for three days to our clinic on the back of a donkey, in an open coffin. For most of the journey, he had been delirious and had not been taken out of the box. On arrival at the clinic he was semiconscious, dehydrated, sodden and stinking of stale blood, pus, urine and faeces. Luckily, we were able to clean him up, resuscitate him, complete the amputation, treat his infection and he survived. The terror in the thought of falling off my horse, sustaining a compound fracture of my leg and being carried for days, back to the clinic in a coffin was enough to firm my grip, steel my determination and hang on to the horse until it came to an exhausted stop.

'Hunji, let's not do that again, OK?' I was not amused but could not get angry at his childish antics and glee.

'OK Doctor John,' he smirked.

Did you realise it would be so dangerous John?

Not until the gallop. Hanging on to that horse for life and limb was a dire lesson for me in risk management. That flashback to the man with the blown-off foot squarely scared me and highlighted how stupid it was to travel in such remote places with no thought of the risks.

But hell, it was a lesson worth learning. That day, riding in the mountains, and several more that followed, were highlights of my mission. I knew I could not remove all danger but I could reduce the obvious risks and set my intentions that I would be safe.

I emphasised to Hunji my limitations as a rider. He ensured that in future, as we wended our way among the remote villages, I rode a more subdued horse. He taught me how to canter and gallop, initially on uphill sections enabling me to pull the horse up more readily. It was not long that I was galloping again but never in my earlier rodeo leg-flapping style.

It became routine for me to complete a risk assessment for any future forage into remote regions. Risk can never be removed but taking time to imagine what might go wrong at any time allows simple protocols and precautions to be implemented and reduce obvious disaster. But the exhilaration of my riding adventures in the Afghan mountains highlighted to me that if we live our lives too carefully, we may have no life at all.

MAZAR-I-SHARIF, NORTHERN AFGHANISTAN
November 2000
Field Coordinator, Médecins Sans Frontières

'We've been invited to witness a bonfire of marijuana by the Taliban. Anyone interested?' asked Julien, the Head of Mission.

'You're joking?' queried Stefan

'Not at all. Apparently, the Taliban want to convince the world that they are anti-drugs and do not finance their military campaign by its sale. Some Taliban public relations bright spark has thought up this idea as a stunt.'

'I'm in.'

'So am I.'

'Me too.'

It might be PR stunt but it was so bizarre that no one wanted to miss out.

Julien briefed us before we departed for the event.

'The delegates from the UN mission have also been invited. We've all been specifically asked to bring our cameras even though officially they are prohibited.'

86

'That seems logical. You can't have a PR exercise without a picture. Ha ha,' cajoled Stefan.

'That might be so,' counselled Ewald, 'but we do not want to be party to this PR exercise. Any photos taken must be for personal use only and not sent anywhere for publication. Do you all agree?' Everyone nodded.

The six of us jumped into the cars and we drove through the city to the arranged site on the outskirts.

We knew we had arrived when we spied the pile of marijuana plants, four metres round and two metres high. Several young Taliban, straggly, dark beards, black turbans, baggy pants, black blankets thrown over their knee-length dresses with AK-47s slung under their arms, were slouching next to their utility cars. We jumped out of our cars to be greeted by Mohammed, an elderly man similar in appearance to Gandalf the Wizard, his wrinkled face, pointed grey beard and long fingernails adding a mystery to his welcome. He led us to a table behind the bonfire. Five bulging sacks sat on the ground alongside a table on which lay five smaller packets of white powder. 'Each large sack contains fifty kilograms of hashish. The smaller packages each hold one kilogram of heroin,' Mohammed explained. 'We will burn it all. We do not promote the production or sale of these drugs.'

'Here come the UN,' announced Martin, the medical coordinator, as a white four-wheel drive car emblazoned with the blue UN logo parked alongside our cars and three of their delegates emerged. We knew them well and they soon joined us.

Opening one of the large sacks revealed it to be full of pungent, dark brown hashish powder. The smaller bags contained a fine white powder. It seemed all too surreal, inspecting such a drug haul as guests of the Taliban. We started to giggle and laugh. Someone threw a handful of hashish powder at someone else. Someone else retaliated. A childish battle developed and hashish powder filled the air. A couple of us rubbed some heroin into our hair to prematurely go grey. A cloud of insanity prevailed.

Sanity was firmly re-established when Mohammed-cum-Gandalf returned, politely coughed and looked at us sternly over his glasses like a disappointed parent. All the frivolity instantly terminated. Without any further formality the sacks and bags of hashish powder and heroin were placed on top of the bonfire, saturated with kerosene and the fire was lit.

We all stood back to watch… downwind.

HINDU KUSH, north of SAR-E POL, NORTHERN AFGHANISTAN
November 2000
Field Coordinator, Médecins Sans Frontières

'We've got to go,' I snapped. It was long after ten o'clock, our planned departure time.

'But we can't, there's still a long queue outside,' countered Charmaine, a Belgian nurse accompanying me on this exploration. She stared at me with pleading eyes, her short brown hair framing an angelic face that was distressed by our dilemma.

'And it will only get longer as the day goes on and word gets out we're running a clinic,' I insisted but regretting my shortness.

It had started as a goodwill gesture, a 'thank you' to the village, Laghman, who were so accommodating to us. Afghan hospitality is legendary. We had arrived unannounced the previous evening, seeking overnight shelter on our way up the valley to the distant mountains where we planned to run a nutritional survey. A delegation from the region had visited our coordination office in Mazar-I-Sharif, complaining that drought had caused major crop failures in the region resulting in severe malnutrition amongst the children. They requested food support. Ewald, the Head of Mission, had tasked Charmaine and me to visit the region to assess the severity. Doctor Basir, my national counterpart, and Kassam, a local nurse accompanied us as interpreters and assistant. We had driven for two days along the long-neglected, cracked, pot-holed main highway turning off on to dusty, dirt tracks that passed through primitive oilfields where myriad antique rocking oil wells, their gases shooting flames ten metres into the air, looked like a scene from *Mad Max*. Ferocious Afghan hounds, a metre high, ran beside the car, foaming at the mouth, barking and snarling discouraged us from even thinking of stopping and taking a photo.

Ahead, northwards, lay the Hindu Kush, the extension of the Himalayas that fills the centre of Afghanistan. Hopefully, we would arrive at our destination in their foothills later in the day. If only we could leave?

When we had arrived the previous evening, the whole population of the village, wide-eyed and curious, had emerged from their mud houses to observe and greet us. We were a novelty. No Europeans had visited the village since before the Russian invasion, over twenty years earlier. The children, wearing a combination of shy looks and giggling grins, enthusiastically escorted us to the house of the head elder where, cross-legged, sitting on homemade carpets, we met with all the village elders. The mandatory green tea was served as refreshment whilst I explained the purpose of our journey.

With formalities finished we were given a tour of the village, one of the prettiest I had seen in Afghanistan. Narrow canals of running water, fed from the near-by river through age-old levies, ran alongside paths lined with budding apricot and plum trees. Waterfalls spilled into ponds for the goats and cattle. A wooden water chute plunged into the flourmill, its raging torrent powering an ancient millstone within to grind the harvested grain. The cogs of the mill's workings were hand hewn from solid timber tree trunks with the precision of a modern engine. Fine particles of flour filled the air. Patterned flowerbeds embroidered in deep reds, vibrant yellows and violet purples peppered the spaces between houses. The colours, the perfumes, the gurgling and splashing of water all created a lush garden paradise.

As the sun set, we again sat cross-legged with the elders eating a generous meal of rice, laded with raisins and laced with bones heavy with mutton meat. It was during the meal that one of the elders mentioned, 'Doctor John, my son has a bad cough. Could you examine him before you leave in the morning?'

How could I refuse?

When we awoke with the rising sun flooding our room the elder was waiting outside our door with his son. I was a little dismayed that behind him several other villagers were waiting too.

His son had a severe chest infection and I could provide an antibiotic from the few medical supplies I had packed for our personal needs. As he left, he again asked, 'Doctor John, would you mind just seeing a couple of other children before breakfast?'

How could I refuse?

The problem was that the crowd outside kept growing. The word was out. There had not been a medical doctor here for decades. Everyone would want to come and test this western medicine. I did not have the equipment, supplies, medication or the time to continue. We had to leave.

I summoned the elder and explained our dilemma. He was polite, accepting but visibly disappointed. I promised to return at a later date and run a clinic. He visibly chuckled with delight.

After hastily packing the car we at last drove off. A hundred disappointed faces stared back at me. What had started as a favour had backfired into a public relation's disaster. Would we ever be welcome again?

And were you ever welcome again? Did you ever go back?
When I returned to Mazar-I-Sharif and told Ewald, the Head of Mission, what had happened he was... dismayed is putting it lightly... but he did quieten down after hearing the full story.

'Never make a promise you cannot fulfil,' he counselled. 'The people here are hardy. They can take bad news, harsh decisions, and tough outcomes. If you had refused to see anyone more than the elder's son, saying you had no supplies, they would have accepted it thankfully. But to gain their trust, you must keep your word. If you do not go back, our reputation will be forever tarnished.

'You tell me that the malnutrition survey you completed has failed to show any significant malnutrition in the mountains and does not merit intervention... but you must a least return to the village and run one clinic.

Good work by the way.'

And did you go back?
I was struggling to find time to visit the village when luckily... well not so lucky for some... there were reports of an outbreak of what could have been cholera in a village in the same valley.

Ewald tasked me to visit the possible epidemic with a small team and set up a cholera intervention. Whilst that was being implemented, I took a day to visit Laghman, which was only an hour's drive. I fulfilled my promise and ran a full day's clinic.

The elders were delighted. I spent another wonderful evening eating and conversing, strolling through the water gardens, enjoying the unique ambience. They asked if I could return regularly. I explained that, being out of our regular operational range it was not possible. They smiled, shrugged and nodded, *Insha'Allah* (God willing).

It was a valuable lesson, not just for humanitarian missions but also for life... not to make any promises you cannot fulfil... to anyone... particularly your children. The betrayal of a broken promise is far more damaging than the disappointment of a realistic expectation.

In the mountains north of MAYMANA, NORTHERN AFGHANISTAN
December 2000
Field Coordinator, Médecins Sans Frontières

I was high in the Hindu Kush, the mountain range that bisects Afghanistan, walking between the tiny villages, huddles of rectangular mud buildings that nestle amid its deep valleys beside rivers that irrigate their few crops. The trip had only been hurriedly planned three days earlier.

'John, there's a rumour of an outbreak of a haemorrhagic fever in the hills north of Maymana. Are you interested in investigating?' Stefan, the new Head of Mission, asked me whilst eating breakfast in the MSF coordination base in Mazar-I-Sharif.

'Too right.' I had nodded excitedly at the opportunity to explore the remote rugged mountains.

'Bruno and Doctor Qamar can accompany you.'

I enjoyed the company of Bruno, a Belgian nurse. He was quiet and self-contained with a dry sense of humour and quick wit. Security protocols demanded a minimum of two expatriates on any journey far from the base. Doctor Qamar, one of the national doctors originated from the Maymana area and knew the region well. He would act as our guide and interpreter.

We overnighted in our Maymana clinic after enduring the tedious ten-hour drive along the potholed and broken highway. Doctor Qamar organised the equipment and supplies before we set out on our exploration the following sun-drenched morning. Heading north towards the snow-capped mountains, our Toyota 4WD car could only carry us the few miles to a village nestled at the base of the mountains where the flat-bottomed river valley narrowed, its backdrop of vertical cliffs converging to a narrow gorge whose entrance was shrouded in shade; forbidding, dark and mysterious. All transport past this point could only be on foot.

I sat cross-legged on the mat and sipped green tea with the elders of the village, a cluster of rectangular, flat-roofed, mud-walled buildings, the typical building design of the region. We met under a copse of leafless poplar and willow trees that grew beside the village. The branches cast speckled shadows from the wintery sunlight over the dusty ground. I told them of our mission to explore the mountains for a possible epidemic. They too had heard rumours of a strange illness and nodded. Doctor Qamar sat close to me, leaning forward, interpreting my every word and their replies. He was well known and trusted by the elders who were eager to help and instantly provided us with local guides and six donkeys to carry our luggage. As well as our personal items we carried medical supplies for emergencies, a satellite phone for communications and a generous supply of food to feed our party and share with the villages that would accommodate us. It was all arranged in an hour.

Walking into the deep shadows of the gorge amplified the winter chill and I shivered both with cold and excitement, appreciative of the thermals I wore under my clothes. The winter snows had thankfully had not yet arrived or our present task would have been impossible, the route made impassable by snowdrifts. The path, hemmed in by the gorge's sheer vertical walls, initially crisscrossed the river that now trickled between the rounded river rocks of its bed, a trickle that becomes a raging torrent of angry white water that thunders through the gorge when later fed by the spring's melting snows.

The stony path, long worn by human feet and donkey's hoof, began climbing the valley's walls, narrowing to little more than a goat track with a precipitous fall beside. Being a smoker Bruno had found the climbing hard work and had decided to ride a donkey. I declined and enjoyed the warmth of the exercise. I picked my way carefully, avoiding peering down the cliff face, instead focussing on the donkey ahead who, despite its load, found its footing with ease.

From the crest of the cliff a spectacular vista of the flatlands and valley that we had left behind was visible. Ahead of us lay undulating sombre brown hills reaching out to the mountains ahead, their distant peaks sparkling with snowy whiteness.

Fortunately, we reached our first mountain village as the sun abruptly dropped behind the hills when darkness descended and the air temperature plummeted. Despite our hasty planning and sudden departure, we were expected. There were no phones or electricity but I suspected radio communication existed between the villages. The mosque, a long, low mud building towered by a lone minaret was opened to accommodate us and its kerosene heater fired up. A pile of rich-maroon elongated cushions, their braided fabric faded and worn, made perfect seats and mattresses. No sooner had we sat down to hopefully relax when the doors were thrown open and the village elders gathered, throwing off their *patoos*, and sat in a large circle. Sipping the mandatory green tea, I reiterated the rumour and our plans. They too had heard stories of a haemorrhagic fever deeper in the mountains and promised to provide us with local guides for the next day before rushing off to their homes for their evening prayer.

My hopes for a restful evening were dashed when the doors were again thrown open and wide metal plates, heaped with rice and mutton, were placed on the floor by the young men. The elders returned and we all sat in a circle and ate with our hands to our fill. Despite the wide chasm between our cultures and customs the conversation was lively and humorous. It reinforced to me that expressions, gestures and laughter are the shared languages of the world.

It was late when they tired of our novelty and I fell into a deep sleep enveloped by the silence of the mountains.

The village sprang to life at dawn. After a hasty breakfast of flatbread and green tea that magically appeared at our door, we recommenced our exploration.

Our entourage, now expanded to a column of twenty men and eight donkeys, was enveloped in a cacophony of excited banter, shouted orders and stubborn braying. At every village the story was the same. They too had heard the rumour and pointed us deeper into the mountains. At every village, we acquired more guides and groupies. The party was beginning to resemble a military parade.

My mind wandered in history... one of Britain's worst military disasters was the British retreat from Kabul 1842 during the first Anglo-Afghan War. A column of four thousand five hundred troops and twelve thousand civilians retreating from Kabul was annihilated by ambush, frostbite and exposure. Only one European (the assistant surgeon) and a few Indian sepoys reached Jalalabad... I scanned the hillsides imagining the ease of ambush and the danger of exposure but was confident that we were safe. The fighting in the present civil war between the Taliban and the Northern Alliance was hundreds of kilometres distant on the other side of the country. Even the influence of the ruling Taliban did not extend into this mountainous region. But there was still unexpected danger...

The next village en route was unusual for it was sited high on a ridge, half way up to the valley's side, well away from a river.

'I'll walk up with Doctor Qamar as my interpreter. Everyone else can rest by the river. There's no point us all traipsing up and down,' I suggested. No one objected for the winter sun was warming when sheltered from the katabatic wind on the valley floor.

Doctor Qamar and I set off up the path that traversed the valley side then cut back to reach the ridge. I wanted to be up and down quickly allowing a rapid transit and turned off the path to head straight up the hillside. The route was steeper but shorter and would save time. Doctor Qamar silently followed.

Halfway up the climb, I heard shouting. Looking up, a figure, silhouetted on the ridgeline, was madly waving and shouting. 'What's his problem?' I asked Doctor Qamar.

He listened intently for a few seconds and turned pale. 'He doesn't have a problem, Doctor John, we do. This is a minefield.'

My feet froze. I again recalled the story of the patient who had been carried for three days in a coffin to the Maymana clinic after standing on unexploded ordinance and losing his left foot. I did not want to be a repeat.

'What shall we do Doctor John?' Doctor Qamar squeaked. I pondered. I could not believe this was a minefield. There must be unexploded ordnance here, probably from the Russian invasion. Who cared? It can still explode and kill me. We had to walk out. I decided to retrace our steps back to the path and explained the plan to Doctor Qamar.

'I'll walk back and you follow in my footsteps.' I had created this fiasco. The least I could do was to go first. 'That's good Doctor John... but Doctor John?'

'Yes?' I questioned.

'You have longer legs. Can you make them shorter?'

I laughed, 'I'll make my steps shorter. I want to keep my legs long.'

Needless to say, we arrived back on the path with immense relief. With a renewed resolve we again set off up the path to the village. Here I learnt that the village had been a hideout for Mujahedeen fighters during the Russian invasion and was attacked on several occasions by helicopter with many of their rounds falling short and failing to explode.

They too had heard the rumour of a 'bleeding fever' and pointed us deeper into the mountains.

So why tell this story?

I broke a fundamental security rule. Never take shortcuts. It was stupid and irresponsible. Even worse was that I had put Doctor Qamar's life in jeopardy.

I'm embarrassed to say I had broken other security rules a few weeks earlier when I missed a routine radio check whilst crossing the desert in a sole vehicle. It was routine to dismantle and hide the UHF aerial when travelling in the desert to deter bandits. Radios were in high demand. Having safely crossed the desert I delayed making our routine radio contact with base. It was a bother to stop and set up the aerial. I knew we would arrive back within an hour and I could report in then.

The radio controller at base was more diligent. He noted our overdue call and alerted the Head of Mission who, knowing the danger of the terrain, had dispatched a search party. Fortunately, we met them on the road as we drove into Mazar-I-Sharif. I rightly received a stern warning from Ewald for my negligence and I vowed to be vigilant in the future. Now I had broken the rules again, this time with potentially far more serious consequences.

Why do you think this happened again?

The problem about working in dangerous areas is 'security creep'. After a while any potential danger which does not eventuate becomes routine, the abnormal becomes normal, the precaution becomes an annoyance. What was bizarre and threatening on arrival becomes commonplace and ordinary. This alters our perception of danger. Armed roadblocks and patrols become the daily reality, crowded marketplaces seem harmless and benign, sandbagged doorways, taped windows, guards at every gate are expected. As a result, we normalise risk and take shortcuts in security protocols and procedures, in this case leaving a well-defined path. We downgrade risk assessments considering the risk assessors have over stated the danger.

In my embarrassment, I did not report this incident… but I had learnt my lesson… thankfully without killing anyone… I gave myself a stern warning and never took short cuts in any way again.

I also volunteered to coordinate the regular monthly practice for team evacuation from our compound in Mazar-I-Sharif, simulating our response to an extreme threat such as an impending attack on the city or a nearing war front. We practised packing the cars with critical equipment, securing our prepared grab-bags of personal effects, hiding files and non-critical equipment in concealed hidey-holes. Everyone followed pre-determined responsibilities and actions. With practice, the evacuation only took half an hour from the initial call to actually driving out of the gates. It was a useful tool to both make the escape schedule efficient but also to remind us of the daily reality of the surrounding dangers and the volatility of the region.

And did you find an epidemic of haemorrhagic fever?

No, there was no infectious epidemic. It was even more interesting. We arrived at one village where several people were suffering extreme weakness, bruising and bleeding gums… but they had no fever. After examining several patients, I made a diagnosis although I had never seen a case before. I was certain it was scurvy, a lack of vitamin C. Many crops had failed in the drought, especially green vegetables and fruits, a common source of the vitamin. The main source of calories had been bread and vitamin deficiencies were common.

After my return to base I organised for two national nurses to return to the region to educate the locals about vitamins and their sources and distribute vitamin C tablets to tide them over until the next harvest.

MAZAR-I-SHARIF, NORTHERN AFGHANISTAN
December 2000
Field Coordinator, Médecins Sans Frontières

I was squashed beside Doctor Basir and a case of medical supplies on the back seat of the Toyota 4WD car, heading west out of Mazar-I-Sharif to visit one of our feeding centres. An earlier nutritional survey of the region had identified this area to have a high malnutrition rate in the under-five-year-olds. Doctor Basir and I had set up a supplementary feeding centre where the children were seen weekly, weighed and given a week's supply of food to complement their diet. I tried to visit every month to support the regular national staff.

'Do you have the travel permit, Ashid?'

Ashid, the driver sighed, 'Yes Doctor John, that's my job.'

'Sorry but we're near the checkpoint.'

I was anxious. All travel outside the city limits needed a travel permit from the Taliban authorities. It was essential it be ready. But there were other dangers too.

Our route took us past the Qala-i-Jangi ('the war fortress' in Persian), an old military base surrounded by high mud walls interspersed with observation towers, and now, allegedly, an Al-Qaeda terrorist training camp. We often saw the sun flash from binoculars studying our passing car.

'Roadblock ahead,' announced Ashid. 'It's not Taliban. They could be Uzbeks from the training camp,' he nervously added.

On the road outside the fort lay an informal roadblock manned by four bearded men, black turbans flowing from their heads and a black shawl thrown over a shoulder. Their AK-47 guns were pointing at our car.

We stopped and I rolled down my window. The gun pointing at my head dropped and one man approached rubbing his fingers together, demanding money.

My mind wandered... I had recently started playing a game called 'What would Billy say?' I loved the humour of Sir Billy Connolly, a Glaswegian comedian who has a spontaneous, twisted, irreverent humour that can make fun of any situation. When I was scared, troubled or embarrassed I would think, *What would Billy say? How would his humour view the event?* Sometimes I had an instant hit. More often it took a day or two to think of a comment. Sometimes it was funny. Sometimes it was not so funny.

My mind had an instant hit. *Which classes are you missing today mate... bomb-making, grenade-throwing or shooting innocent people?*

I inwardly smiled until my sense of humour evaporated looking down his elevated gun barrel. My humorous distraction had been short but his patience was even shorter. Doctor Basir eyed me suspiciously.

My mind quickly refocused. We had been issued with a small wad of money for such an emergency and I handed it over. He looked unhappy at the amount and put two fingers to his mouth demanding cigarettes. I shook my head. 'I don't smoke', I foolishly added. His look was malignant but luckily another car was approaching and with the realisation of easier pickings he waved us on.

Our relief was short-lived. The official Taliban roadblock lay only a couple of kilometres ahead sited strategically before the road crossed the Darya River, where it narrowed beside the remnants of the ancient city's mud walls.

A rope blocked both inward and outward lanes. A rectangular mud-walled gatehouse, the size of two sentry boxes, set with a small observation window sat on the opposite side of the road. We stopped. A young Taliban soldier strolled over to Ashid who silently handed him our permit. He peered through the window scanning all our faces, his eyes widening at my white, stubbled face. His eyes fell whilst he slowly unfolded the permit, examined it minutely for a few seconds, turned around and walked over to the gatehouse. I smiled inwardly. He had been scrutinising it upside down. We waited... and waited...

A beaten-up, worn-out taxi, wings dented, paint faded, windscreen cracked like a giant spider's web, drove up to the roadblock opposite our car and stopped. There were two passengers in the front passenger seat, four on the back seat, two inside the open boot and one perched on each wing, leaning on the roof pillar and holding on to the overloaded roof rack. Another Taliban soldier strolled over, scanned each passenger, examined the travel permit and loitered to the gatehouse.

We all continued to wait.

In a flurry of haste, a soldier stormed out of the gatehouse summoning two other sentries to follow him to the taxi. Flinging open the back door they dragged an old man by his arm on to the road and started to kick and yell at him. The man's turban fell off and he curled up to protect himself but they continued to kick and hit him with their rifle butts.

I tensed and felt I had to do something.

'Don't move Doctor John. If you interfere, we will be beaten too. Maybe not you, for you are a Westerner but Ahmed, Kareem and I will be. You may be deported.'

'Why are they beating him?' I whispered louder than I intended.

'Maybe his beard is too short. It must be ten inches long.'

'Is that all?'

'Maybe the soldiers are bored?'

I sat rock still, tense as a board, every fibre wanting to interfere.

The old man's head was bloodied, his *parahan* or shirt was widely torn. He was unmoving. The soldiers tired and with one final kick laughed amongst themselves and moved back to their observation posts.

Two men from the taxi's back seat raced out and tended the unconscious body.

'Do not help Doctor John. We must stay in the car,' commanded Doctor Basir. I knew he was right. I could not endanger my staff.

I watched as they lifted the beaten body back into the taxi, resting it across their laps on the back seat.

The soldier returned from the gatehouse and sauntered to our car, returned our travel permit without comment and signalled to the rope keeper to drop the rope. We drove out.

How do you cope with situations like that?

I cried with frustration and anger that night. It is so unjust to witness such unprovoked aggression against vulnerable people and be able to do absolutely nothing. I felt impotent and cowardly even though I knew I could not help.

I would repeat and repeat my self-talk... *this will happen whether I am there or not... this is the 'what is' of life. I have to accept it. I cannot change it.*

Before I fell into a troubled sleep, I wondered *What would Billy say?* I imagined him jumping out the car and in his broad Glaswegian accent, shouting, 'Hey, you gits... stop that. Of course, the beard is short. That's my mother.

In the mountains north of MAYMANA, NORTHERN AFGHANISTAN
February 2001
Field Coordinator, Médecins Sans Frontières

'Doctor John, Doctor John, Doctor John,' echoed adoringly between the towering valley walls, cried repeatedly and in unison by the village's population who all stood tall with one arm aloft in salutation. They lined the rocky track as I entered the remote Afghan village astride my sturdy mountain stallion at the head of my column of guides, porters, interpreters and pack donkeys laden with baskets of medical supplies, food and camping equipment. We were high in the snow-capped mountains of northern Afghanistan, a five-day hazardous trek across raging torrents, up vertiginous, narrow ledges that clawed their way up steep valleys and across mountain passes from one valley to another to bring much needed medical supplies to a destitute population. It had been a hazardous journey across the mountains evading Taliban patrols, sleeping during the day and travelling in the shadows of the night. Now we had arrived.

I suddenly woke up and realised it was but a dream. In reality, I had recently returned after trekking in the Hindu Kush Mountains of northern Afghanistan, exploring the region for an outbreak of a haemorrhagic fever. For five days we had trudged from village to village, asking questions, examining any sick villager. We had found no epidemic. I had no horse. I was on foot alongside my guide, interpreter, six pack donkeys and several stragglers. Many of the villagers had indeed looked at me but in silent curiosity, fleeting suspicion and probably a withheld amusement. They had not laid eyes on a European for over twenty years and for them, if nothing else, I was an oddity and novelty.

Did you have this dream often?
No, just a few times over the ensuing months.

What is its significance?
I think it was just an emergent boyhood fantasy. 'Lawrence of Arabia' was a boyhood hero. I first read of him in a book of British adventurers whilst in primary school. I was mesmerised. A misfit British army officer stationed in Cairo, he was seconded to liaise with the Arab desert tribes and assist them to fight against the Turks in Arabia during the First World War. Practically single-handedly he managed to unite the Arabs into a formidable army. He accompanied them as they blew up the Turkish supply train lines and attack Turkish strongholds. He was instrumental in their capturing the fortress port of Aqaba on the Red Sea, crossing the impassable Nefud desert with an Arab army to surprise the garrison by an attack to the rear of the city whose guns all pointed out to sea. He later accompanied the Arab army as it entered and occupied Damascus before the arrival of the Allied forces.

He was a loner, independent, resilient and rebelled against authority and deceit. He was devastated and felt totally betrayed when his commander, General Allenby, of the Allied forces, reneged on his promise to give independence to the Arabs for their uprising against the Turks.

So, you identified with him?
Yes, I resonated with his rebel and loner archetypes. I respected his sense of fair play and honesty. Naïve and idealistic maybe, but I was just a boy.

When the Oscar-winning film *Lawrence of Arabia* was made in 1962 I was in heaven. The scenery was stunning, the characters captivating and the story sensational. For me, fiction could not have been more thrilling, intriguing or exciting. In the film, Laurence is acclaimed as he rides his camel into a wadi, lined by adoring tribesmen all calling out his name. Hence my 'John of Afghanistan' dream. It was just my inner child ignited by actual events.

I suppose my inner child is still thriving on adventure. My missions have been the perfect vehicle for me to access out-of-the-way, beyond-the-*Lonely-Planet* locations. It is one reason that I volunteer for them. Maybe I don't want to grow up yet. Being an adult seems to be little fun. I find it rejuvenating to see the magic, adventure and fun in life, not only on missions but also in normal daily living. We don't stop playing because we get old; we get old because we stop playing.

'Doctor John, there is a delegation from the Chimtal region who want to ask for medical help. Can you see them?'

'Of course.' I was at my office desk in our compound in Mazar-I-Sharif writing a report on a recent nutritional survey. Any distraction was welcome.

Four elderly men entered. Their faces were etched with wrinkles and framed with stringy white beards. All were clad in the customary *shalwar kameez*, or long shirt and baggy pants with a *waaskat*, or waistcoat, and white turbans on their heads. I stood up to greet them.

'*As-salamu Alaykum,*'

'*Wa'alaykum s-salam,*' they chorused.

'Please come and sit.' As Doctor Basir interpreted my comments I indicated two couches beside a central coffee table. I pulled my office chair around the desk, Doctor Basir sat in a single chair, Kareem, the national nursing coordinator, brought in an ever-ready jug of hot green tea and poured everyone a cup. I waited. It was not polite to rush.

'You have travelled far,' I opened. Doctor Basir automatically interpreted. We had formed an easy working relationship and mutual trust. He needed no direction.

'It is far, but not too far,' one countered.

'You are welcome,' I continued not wanting to ask their purpose.

'We have seen your medical clinics in the city. They are highly regarded. Our region has no clinic. We ask that you help our people,' he continued to highlight the dire need of his people and plead for our help. I listened sympathetically but offered no encouragement.

'Thank you for coming. We will consider your proposal.' I had learnt not to make promises, give expectations or impart impressions. They were poker-faced too. The following silence was a signal for them to rise and, after many wordy farewells and handshakes, they departed.

'What do you think Doctor Basir?'

'I know the region well. It is not too far from the city. There are several surrounding villages. A clinic there would service many people.'

'We have funding to open new clinics. Let's go and have a look.'

The following week we toured the region. The dirt road paralleled the Balkh River where ancient irrigation channels fed water to the adjacent fields and painted a mosaic of green fields. The other side of the road contrasted a dry brown dusty landscape dotted with mud-walled compounds. One large elongated building stood above the smaller houses. It was derelict but seemed strongly constructed and I wondered if it would be suitable for a clinic.

'Stop the car. I want to have a look.'

Majeed, our driver, slammed on the brakes. I jumped out, leapt over a low wall, across the overgrown garden and pushed the door. It creaked open and I entered the building. Doctor Basir followed. I walked through the various rooms, paced out the rough dimensions and jotted notes.

'This would be perfect,' vocalising my thoughts to Doctor Basir. '... males that end, females this end, dividing wall here, lots of side rooms for consulting and dressing areas.' I didn't linger for we were pressed for time.

Whilst standing in the doorway having a final appraisal, a young man on the roadway started to scream. My heart sank. Who had we offended? Doctor Basir listened.

'Doctor John, this used to be the Russian army command centre.'

'That's interesting but why is he so angry?'

'He isn't angry. He is scared for us. The grounds are mined.'

My heart sank. *Not again*, I mused. I had not imagined there could be such a danger. There were no warning signs.

Doctor Basir and I looked at each other.

I decided. 'We'll go back along the same line we entered. I can see our path through the weeds. I'll go first. You follow in my footsteps.' It was easier to just do it than discuss it any further.

It was only thirty metres but with every footfall my heart hammered, my nerves sparked and my muscles tensed in anticipation of standing on a mine. I kept my steps short.

On the roadside, we hugged each other with relief.

The meeting with the elders was hilarious. News of our blunder spread before us and everyone thought it funnier that falling off your donkey, such was Afghan humour. I would later ask the local demining team to check and clear the entire grounds before we could open a clinic. They would find six mines.

Before I could expand our medical services with a new clinic and have a regular daily travel permit, I needed written permission from the Taliban administration. I had sent several letters but received no reply. Arrangements for the clinic were advancing quickly. Doctor Basir identified suitable staff. Equipment and medications were stockpiled. The grounds were cleared of mines and the building renovations were complete. The village elders were impatient.

In an attempt to speed up the process I organised an appointment with the regional medical director, Dr Rashmid. I had met him once before. He was a Taliban appointee, very fundamental and surly. His fluffy black beard and bushy black eyebrows merged with his black turban to frame his dark eyes, ridged nose and firm mouth that pursed with determination. He would not be easily persuaded.

On arrival at his office, I was surprised to be led straight into a long-carpeted room. He was already meeting with about twenty of his staff and on observing our entry he indicated for Doctor Basir and me to sit with the staff on the floor in a large semi-circle around his desk. It was not a good omen. He did not miss a word of his speech. An elderly guard brandishing a K47 machine gun over his shoulder laid mugs of green tea and a plate of boiled sweets in front of us.

Doctor Basir interpreted, 'He is decrying the western powers as corrupt and perverters of Allah. He says they are all greedy, drunkard, sodomising and sinful and only want our money, gas and oil. Their women are harlots, dress skimpily and beg for sex. They have no real god and worship false idols and money.'

The tirade went on and on and on. After a few minutes, I stopped Doctor Basir interpreting and sat quietly, staring at the carpet in front of me, sipping the tea and sucking on the sweets, realising this was a waste of time but unable to get up and go. After an hour my bladder was uncomfortable. After two hours it was bursting. After three hours I was in agony.

In my foggy, bored and befuddled reality I realised the tirade had stopped. Everyone was standing and filing out of the room. I hastily stood up and was heading to the door when Doctor Rashmid cried out, 'Ah, Doctor John, I will see you now.'

All I wanted to do was empty my bladder but somehow found the control to turn back to his desk.

He stood up and walked around to shake my hand.

'I 'ave a small favour to ask from you, Doctor John.' His English was stilted but understandable.

'My car, a Toyota, has broken its alternator. With UN sanctions I cannot find a part. Can you help me?'

I was a little taken back, not knowing how to react... until divine intervention sparked an inspiration.

'I would love to help you, Doctor Rashmid... but I am so busy trying to get permission for a new medical clinic in the Chimtal region that...'

'Ah yes, of course,' he murmured whilst looking up at the ceiling and thinking... but that is no problem. I will get my secretary, Kamal, to type a letter of permission for you.'

'Can he do it now so you might also sign it? It would save you so much time,' I suggested hopefully.

'Of course,' he sighed gently. He called his secretary who was lingering behind him and snapped instructions.

'I am sure I can organise our logistics staff to import an alternator for you.'

'That is good. *Asalam-o-Aalikum*,' dismissing us (that is the way of the prophet).

I hurried out to find a toilet.

I left with the signed permission.

Did the director get his alternator?

Yes, the logistics staff sourced a new alternator in Pakistan and flew it in with our supplies. I insisted on personally paying for it. I did not want MSF donors to be paying bribes but I reckoned, rightly or wrongly, two hundred American dollars for opening a new medical clinic to serve over five thousand people was a bargain.

SYDNEY, NEW SOUTH WALES, Australia
May 2001

Was coming home from Afghanistan difficult?

You could say that. After a twenty-eight-hour journey, I landed at Sydney airport tired, irritable, lethargic and bloated by the continual input of stodgy airline food. My only thought was of a long steamy shower and sleeping in crisp clean cotton sheets.

Waiting at the luggage console I noticed a customs officer lead his drug-sniffing beagle around the passengers and their luggage. The dog was happily wagging his tail until he came up to me. His tail flopped and he pawed my leg. I looked down into his eyes. He stared back accusingly.

'May I see your passport please?' The customs officer, closely shaven, short-cropped brown hair, crisply ironed uniform asked in a tone that agreed with his dog. I handed it over. He slowly scrutinised it, his eyes frowning as he scanned my Afghanistan, Pakistan and Turkmenistan visas.

'Would you mind coming with me, sir?' It was not a question. 'And bring your luggage with you.' He walked off with my passport.

Hoisting my rucksack on my back and my backpack on my shoulder, I followed. The luggage collection area had fallen silent. All eyes followed the customs officer and his dog and stared accusingly at me, a suspected drug courier.

I was led through a code-operated door and along a corridor into a windowless room. 'Please wait here, sir.' The tone indicated that the 'sir' was purely prescriptive, not polite. I presumed this was an interview room having a central table with a chair on either side. Two other tables were set against a wall. I placed my luggage on them and sat on a chair.

I waited… and waited more.

Two burly customs officers walked in. One had a big nose and cauliflower ear. I guessed he was an ex-boxer. His neck was flabby. His uniform bulged around his middle. He had not sparred for a long time. I calculated he had lost most bouts. He sat opposite me at a central table. His offsider had shoulder muscles bulging his shirt and a neck wider than his head. I guessed him to be a gym junkie on steroids. He stood to one side and leant against the wall.

Tweedle Dee and Tweedle Dumb? I wondered. 'Big Nose' and 'Muscles' I concluded.

'Why would our dog be interested in you, Doctor Parker?' Big Nose asked whilst perusing my passport.

'I've no idea,' I replied.

'Are you sure there is nothing you wish to tell us at this early stage?'

'Nothing,' I muttered, noting his implication this would be a lengthy affair. My mind was racing as to why the dog had sniffed me out.

I intuitively realised that Big Nose and Muscles would be aggressive, authoritarian and intimidating and any attempt to be friendly would be counterproductive. I decided to be minimalist and diminutive.

'You have visas for Pakistan, Afghanistan, Turkmenistan and Tajikistan. Why would you be visiting these particular countries?'

I explained, 'I've been working in Afghanistan, transiting via Pakistan. We had visas for Turkmenistan and Tajikistan in case we had to escape the country overland.'

He was not impressed or seemingly interested.

'Do you mind if we examine your luggage?' Again, it was not a question. I shrugged, 'OK.'

'Please open your rucksacks.' I complied. For the following forty-five minutes, they completely emptied both bags, feeling the lining, the seams, every strap, examining each item of clothing, shaking out the contents of my wash kit, my shaver, my laundry bag, squirting out the tube of toothpaste. My *pakols*, the round traditional Afghan hats that I had bought as souvenirs, merited extra attention with their rolled edges and braided seams. The floor became a sea of strewn possessions.

They finished, looked at each other and walked out without comment. Muscles returned a few minutes later with a gown. 'We wish to examine your clothes. Please change into this and leave your clothes on the table.' Handing me the gown he walked out. I stripped, folded my clothes on the table, sat down and waited… and waited. They returned and without comment minutely examined every article of clothing.

As I sat, naked but for the gown, the penny dropped. I had been wearing my jacket at the Taliban's drug bonfire when we had the hashish fight and I was using heroin to grey my hair. Despite having worn it regularly and despite it having since been blasted by wind, rain and snow, some particles of hashish or heroin must have become embedded in the pockets or implanted into the lining or seams.

I was faced with a dilemma. Should I now tell these two condescending dolts, 'Oh Officer, I think I may know why the dog sniffed at me? There could be minute quantities of hashish and heroin on my jacket. I was wearing it when I attended a bonfire of marijuana, hashish and heroin with the Taliban in Afghanistan.'... or should I remain quiet?

I was also wondering if they would extend their search to my body cavities.

I decided to stay quiet.

At last they finished and without comment left the room.

Big Nose returned after a few minutes. 'You can get dressed.' He left the room.

With relief that I would not be intimately assaulted, I hurriedly dressed and waited... and waited.

Big Nose returned. 'You can go now.' Without any direction, explanation or apology he walked out.

I hastily stuffed everything into my bags and walked back down the corridor. A door automatically opened into the luggage collection area.

Head down, but inwardly daring any challenge, I walked the green 'nothing to declare' customs exit line. The Custom Officers must have been forewarned for I glided through and escaped out of the double sliding doors into the Arrivals Lounge. As relief flooded my mind I decided there and then to burn the jacket. Next time they might be more thorough.

But apart from that adventure, was coming home from Afghanistan... I mean, settling back into home life... difficult?
Returning from Goma had been difficult but at least I had a home, a job and a social network to support me. This time I had burnt all those bridges before leaving for Afghanistan. I returned homeless, unemployed and single. I was lost, forlorn and despairing. I felt I had fallen off the edge of the world. It was the lowest ebb of my life.

In what way?
I had been living an exotic, exciting and enriching adventure, high on adrenaline for a year. I had been working in a close-knit team who all shared the same experiences. I had a base with all the comforts of home; cooked meals, house cleaning, laundry, transport were all supplied. Suddenly... nothing... no... worse than nothing... life was drab, dull and dreary.

Instead, I was faced with finding somewhere to live, to shop for groceries, prepare food, wash clothes, and clean floors. It was daunting... with no energy or enthusiasm to overcome it.

I was an adrenaline addict and suffering withdrawals... an emptiness interjected with a gnawing need for more exotica and excitement. No wonder so many people head off to another mission for another 'fix'.

So how did you cope this time?
I hit the bottle... to dim the drudgery and despair. Alcohol is a great drug to numb reality and give temporary respite. Alas, it has its downfalls. I was thankfully

supported by a couple of friends who offered me temporary accommodation. I shamefully admit they tolerated my thoughtless, drunken behaviour that no friends should ever have to endure. I think I deteriorated faster than I could lower my standards. I am eternally grateful to them that they stood by me.

How else did it affect you?
I struggled with ordinary daily tasks: to go shopping, to cook and to launder my clothes was at times overwhelming. Walking along supermarket aisles crammed with myriad brands of every item seemed indulgent and indecent.

My concentration span collapsed. I couldn't focus on a storyline, fixate on a page or add up a sum. My energy level plummeted. I struggled to complete simple tasks, was easily distracted and forgetting to finish. Alongside all this confusion, amid all the loneliness, I was overwhelmed with anger.

What made you so angry?
Initially by the lack of gratitude of people in general. No one appreciated their security, their freedom, their wealth and health. They had no concept of what it was like to live in an oppressed society where speech, religion, politics, dress code, behaviour were closely restricted and regulated.

The local TV news was crammed with people whining about petty issues; waiting thirty minutes for an ambulance, the cost of public transport or hoons doing wheelies outside their houses. I mean... get real... this was all first world trivia... no one walked a kilometre to collect water... or carried a child all day to see a doctor... or had militia running wild; shooting, looting and raping.

Then there was the 'the stuff' that filled everyone's houses. It sent me ballistic. To see so many possessions cramming cupboards, drawers, lofts, garages, most of which were never used... possessions for status and security, novelty and nicety, bought on a whim rather than for necessity and practicality.

And finally, the obscene waste that's endemic in our society; throwing out anything that was worn or torn, faulty or broken, out of fashion or fad; dumping food past its used-by-date; excessive use of water, electricity, and fuel. It seemed sinful.

The transition of moving from an impoverished country where every commodity is valued, repaired and recycled to one that mindlessly accumulates, carelessly consumes and then wantonly discards was too much to tolerate.

How did you cope with all this?
I withdrew. I crawled back into my hole.

Can you be more specific?
I was unable to communicate with anyone. It seemed no one understood or even cared where I'd been or what I had done. Many thought I was weird going off to the other side of the world to help the poor... why not stay in Australia and help the poor here... and where is Afghanistan... and who gives a toss what happens there?

Many were completely indifferent to the injustices and hardships that I had witnessed. They were focused on their lives, their neighbourhood and their issues. After listening to me rave on for a couple of minutes, their eyes would wander and glaze over with boredom, embarrassment even. I was left feeling intrusive, a zealot and an idiot.

A couple of friends avoided me totally. They later confided that they had felt jealous of my adventures and I made them feel inadequate. It was bizarre. I was so self-focused and indignant that I had little insight. I found it easier to keep to myself and avoid meeting others.

Did no one acknowledge you?
Paradoxically when I did receive some praise, I felt unworthy. I was sometimes elevated to hero-status but I did not feel the hero. I felt an imposter and was unable to accept such a compliment. To do so seemed hypocritical. I had travelled to Afghanistan for selfish reasons. The real heroes were the national staff whom I had left behind. I had visited for only a few months and had returned to the luxury, safety and comfort of Australia but they... they had to remain and continue the work. I felt I abandoned them. What right did I have to complain about my circumstances? I was the lucky one.

So, you were suffering withdrawal anxiety, anger, frustration and guilt?
Yes, as well as the nightmares, flashbacks, lethargy and insomnia. I was a mess.

How long did all this persist?
A few years. I found a room to rent on a quiet horse stud in the countryside on the outskirts of Brisbane. Helping with the horses gave comfort. Whilst I fed, brushed and mucked them out they seemed to sense my distress and would stare at me, shake their head and nuzzle my face lovingly. I would tell them my stories feeling secure in their confidentiality. They gave me my first smile.

I found a part-time job in a skin cancer-screening clinic in the city. The work was routine and straightforward. It was a safe start.

My poetry failed me. I tried to write and express myself but nothing flowed and what I wrote was forced, stifled and unsatisfying. I gave up trying.

As I began to settle, I met an old friend and we became close friends. She was very understanding and allowed me to gently download many of my feelings. She was supportive, fun and a safe conduit to release many of my frustrations. We eventually became partners and I began to settle into a relationship... but I knew I could not overwhelm her with my problems.

After a couple of years, I moved to a more fulfilling job in general practice. Ironically, or maybe it was an intuitive need, I developed a special interest in emotional health and collected many patients with similar problems to me: war veterans, accident and abuse survivors. Listening and empathising with their feelings gave me comfort. I could connect with their pain. But it's easy to see other people's issues and nigh impossible to see your own.

Over time my energy improved. I was less distressed and angry about the injustices and apathy of the world. My sleeping improved, my flashbacks and nightmares receded and I became less irritable. Whether it was Mother Time easing my distress or having a more fulfilling life I did not know, or care. I began to think I was back to normal.

Did you seek professional help?
Alas, no. MSF did offer free psychologist consultations on my return but I shunned the idea. They were still taboo. I was convinced my problems were temporary and I could overcome them. I was in total denial I had any serious ongoing malfunction. I convinced myself that this was a natural reaction to my mission and

would resolve itself. I did manage to curtail my excessive drinking and contain much of my anger but in hindsight, it was only buried and not resolved. It was the best I could do.

And it obviously was not good enough for my relationship started to falter and again, after five years, I found myself single. It seemed the right time to go on another mission.

SUNSHINE COAST, QUEENSLAND, AUSTRALIA
April 2006

'I have the perfect mission for you, John.' Theodore was returning my call to MSF headquarters in Sydney. 'There has been a team deployed to Northern Nigeria to assist in containing a meningitis epidemic and they desperately need a doctor. It should only last three to four months. And by the way, the 'desk' coordinating this mission is based in New York where you'll debrief after the mission. Are you interested?'

I sure am. When do I leave?' Being single I could decide instantly. I knew my employers would understand.

'Tomorrow morning. I'll arrange any necessary vaccinations as you pass through Sydney for a briefing. We will fly you straight to the field as time is critical.'

'I'm on my way.'

John, before you continue your stories about your missions, I'd like to ask you why you decided to go on another mission? You had already suffered two traumatic episodes causing severe, prolonged periods of dysfunction and disruption. Then you proposed to repeat it.

A fair question that I've often asked myself.

Firstly, time can dissipate the pain and amplify the joys of past experiences. Why do so many women continue having babies after suffering problematic pregnancies and traumatic deliveries? The ongoing joys of the baby far outweigh the fading memories of the delivery. So too the adventure, excitement and exhilaration of missions were rich memories that overwhelmed those of the misery and malfunction after returning.

Secondly, before my first mission I'd spent fifteen years working long punishing hours as a country general practitioner, giving anaesthetics, delivering babies, setting fractured bones, consulting with patients six days a week. I was on call for emergencies every second night and weekend. Patients were generally becoming more and more demanding and less appreciative of my efforts. I was becoming disillusioned with their discontent and handing out more and more pills for conditions caused primarily by poor personal choices: dreadful lifestyle, a rubbish diet, smoking, inactivity and excessive alcohol. I remember looking into a mirror at the end of one long busy day and thinking, *You're the sickest patient I've seen all day.* I had a heavy cold. I thought, *Wouldn't it be wonderful to give the necessary to the grateful and not the unnecessary to the ungrateful.*

Thirdly I am an adventurer. I don't know if it is one of my archetypes or was nurtured in my childhood by reading Enid Blyton's *Secret Seven,* Captain Johns' *Biggles* adventures, Eric Leyland's *Flame* and Dan Dare in the *Eagle* comic?

As a teenager I hitchhiked solo around Britain and Western Europe. When a medical student, I scuba dived, parachuted and ventured to Kathmandu in Nepal and Mombasa in Kenya for my elective medical terms. Once qualified as a doctor I worked in Gibraltar on the southern tip of Spain and then travelled to Queensland in Australia to dive the Great Barrier Reef. I never returned to live in the UK. I have always sought adventure. Life is so exhilarating living off the edge of your comfort zone.

Certainly my 'enchanted child' archetype was active. I still dreamt of boyhood adventures and my missions fulfil these fantasies as I described in my 'John of Afghanistan' story.

Do you think you have the saviour or activist archetype? Do you want to save the world?
I used to join protest marches against the nuclear bomb and Vietnam War and I certainly admire activists. The young Pakistani girl, Malala Yousafzai who was shot in the head by the Taliban for going to school is wise beyond her years. Her active campaign and thrust for universal education, especially of young girls, as the key for strengthening human rights, extending birth control for population control and boosting economic development is having a profound effect.

I fully appreciate that only radical action will change injustice. Slavery wasn't abolished, women didn't get their vote, people of colour didn't get their civil rights and corporations did not become environmentally considerate by everyone being moderate and reasonable. Moderation and reasonableness do not move the inertia of institutions, the stagnation of incumbents or the greed of industry. They need to be levered, intimidated and shamed by confrontation, exposure and public opinion.

But I don't have that energy or enthusiasm anymore. Thank god there are others who do.

What you seem to be saying is that you were a disillusioned doctor, an adventurer following childhood fantasies and a burnt-out-activist.
I hadn't categorised it quite like that before but... yes.

Tell me more about this mission.

NORTHERN NIGERIA
MÉDECINS SANS FRONTIÈRES
2006

'Doctor John, the expatriate nurses are being a pain and demanding we buy equipment for the vaccination program that just isn't available. They want freezers to make ice but here in northern Nigeria there are none to buy.'

'Doctor John, the logisticians say there are no freezers available and the financial controller tells me there is no money to hire vaccination staff. How can we make ice packs for the cold boxes? There's no way we can run a vaccination program.'

'Doctor John, the national doctors will not work at night and patients arriving after hours sometimes have to wait till morning to be seen. Some are dying before that happens. They say they do not want to help with the vaccination program.'

'Doctor John the cash flow is not working. The coordination team in Abuja are sending money to the local bank every two weeks but it is not enough.'

I had just arrived in Dutse in the Jigawa state of northern Nigeria, exhausted, jet–lagged, bleary-eyed and road-weary after a forty-six-hour flight from Sydney, Australia to Abuja in Nigeria via Dubai and Johannesburg followed by a ten-hour drive in the back of a Toyota truck. I could hardly keep my eyes open.

En route, at Dubai airport, I had received an email informing me that the field coordinator of the mission had urgently returned to the Canada for personal reasons and asking me to take the role the field coordinator instead of doctor. The email concluded 'this is a sensitive mission'. I wondered what being a field coordinator for a 'sensitive mission' involved?

In Johannesburg I had phoned the MSF office in New York where the 'desk', the team that coordinated all the missions in Nigeria, was located, for clarification.

'John, as you know, Nigeria is in the malarial belt, a band across Sub-Saharan Africa, where meningitis is endemic every dry season. Every ten years or so there is a mega-epidemic, killing tens of thousands. This epidemic threatens to be one. We want to contain it quickly before it can spread widely.' Marie, a member of the desk, was effusive.

'Yes, I know all that. I was briefed in Sydney,' I impatiently replied.

'But it's more complicated. We were operational in this region ten years ago when there was a conflict with the Pfizer pharmaceutical company. They flew a research team into the same town, Kano, to trial a new experimental antibiotic called trovafloxacin or Trovan, comparing it to another antibiotic, ceftriaxone. They even used the same hospital as us, commandeering two medical wards for their exclusive use. The problem was they allegedly did not obtain informed consent for the trial and used a smaller than recommended dose of ceftriaxone, allegedly to skew the results in favour of Trovan. It was claimed the families of the sick children did not know they were being used as guinea pigs. Eleven children died in their trial. It is alleged that when it was obvious their experimental drug was not working, they did not revert to the standard drugs. After several years the case was settled out of court for seventy-five million dollars with confidentiality clauses.

Unfortunately, religious fundamentalists used the alleged deceit as an example of 'western intervention' to 'sterilise the population' and linked it with local vaccination programs. It maybe is one reason that polio has not yet been eradicated from the region. The same brush tarnished MSF. We want to regain our reputation of integrity and independence. It is important that this campaign is well managed and successful. No pressure, eh John?'

I had reluctantly accepted. Now I was faced with a team rampant with discontent and dissatisfaction. All I heard was complaints and I didn't even know who was complaining!

'I'm going to get some sleep. Can you call a meeting of all staff, expatriate and national, for five o'clock this afternoon? No excuses not to attend. I'll sort it out then,' I spoke to Amy, the American logician. She nodded agreement.

Despite collapsing exhausted into bed, sleep eluded me. Our accommodation and administration office had been established in a dilapidated, downtown motel. Road noise boomed, the en-suite stank, the ceiling fan clanked, the mattress was a bed of rocks and my pillow smelt of cat's piss.

I tossed and turned, my mind struggling with the challenges ahead. Our mission was to support three hospitals in neighbouring towns to treat the hundred new daily cases of meningitis, as well as to implement a vaccination program to contain the spread of infection. It had to be done quickly. I realised I had to resolve the team's problems and make things happen before the epidemic extended to other regions.

'Hi everyone, I'm Doctor John,' I introduced myself to the five expatriate and fifteen national staff who were sitting and standing around the table at the head of the driveway, the coolest spot in the motel. The day's heat was beginning to dissipate. Everyone looked at me suspiciously, shuffling in their seats, standing tensely, unsure what to expect. I asked everyone to introduce himself or herself. With the niceties over I cut to the chase.

'I hear we have numerous problems. Can each department head tell me what's going on so I can help sort them out?'

Deadly silence followed. No one wanted to open the floodgates. Doctor Rami, the most senior local doctor, preened in pressed trousers and a white shirt spiked with a bright yellow tie spoke first. 'Doctor John, we are expected to work at nights but we have no transport to get to and from the hospitals. We cannot afford taxis every day. Also, we are told we must give vaccinations but it is not our job.'

Pierre, a French logician, straight shoulder-length hair, a heavy stubble on his chin, dirty jeans and grimy MSF T-shirt snapped, 'Doctor Rami we now have extra cars that can transport you. All you have to do is ask.'

Jean, a frizzy-haired Canadian nurse with a band around her forehead to hold it high, butted in, 'You won't be giving vaccines, you'll be supervising the vaccinators and ensuring the vaccines are properly stored, drawn up into syringes and given according to the protocols. That is your job.'

Doctor Rami was startled by the facts. 'Oh. Then there is no problem. I will roster a night shift and we can lead the vaccination teams.'

Jean continued quickly, 'But for the vaccination program we need hundreds of ice packs to keep the vaccines cool in the cold boxes each day. I estimate we need twelve chest freezers, but the logicians say there are none to be bought locally.'

Thiepe, one of the national logicians who looked too young to be working legally for us, raises his hand, too shy to interrupt. 'What is it?' I ask, hiding my ignorance of his name.

'Why buy them? Last year I worked just across the border on a vaccination program with MSF in Chad. They have lots of freezers in storage. Why not borrow them? I know the local logistician.'

'There might be importation problems... moving them across the border. It's not as easy as you think Thiepe,' Pierre added. 'I can check it out tomorrow.'

'I'll do it tonight,' Thiepe insisted. 'My uncle works in customs on the border. For a small bonus I am sure he can arrange easy passage,' he smiled, knowingly.

Kelly, the American financial controller joined the fray. Her face was strained, her eyes puffy and bloodshot from many late nights

'There is insufficient cash to cover all these expenses. Head office is already transferring the maximum allowable amounts to our account. How can we pay all the extra vaccination staff? It is in the budget but is not to hand.'

'Any ideas how this can be managed?' I was still tired and had no ideas myself.

'If Head Office opens a second account with a different fund name, it would give me twice the cash. But I do not have the authority.'

'Do I?'

'Yes, as field coordinator you do.'

'Then do it.' I shrugged with my best French impersonation.

Everyone laughed. 'Any more urgent problems?'

All silence.

'Before we finish can I urge everyone to be polite and respectful of each other? You have all been working under pressure and achieved a great deal. The pressure is going to continue and even increase and we need to support, not undermine, each other. Once something is said it cannot be unsaid.'

I had a new page of A4 printer paper in my hand and screwed it up tightly.

'If you screw up an unused piece of paper it will never ever be the same again.'

I flattened the paper on the table and smoothed it out.

'No matter how much you press it out it will always be wrinkled. Please be thoughtful of what you say. Words cannot be undone, even after an apology.'

There were numerous gasps of amazement as the analogy sank in.

You got off to another good start John?

I did. I had fallen on my feet. As I left the meeting, I overheard one of the national nurse's comment, 'Doctor John sorted everyone out quickly.' Everyone thought I had run a great meeting, that I had solved their dilemmas. Little did they realise that I had done nothing but listen. Even that had been challenging with my eyes heavy, head throbbing and feeling like a wet rag.

I was fully aware that they had solved their own problems with the age-old technique of communication and co-operation. It was a startling lesson for me. I would say it was an AHA moment of my leadership life. I had arrogantly thought I would solve the problems but it had all happened despite me, not because of me. My non-interference had been a positive.

I did not tell anyone of my revelation. Sometimes it is satisfying to bask in the glory, even if undeserved.

I ran a similar team meeting every week.

She took her last gasp. She was only three years old, a skinny underweight girl, with long tightly braided hair, a faded pale green dress that was frayed around its hem loosely covered her body, two sizes too large. She had severe meningitis. A plastic bag of clear intravenous fluid hung above her head regimentally giving fluids and antibiotics, drop by drop, through a dangling tubing into her arm.

Her mother, sitting on a stool beside the bed nursed her on her lap. The girl's head limply extended over her mother's elbow, her dry eyes staring wide and unfocused on the water-stained, peeling cream paint of the ward's ceiling, unfazed by the single bright light bulb with its broken dirty-white plastic shade overhead. She gasped a breath then lay still, not breathing.

The other mothers in the ward, their children also sick with meningitis, sat beside their child's bed, heads bowed but silently watching the drama... and waiting... and hoping their child will survive. Several heads peered nosily in through the cracked windowpane, relatives from the village who waited in hope, waiting, like us all, for another breath, any sign of life... but the silence kept on counting the seconds.

Her father, resplendent in a bright blue *agbada*, the traditional dress of Northern Nigeria, a round red *fila* on his head, stood beside his wife, hand on her shoulder, looking down at his dying daughter, his head fallen, his shoulders slumped, his heart heavy, a tear trickling down his right cheek.

I stood close beside him with Angelina, a plump national nurse, her frizzy hair crowned with a starched white cap, like a princess's tiara. Her usual beaming smile had shrivelled to tight tense lips whilst we watched the girl die. We had been waiting for over half an hour, supporting the parents but still waiting for the inevitable. The family had arrived too late for our treatment to have an effect. Her parents had walked twelve hours to bring her to the hospital, twelve long hours that allowed the infection to flourish and inflame the brain.

It is in these moments of deep sadness and despair my mind mists... then wanders... Billy has nothing to say...

Then, in my mind's eye...

The door opens. A tall man wearing a pin-striped suit and bowler hat clutching a worn black leather briefcase and a black rolled-up umbrella with a polished wooden handle enters... an English civil servant with a Monty Pythonesque tinge of John Cleese.

'I'm from the Ministry of Living and Dying and I'm here to collect the dying tax. Under 'The Dying Before Time' Law of 1823, statute 15, article 16b, clause 541i you must pay a hundred pounds before dying... but for children under five years of age, there is a thirty per cent discount which brings it down to seventy pounds. Once this is paid, she can die.'

We are all flabbergasted and stand with our mouths open.

'But... but we are very poor and cannot pay such an amount,' stammers the father.

'What... what... poor you say... well under sub-article 23C, there is a compassionate clause allowing a further reduction to fifty pounds.'

'But you don't understand. We cannot pay fifty pence, never mind fifty pounds. We have no money.'

'What? ...have no money you say... mm-mm-mm-mm... you can always pay on credit card.'

'No one has credit cards here,' I explained. 'There are no banks, no ATMs here.'

He becomes quite agitated and coughs nervously. 'Well, she cannot die then... no tax paid, no release.'

'Doctor,' looking at me, 'Doctor, I order you to cure this child immediately. She is not allowed die.'

I shrug and turn up the drip, the little girl wakes up and smiles, her parents grab her and they all hurry out of the hospital... to live happily never after.

I inwardly smiled as I re-emerged into reality... but my heart was as sad as ever.

I leant over and felt for a pulse in the neck but it was absent. Gently closing the little girl's eyelids, I turned off the drip and told her parents it was over and how sad we were for their loss before writing the declaration of death in the medical notes.

Angelina removed the tubing, and wrapped the small body in a blanket for the family to carry to their village for burial. She organised for the bed to be sanitised and made ready for the next admission already waiting at the door.

I remembered her name was Nambia. I didn't want to know it, but something in me made me take note. She was just another kid dying of a preventable, treatable disease... but she wasn't... she was Nambia.

Another child's death, John. They obviously greatly distress you.

Yes. It is something I will never get used to. They eat away my soul, each one nibbling my resilience and eroding my resolve. Using black humour at times helps me cope. My partner was shocked when I later told her this story. 'You can't write that. It will upset too many people and make you seem insensitive'. But it's what I do. For a few minutes it trivialises death and distorts disaster as well as ridiculing the taxation department, a touch of *Yes-Minister*-humour. I find myself inwardly smiling with its absurdity, distracted by the ridiculous and enjoying a moment of escape before I'm yanked back into reality, like stretching a piece of elastic which reaches its limit and snaps back to original length. It is but a temporary respite. Sometimes I think I must be abnormal and feel guilty. Am I?

No, John. Dark or gallows' humour is a well-documented and common cognitive behavioural strategy used by professionals, especially journalists and emergency responders exposed to extreme events as you have been. It's thought that even during these brief interludes of dark humour your perception of the moment changes; fears are defused, horror is normalised and catastrophe is contained. The heart slows and the blood pressure falls. It has a calming effect albeit temporary. But as one journalist commented, he preferred jokes to drugs to cope!

RINGIM, JIGAWA STATE, NORTHERN NIGERIA
April 2006
Field Coordinator, Médecine Sans Frontière

'Doctor John, we have a royal audience with Emir this morning.' Doctor Hakim, the local Medical Director jubilantly announced when we met in the early morning. 'He has strong local influence. His support will give the vaccination campaign great prestige. Quick, we must go now and not be late. An audience is a great honour.'

As we drove to the palace he continued to elaborate. 'The Emir is the traditional prince of the region. Since colonisation by the British in 1897 and independence in 1960 the country has been frequently re-divided into many administrative states. The original emirates created when the Fula overthrew the Hausa Sultanates in the nineteenth century became defunct. Although the Emir now has little political power the whole population holds him in the highest of esteem.'

'How is he addressed? Are there special protocols to follow?' I asked feeling unprepared for the meeting.

'Don't worry Doctor John. I will tell you as we go.' But his voice wavered with anxiety. I was intrigued.

Mud brick walls, three metres high, painted a royal cream, reinforced with white concrete pillars rose above the surrounding mud hovels. 'That's the palace compound,' Doctor Hakim volunteered as our car turned and cruised around the intervening houses. An imposing pair of solid wooden gates, each six-foot-wide, formed a peaked entrance over which an ornate covered balcony, capped with a flagpole, stood tall like the bridge on a ship's hulk. In one of the main gates, a small door was recessed.

The tradesman's entrance? I pondered.

We parked nearby. Doctor Hakim knocked firmly with his fist. The little door opened and a stick-like man, skinny as a beanpole, wearing a flowing white caftan, his head capped with a simple *hula*, jumped out. Hakim spoke quietly with him, shaking hands and enquiring of his family and health, a prolonged formality that all greetings encompass in this part of the world, before introducing me. 'This is Mr Salim, the Emir's personal secretary.'

Salim looked at me then smiled, his small trimmed moustache widening with his grin and splitting his round face into two. His eyes, initially squinting through John Lennon glasses, opened wide and sparkled. 'Welcome Doctor John, you are very welcome,' and shook my hand with gusto. 'Follow me.' Quickly pivoting like a ballerina, he jumped over the door's step and disappeared like the rabbit in *Alice in Wonderland* down the rabbit hole. I followed with Doctor Hakim close on my heels.

We entered a courtyard hemmed in by the palace's walls and stifling in heat and glare. It was thronged with people huddling close together in small groups. Some had constructed shade using sarongs and sticks to protect against the intense sun. Anticipating my question Doctor Hakim explained, 'they are all subjects waiting for an audience. The Emir may not have legal powers, but many traditional folks seek his guidance and arbitration.'

We weaved our way through narrow aisles formed between the various groups and passed through two tall thin doors studded with metal stars, to enter the foyer of the palace. High ceilings and shuttered windows cooled the air and shaded the glare of the sun. The walls were bare of adornment. Pale green and cream paint was fading and in parts peeling. But my attention was drawn to the carpet of people sitting on the ground, covering the entire floor. I wondered how we would cross.

'They too are waiting for an audience,' Doctor Hakim whispered over my shoulder. I was flabbergasted. 'How long do they have to wait?'

'Some wait several days,' he explained.

It was like magic. Walking into the foyer behind Salim, a pathway opened through the crowd of seated bodies, like the Red Sea parting for Moses! There was no noise, no discussion, no awkward shifting or shuffling. After passing, the pathway closed as if it never existed. I felt a little guilty that we were pushing through. Doctor Hakim must have sensed my discomfort. 'We have an audience. The people will wait their turn,' he reassured.

'We are approaching the anteroom,' he whispered. Two more tall, narrow, star-studded doors lay ahead. On either side stood a burly, bearded guard, both over six feet tall, dressed in flowing white satin shirts whose sleeves flared at the elbows, bright pillar-box red embroidered waistcoats with golden buttons and baggy white satin pants tucked into knee-high tan suede boots. Their heads were crowned with a tall white turban that magnified their height and intimidation. But what caught my attention was the scimitar that hung from the shoulder strap and sat on the hip to reach the ankle. My mind thought of *Sinbad the Sailor of the Arabian Nights*.

Following Doctor Hakim through the doors, I glanced sideways into one of their faces. There was no reaction, no flicker of an eye, a face set in stone staring stoically straight ahead.

The anteroom was high ceilinged and narrow, its walls sparsely hung with faded tapestries. The floor was crammed with more bodies waiting, their density increasing as we neared the Emir. 'They are waiting for an audience too?' I asked, more comment than question. Doctor Hakim nodded. The magical path continued to open and close around us as we glided through the human congestion onward to two more star-studded doors guarded by two more static sentries.

From the gloom of the anteroom, the throne room erupted with light from a magnificent central dome that soared overhead. The Emir was perched on a richly embossed cream velvet-lined throne, its arms, legs and outer surround finely carved and gilded with gold. It was set on a dais that overlooked the room. Although his body was elaborately dressed in a gold-embroidered, deep-blue satin *babban riga* (a flowing robe) over a plain white *jalabia*, it was his Tuareg-style turban that drew my eye. Its *tagelmust* (veil) was of fine chiffon and pulled beneath his chin creating a wispy-bearded frame to his weathered face, softened by a pair of spectacles. Two corners of the veil, tied above the turban, sprouted sideways like animal's horns.

As I approached the dais, he waved me to one side, indicating to sit on a couch set at right angles on another dais to his left side. I climbed up and sat down. He acknowledged me with a flash of his eyes then focused on Doctor Hakim who had sunk to his knees in front of the Emir and like the rest of the audience in the room, crouched prostrate on the floor, face downcast. He started his introduction that he later told me explained the organisation of MSF and our wish to vaccinate the area against meningitis to control the present spreading epidemic. The twenty minutes of explanation gave me ample time to gaze around. The couch on which I sat was of a finely woven braided tapestry, thread-bared and faded by decades of use. The dome above was intricately decorated with diamond-shaped panels that were inset, each painted green, red and gold. The lights set around its base flooded light upwards highlighting the layered insets.

Doctor Hakim stopped talking and the silence was deafening. The Emir seemed caught up in his thoughts. He turned to me and in a sharp crisp Oxford-English accent said, 'You are very welcome Doctor John. I am highly appreciative of your vaccination campaign and will give it my full support. Where are you from?'

Taken aback by his uppercut accent and his instant support, I managed to modulate my voice, 'I was born in England but have lived in Australia for thirty years.'

'I have been to Australia... four times, I think. It is an amazing country.'

'Thank you, sir. Which part did you visit?'

'Sydney mostly. I stayed in Kings Cross. Plenty of atmosphere there.'

As Kings Cross was better known for its prostitution, drug addicts and gay community, I was unsure how to respond. It must have shown in my face for he chuckled.

'A friend has a penthouse luxury unit there that he lends to me. It has a glorious view over the harbour.'

We spent the next ten minutes talking about Sydney and Australia.

He stood and stepped off the dais. I mimicked his actions and we met in front of the throne. He extended his hand and we shook hands... but he did not let go and continued to chat. I glanced around and the whole room was still crouched with faces turned to the floor. We talked for another ten minutes; hands clasped. With a final firm shake, he let go. I smiled, thanked him sincerely for his support, turned and walked out. I sensed Doctor Hakim at my back. The magical path opened up even wider than our entry. My rapport with the Emir must have spread afar for I seemed to be revered by my association. I felt like Prince John as I dreamily walked back to the courtyard, out the gates and back to the car. Doctor Hakim was silent.

'That went well. Thanks for your organisation and assistance,' I reassured him.

He remained silent. I pinched myself. *Did that really happen? Did I just have a personal audience with a prince? Maybe I should have taken a selfie with him? No, that would have belittled the event.* It was ingrained in my memory for eternity.

You have had many amazing experiences on your missions, John. Have they inspired you?

No... and yes... I savour them, like enjoying a gourmet meal. There have been moments of silliness and surreality, of magnificence and, at times of magic. Moments when I pinch myself and think, *Did that really happen?* They did but they were only moments, great for dinner party stories, book chapters and fond memories.

I've been blessed in having these opportunities to experience these extraordinary moments... but my challenge when I return home is to archive them and begin to appreciate the 'ordinary' moments, to find the magic and mystery of everyday life and not allow it to be lost and blurred in a mindless frenzy of activity and distraction. Einstein's quote: *There are only two ways to live your life: as though nothing is a miracle, or as though everything is a miracle,* rings true to me.

And how do you achieve that?

It seems simple but it's not easy. I often struggle. I am learning to run with life in the slow lane; to become more mindful each day; to appreciate the regularity and routine; to feel grateful and blessed for all I have, my health, wealth, and safe environment; to reflect on my small daily meaningful accomplishments; to create frequent, simple but special moments that add spice to the day, walks in the park, a swim on the beach, meeting a friend, cooking a recipe, reading a poem.

Life isn't meant to be one long extraordinary adventure or party. It is something even better that lasts after the adventure or party are over.

DUTSE, JIGAWA STATE, NORTHERN NIGERIA
April 2006
Field Coordinator, Médecine Sans Frontière

'You can't be serious, she's a woman.'

'Coming from you Amy, that's a bit rich.'

'No, you misunderstand me, John. Of course, Natalie is the best person to be the operational manager for the vaccination program, but promoting a female nurse above the national male doctors will be a huge insult to them and they will not cooperate. Culturally it won't work. Why don't you be the operational manager?'

'I'm too busy overseeing the whole medical program and finances. I need an operations manager to coordinate and supervise the vaccination program. All the expatriate nurses have left. They've completed the planning and ordering of supplies but now it needs a competent manager and Natalie is the obvious choice.

'I'm naming Doctor Rami as the head of the project. That will save face but I told him that Natalie will be in charge of operations, giving the daily orders under my supervision. He knows he isn't up to it. He's basically lazy and happy to have the status without the true responsibility. The male nurses do not have Natalie's organisational or people skills. She will handle them well. I don't see a problem. I know it's not fair that Natalie will not get her full recognition but as you point out unless we 'save face' the whole arrangement will collapse. I've already spoken to her and she is happy to get the experience.'

'If you think so. I'll make sure the national logisticians know she's the boss and is to be followed ... or answer to me, another woman! If she can pull it off it will be a great symbol of female emancipation.'

'That's why I want it to happen.'

So how did it work out?
Overall brilliantly. Natalie was highly effective; persuasive, complimentary but assertive. She soon had all the vaccination and logistic teams under her spell. A few male nurses were sulky for a while but, knowing that both Amy and I were supporting her, they became compliant.

I was beginning to realise how much I enjoyed mentoring others. Giving away control, particularly to a female national nurse, was a great thrill

Being free of operational details, I was free to deal with any major problem that reared up unexpectedly. And they did.

DUTSE, JIGAWA STATE, NORTHERN NIGERIA
April 2006
Field Coordinator, Médecine Sans Frontière

'What do you mean we cannot import the vaccines; they are already in Abuja?' I was astounded.

'I know how infuriating it must be. It took us a month to find a quarter of a million meningitis vaccines. There is a world shortage and we eventually were able to divert them from another less urgent program, but they expire in nine months,' Maxine, the medical coordinator in Abuja was as furious as me.

'So, what's the problem? We're going to use them within a week.'

'Yes, but Nigerian law demands all imported medications must have an expiry date greater than one year ahead so the vaccines are technically illegal and they will not grant an import license.'

'Who's 'they'?' I was curious.

'The customs officials. We suspect they are priming us for a bribe but don't quote me on that.'

'Can't you go over their heads, to government levels? We are about to start training the vaccinators and plan to begin vaccinating in four days.'

'Yes, the MSF desk in New York is lobbying via their UN and government connections but this takes time. Nothing happens fast. Can you confront the local officials with the urgency?'

'I've already seen them all to get their support for the program but I'll keep pushing. I'll insist that they at least have the vaccines transported to Dutse pending approval. That may save a couple of days. I'm not going to cancel anything until the last moment. I don't want to lose our momentum. We don't have the time to delay the vaccination program. The meningitis cases are rapidly spreading and will soon break our vaccination programme boundaries.'

So, what happened?

Natalie continued with all the preparations and training. I visited our local medical and government officials to explain our dilemma and asked them to intervene. Everyone seemed amused by the standoff, as if implying, *What did you expect? This is Nigeria...* but when I reminded them of the number of meningitis cases and deaths their community was suffering, they changed their attitude.

The local custom man was fishing for a bribe, saying he could maybe hurry things along but it was very costly. When he realised I was not going to pay and threatened to tell everyone he was blocking the release of the vaccines causing multiple deaths, he quickly backed off.

And...?

And the afternoon before we were due to start vaccinating, the permit was granted. The vaccines had already been transported to the local custom offices and we could access them immediately.

I felt triumphant and relieved. The previous three days had been stressful, sleepless and draining. I had not told anyone else in the mission of the possible delay or the possible collapse of the program. I did not want to squash their enthusiasm or lose heart. It was a lonely time. I had no idea what had swayed the decision but did not care. We could start vaccinating the next day as planned.

Far outside RINGIM, JIGAWA STATE, NORTHERN NIGERIA
May 2006
Field Coordinator, Médecine Sans Frontière

The four young women, dazzling in brightly patterned colourful abayas, were rhythmically and tirelessly pounding their great pestles deep into the mouth of a wooden mortar. Each stroke reached high overhead and flowed like a surfing wave, crashing down in a silky sequence to crush the millet into flour. This technology was ancient a millennium ago and I watched in fascination and admiration, a symphony of graceful motion. Toothless crones, their heads covered with brightly patterned shawls, squatted on the ground beside the mortar, like witches around a cauldron, and I could hear their tireless commentary, cackling laughter and squeals of excitement. I guessed they were discussing me.

We had arrived at the village, deep in the arid, dusty savannah, far from any town, in the simmering, stifling heat of mid-morning as part of our meningitis vaccination program. It was but a small cluster of mud-walled, thatch-roofed huts. A wall of sticks, two metres high, surrounded the huts and extended around an adjoining animal enclosure where six wasted cattle sat in scrappy shade chewing their cud, their ribs prominent on their fatless bodies, their tails continuously flicking over their nether regions to waft away the teeming flies and stir the heat.

'Doctor John, we have run out of vaccines. The local population in the outlying villages is much larger than our estimates. There are still many waiting and arriving. What can we do?' Sasha, the nurse in charge of the vaccination team, was stressing. Her voice wavered with the strain and sweat dripped from her heavy brow down a snub nose to her chin.

'Take some deep breaths, Sasha. We will manage. What do you suggest?'

'Can we have more sent from the base?'

'That would take the rest of the day. It is too far?'

'I could radio the other teams nearby and see if they have a surplus? Amid could drive and collect them.'

'Good idea. Give it a go.'

She turned and walked to the radio in the car.

I was just tagging along with the team, taking a day off from the office to see the scenery and give a helping hand. I did not want to be in charge or undermine her authority. My presence was intimidating and I was delighted she had the problem solved. It would boost her confidence.

'Omega team can give us two hundred vaccines. It is quiet over there. Amid is heading off,' Sasha had returned to my side and confirmed her actions.

'Well done. How long will he be?'

'About an hour.'

'Then let us rest.'

We were sitting on a scarlet patterned rush mat in the shade of the spreading branches of a boab tree, its trunk five metres around, as ancient as the local technology. I lay back absorbing the surrounding scene. Fifty metres distant, in the shadow of another boab tree, lay the village men-folk. Some snoozed, some smoked, some chatted. They had left their fields in the heat of the noonday to rest and eat. Under an adjoining tree, the village's children, tots to teens, played together. They had all had their vaccinations and were in high spirits. Many young girls carried their younger sibling in a cloth slung on their hip. Others were skipping and others danced in a ring. A few boys kicked a tightly bound ball of rags in a half-hearted game of soccer. They were all grinning and laughing. An aura of peace and contentment enveloped me.

The headman emerged from the huts to meet with me, formally dressed in a vivid yellow-coloured *babban riga*, a *fula* on his head. His greeting was warm, his toothless smile warmer, his face scorched and aged by the sun. He spoke and Sasha, sitting beside me, translated quietly in my ear. He praised us for coming to his village with the vaccinations. His voice was rich and clear and rang loud between the trees. All the men and women nodded in assent. His wife, petite and wearing a patterned red abaya, brought out tea to drink and a gourd of yak yoghurt. It was tart but delicious and I greedily tasted it until Sasha nudged my ribs sharply with her elbow and whispered, 'They have very little. It is a very special delicacy.' I embarrassingly realised his offer to taste was a gesture of good will, not a free lunch.

I chatted on with the headman who told me of their meagre food stores, their cattle thin and hungry and their harvest dwindled by drought.

'How will you survive the winter?' I asked.

'Insha'Allah.' He smiled and then laughed a huge guffaw. I looked around and saw heads nodding, faces smiling and a close, content community.

It seems to have impressed you, John?

I was impressed. These people were on the edge of survival with no food reserves, only their resilience and faith to sustain them. I was sure many of those children playing under the boab tree would be dead by the following spring yet they were all congregated around the village, happy and content, accepting life for what it is rather than as they think it should be.

Is that how you see it should be?

Not at all, but I was humbled by their contentment and resilience. Their existence, simple and wholesome, is a true testimony that happiness is not created by material wealth or circumstance. In fact, maybe it is just the opposite... that real expectations and acceptance of 'what is' creates mindful peace.

On the other hand, the more we have, the more we expect. The more we expect, the less we accept. The less we accept, the less content we feel. Enough is never enough. When happiness depends on circumstance it is as transient, unreliable and fleeting as the circumstance itself. It is paradoxical and perplexing.

Should we all strive to be 'simple and wholesome'?

Not at all. These people are in a time warp.

After the headman had finished his formal thanks and returned to his hut I lay back on the mat and listened to Mozart on my headphones. I realised how these villagers were deprived of the wonders of humanity, its technology, its explorations, and its sporting, artistic, musical and academic achievements. Living in poverty may impose simplicity and wholesomeness but it is stagnant. There is but one focus – survival.

Nobody wants to live in poverty. Poverty is pervasive, corrosive, progressive and persists for generations. Poverty is not the absence of wealth. It is a malignant misalignment of existence and opportunity.

Poor people spend their time surviving, vulnerable to disease, malnutrition and oppression. They are powerless, unheard and exposed. Any change in circumstance, climatic, political or commercial immediately increases their vulnerability. There is no buffer, no cushion, no insurance between life and death.

Wealth positions you in a depression where everything in life gravitates towards you. Poverty positions you on the top of a rise where everything rolls away unless it is actively grasped and held close. The playing field of life is dramatically and unforgivingly different.

The children of the poor are undernourished, understimulated and underachieved, never to fully develop physically, intellectually and educationally, never to reach their employment potential. This cycle of poverty will disadvantage their children and on it goes.

The eradication of poverty should be a global priority. Everyone has the human right to achieve their potential and enjoy the fruits of our civilisation.

That's very idealistic for you John.

Maybe... but I was seeing poverty full frontal and was both shocked to witness its brutality yet surprised to experience its contented acceptance and submission.

I maybe could only dream of its extinction... but only the dreams you dare to dream come true.

DUTSE, JIGAWA STATE, NORTHERN NIGERIA
May 2006
Field Coordinator, Médecine Sans Frontière

'Doctor John, the vaccinators are going on strike tomorrow,' Natalie delivered the bad news.

'WHAT.' I could not believe it. 'Why?'

'The World Health Organisation is about to launch a routine round of vaccinations for polio, tetanus and whooping cough. Their vaccinators are paid poorly, far lower rates than we pay. Their union is unhappy and is organising the strike. Our vaccinators, being union members must strike too.'

'But that's ludicrous. Don't they realise the meningitis will spread while they are striking and our vaccinators are already well paid.'

'Yes, but they want as much disruption as possible and maybe they think MSF will force WHO to raise their pay levels so our program can continue.'

I was angry. We had imported the freezers and vaccination equipment, acquired the vaccines, battled to have them imported, hired twenty-seven cars and drivers for transporting our teams, trained the vaccinators and been vaccinating for only a week... and now this.

I was frustrated. Just when I thought I was in control of a situation something arrives out of the blue to knock you over.

'Let me think on it. Call a team meeting at five o'clock before everyone goes home.'

The air was electric with anticipation when I arrived. Everyone was gossiping about the strike.

I opened the meeting. 'You've all heard the vaccinators are striking tomorrow. Any ideas on what we should do?'

Pierre piped up, 'We could threaten to shut down our mission and see if the local health authorities will put pressure on the union to stop the strike.'

I countered, 'I've just been to see them and they will not intervene. I've spoken with the union representatives and they will not budge. We cannot walk away from the hospitals we are supporting and let those infected die.' I did not tell them that we had to be successful and gain credibility and respect in the region to redeem our reputation.

The team was silent and sullen. It seemed we had failed.

'I have an idea.' I sparked. 'Are you interested? It will be hard work.' I wanted to arouse their curiosity and enthusiasm.

'Of course, Doctor John. What is it?'

'I want to continue the program without the vaccinators.'

'But we can't do that. Who will give the vaccinations?'

'The nurses and doctors will give the vaccinations. Tomorrow we will train the logistic team and drivers how to set up and help with cold boxes, syringes and the records. It will mean overtime and long days but it can be done.'

I was expecting resistance from the doctors or even the logisticians. I knew the nurses would support me.

'What about our pre-vaccination visits Doctor John? Who will do them?' Thiepe queried.

Two days before a vaccination team arrived in any village our logistic team would visit to inform the elders of our intent, gain their support and ensure the villagers knew of our arrival time. I had learnt my lesson in the consequences of poor communication with village elders years before! This was vital to our success.

'The visits will continue but the pre-vaccination team can be smaller and we will cover fewer villages each day. This is a poker game. We need to be seen to be vaccinating normally but we can scale down.'

I added, 'I reckon if we can continue to vaccinate for two to three days the union will see their members are losing good wages for no advantage and allow them to return to work.'

'What about the drivers?'

'I've just spoken to most of them and they are enthusiastic. Normally they just sit around their cars all day. This way they will earn a little extra money.'

'Let's do it,' cried Natalie. 'We can show the union we are self-sufficient.'

'I'll second that,' shouted Doctor Tofa, usually a mild-mannered, unassuming man.

And was it a success?

It worked like a charm. Give a team a common adversary and they will join together in revolt. The following day was hilarious with the drivers and national logistic staff learning how to hygienically wash their hands, unwrap syringes and needles and fit them together, soak cotton-wall balls with alcohol to fabricate skin-cleaning swabs, open and close insulated cold-boxes to stop the ice melting. Their eyes were popping open with surprise and delight and a constant barrage of laughter echoed round the room. The local doctors lost their hierarchical superiority and joined the camaraderie. A few stayed in the hospitals and covered all the medical rosters whilst the rest joined the vaccination teams, rolling up their sleeves, drawing up the vaccines and helping the nurses to vaccinate the villagers.

The teams left at sunrise and arrived back at base in the dark. Amazingly, in our first two days of ad hoc vaccinating we administered more vaccines that the first two formal days of vaccination. Back at base everyone was high fiving, back slapping and hand shaking to congratulate each other.

After two days the head vaccinator from our team visited me to say the union was now happy for them to work again and they could start the following day.

And did they?

I was tempted to hold off another day and make them wait but I put aside my pettiness and agreed. In fact, a part of me felt guilty that we had used classic strike breaking tactics so successfully and completely abandoned them. It would have been more satisfying to negotiate with the union to find ways we might have supported them but when I initially met with them, they were not willing to listen and I did not have the luxury of time to be diplomatic. Our vaccination programme had to take precedence. We now needed to get back to full operation as quickly as possible. But I did give the drivers and logisticians an extra day's bonus so they would not feel betrayed. They had been pivotal in our plan.

These are the moments that balance out the difficulties and disappointments of other times. I began to realise that it was these close interactions with the staff, particularly the national staff, which gave me the most satisfaction and pleasure.

Why now?

This was my third mission. Goma and Afghanistan had been ego-driven. I was ten years older, more experienced and tempered by life's lessons. Maybe I was growing up?

DUTSE, JIGAWA STATE, NORTHERN NIGERIA
May 2006
Field Coordinator, Médecine Sans Frontière

'Doctor John! Doctor John! Are you OK?'

It was a rhetorical question, for I was laid out flat on the floor of the corridor having collapsed whilst walking towards the toilet beside our office area.

Nathan, a national logistician knelt beside me gently slapping my face.

'Are you OK Doctor John?' His thin face reflected his concern, his brow furrowed, his mouth grimaced and his eyes staring at my face looking for signs of life.

I grabbed his arm and startled him, as if I had risen from the dead.

'I'd feel much better if you stopped hitting me,' I ungratefully complained. 'I'm fine but thanks for helping,' I lied. I felt light-headed, nauseous and dizzy. My bowels were rumbling, dangerously predicting another imminent evacuation.

'Help me up, Nathan, I've got to get to the toilet.'

'You must lie down Doctor John. You are sick.'

'After the toilet,' I demanded.

He pulled me to my feet. My head swam but I leant against the wall and staggered to the toilet cubicle, closed the door, dropped my pant and explosively relieved myself. I felt immediately calmer until I looked down into the toilet bowl and saw it full of blood and mucus. I felt my brow. It was burning and sweaty. I had spent the night visiting the toilet with runny motions, sipping rehydration fluid and swallowing paracetamol tablets to dull the abdominal cramps but it obviously was not enough.

Nathan helped me back to my room where I collapsed on my bed, my limbs feeling leaden, my head throbbing. 'I need an intravenous infusion. Can you call Doctor Najir and ask him to call around? He should be nearby.'

'You need to wash your hands more often Doctor John,' Doctor Najir remonstrated. 'You have dysentery. You are always telling us to do it yet you are the one who's ill. And you work too long hours, eat scanty meals from the market and have no time off. No wonder you are sick.'

Without missing a word of advice, he jabbed a cannula into my arm, connected the tubing and turned on the intravenous fluids. It ran freely and fast.

'I'll give you a litre straight away and then another litre over four hours. You can continue to sip fluid by mouth. That will rehydrate you but you must take forty-eight hours off work. Your body needs rest to recover. Do you hear me, Doctor John?'

'I hear you Doctor Najir.' I felt terrible and had no strength to resist.

'How can you lead the team when you are exhausted? Then you get irritable and impatient. Nobody likes you like that.' I sighed, too weak to comment.

'The vaccination program is running well. You sorted out all the early problems and now we can manage for a couple of days without you. You are not indispensable. Others will rise to the occasion. You will see... if you let them.'

Doctor Najir was on a roll, full of insight and wisdom and showing no mercy.

'I'm prescribing you some antibiotics for the dysentery. You must complete the full course.'

'Yes doctor,' I ceded. It only encouraged him.

'You know that self-health should be your priority Doctor John, yet you ignore it. It is not good enough.'

'I hear you Doctor Najir. Can I rest now?'

'For at least forty-eight hours, Doctor John. Forty-eight hours.'

'You win Doctor Najir.'

Why is this so memorable John? You must have had dysentery in previous missions?

Yes, I had but I'd never had a national staff member dress me down before. I was exhilarated by it.

Why? What was so special?

The national staff, especially in medical emergency missions, is usually very meek and mild. They feel very vulnerable. They value their job and are scared of losing it. Often the income is vital for their family's security and wellbeing. Jobs are hard to find in humanitarian emergencies and MSF pay relatively well, give free medical care, medications and even hospital care to their families.

They have to tolerate a series of expatriate staff that come and go during a mission, each with their individual styles, temperaments and foibles. They learn to keep the peace, tell you what you want to hear and are scared to offend or criticise.

For Doctor Najir to lecture me like this was unusual. I felt proud that he trusted me enough to tell me what I needed to hear. He was a hundred per cent correct. I had not been looking after myself: working sixteen-hour days, eating market foods spasmodically and sleeping fitfully, a perfect recipe to burn out and get sick. I had become irritable and short tempered. I had forgotten how essential self-care is, especially on emergency missions.

It normally takes weeks or months to build up enough trust for the national staff to feel comfortable and secure. I had only been there three weeks. I felt honoured and privileged to be so humbled.

I rested for forty-eight hours, took all my antibiotics and returned to work invigorated and relaxed, determined to practice better self-health.

Dutse, Jigawa State, Northern Nigeria
June 2006
Field Coordinator, Médecine Sans Frontière

'I'm looking forward to flying to New York instead of Paris for debriefing. It's one reason I accepted the mission.' I was chatting to Amy, our American logistician, who had helped run the meningitis vaccination program with me. It was now all over. I intermittently sang the chorus of *New York, New York.*

The number of cases of meningitis had fallen to normal rates. Over a quarter of a million people had successfully been vaccinated in under four weeks, two weeks ahead of schedule. All national staff had been fully paid, the freezers had been sent back to Chad and the rest of the equipment had been packed into a ten-ton truck. We were personally escorting it back to the coordination base in Abuja, a twelve-hour drive. Trucks can go missing.

When we arrived back at the coordination team offices in Abuja, exhausted, hungry and thirsty I was stunned.

'What the hell are you doing here?' I demanded.

All the members of the 'desk' from the New York office were sitting at a table sipping a bottle of chilled Chardonnay chatting with the national coordination team.

'Welcome back Doctor John,' Marie the emergency coordinator smiled. 'The desk team is having their annual visit to Nigeria. It just happens to coincide with your premature arrival. But it's lovely to be here and welcome you. Your mission was a great success. MSF's reputation in Kano has been greatly enhanced. Here, have a glass of wine.' She poured and handed me a generous glass.

'Yes, but I'm coming to see you New York, for debriefing?' I questioned.

'But that won't be necessary now. We can debrief you here.'

'But... but... that's not right. I came here because the debriefing was to be in New York.'

'That might be so... but you have finished early and we are here.'

'But... but...' I gave up, exasperated and defeated.

'... But'... Marie continued... 'but should you be able to pop over to northern Uganda for a few weeks, we urgently need a field coordinator to sort out a few small problems at Patongo... and of course, they would be debriefed in New York.'

I did not know if I was being played like a fish, but heavily suspected so.

'So where is this Patongo and what are these few "small problems"?'

I was nibbling the bait... dangerous!

'Patongo is in northern Uganda. MSF is supporting a government medical clinic in one of the internally displaced people (IDP) camps. They are about to introduce an AIDS testing and treatment program, partly financed by the Clinton Foundation. We need someone to coordinate the program in our clinic and assess if it is viable.'

'But I'm not an AIDS treatment specialist. I've never ever treated a case.'

'We have seconded an experienced national nurse who has been working in our AIDS program in Arua, in Uganda. He will help you.'

'So why can't he do it.'

'John, we need an experienced expatriate field coordinator who cannot be bought, intimidated or threatened by local authorities. A national nurse, although

123

capable, is too vulnerable. Also, he is not a coordinator. You have those skills. The meningitis epidemic just proved that.'

A bit of flattery goes a long way. I bit the bait and was hooked.

NORTHERN UGANDA
MÉDECINS SANS FRONTIÈRES
2006

'John, you have to understand that the humanitarian crisis in northern Uganda is an ongoing symptom of fifty years of complex tribal and political turmoil in Uganda since independence in 1962. We are supporting the government's health clinics in a few IDP camps in the region and our presence is limited but allows us to witness what is happening.'

I was sitting with Francis, the Head of Mission in Kampala, the capital of Uganda, en route to Patongo.

'Tell me more. I have little knowledge of the region and haven't had the opportunity to research it.'

'The backdrop of the crisis began in 1971 when Idi Amin overthrew Milton Obote's government. His dictatorial rule not only ruined the economy but the Acholi and Langi tribes in the north were ruthlessly persecuted because of their support of Obote.

'When Amin was overthrown in 1979, elections re-established Obote as president who then persecuted the Lowera region for supporting Yoweri Museveni's National Resistance Army (NRA) who opposed him.

'Obote was then overthrown in 1985 by Olara-Okello but the NRA pushed him out of the country and Museveni became president. The persecution and human right abuses of the north continued.'

'It sounds like a political not-so-merry-go-round?'

'Exactly, so you won't be surprised that in the north rebel groups started to form to defend themselves against the ongoing persecutions. One group, the Holy Spirit Movement, led by Alice Lakwena, bore no arms, only sticks and stones, believing they acquired protection from bullets by covering their bodies with shea nut oil.'

He continued to explain how this movement was slowly taken over by Joseph Kony who gained a reputation of being possessed by magical spirits. However, he did not depend on shea nut oil alone and recruited former soldiers of the Ugandan National Liberation Front to form the infamous Lord's Resistance Army or LRA.

He attacked and overtook Gulu, a major northern town but as he advanced southwards towards the capital, Kampala, he was forced to retreat. The Sudanese government began giving him military support and sanctuary in retaliation of Uganda's support of the South Sudanese rebels and he continued raiding from the north, terrorising the villages: murdering, looting, raping and abducting children to join his army as child soldiers and supplement his troops.

Francis paused, aware how intricate and involved this background was to absorb. After a cup of tea, he further explained that in 1996 the government created "protected camps" where villagers in the north could live and be guarded from the raids. In 2002 the situation became more dangerous when the NRA, now renamed Uganda's People Defence Force (UPDF), launched *Operation Fist* against the LRA forces hiding in South Sudan. In retaliation, the LRA attacked some of these camps killing hundreds of people and abducting hundreds more children. As these attacks became rampant, more and more protected IDP camps were created and the humanitarian crisis escalated. One point six million internally displaced people were now living in over two hundred camps.

Kony had not only used South Sudan as a refuge but was also utilising the ongoing Second Congo War in the neighbouring Democratic Republic of Congo to forge alliances and refuge. Despite several military campaigns and a failed CIA incursion, he had survived to continue his terror.

Francis paused again, somewhat exhausted but excited by his dialogue. He concluded, 'Negotiations for peace are underway at this very moment, and although very fragile, this stalemate can hopefully be resolved and the population can return to their villages. The crisis is politically created and needs to be politically resolved.'

'So, what's the problem? Why am I here?'

'We are more concerned that amid all this disarray AIDS continues to ravage the population. Estimates vary between six and fifteen per cent of the population are infected but these are unreliable. One survey of sex workers in one town revealed a thirty-two per cent incidence. Maybe this enforced concentration of population is an opportunity for better AIDS education and initiation of treatment. The government is about to introduce an AIDS diagnosis and treatment program, funded by the Clinton Foundation, and your clinic in Patongo is included. We need you to help implement it and assess its viability.'

'But I know nothing about AIDS. I've never ever treated a case,' I reiterated my concern.

Don't worry, Bruno, a nurse from our AIDS treatment centre in Arua is joining you to assist. The program should follow simple algorithms so that any doctor can be involved.

'The major concern is the huge initial surge in the uptake of AIDS treatments allowing the government to claim the overseas grants.'

'You mean getting bums on seats so to speak.' I summarised.

'Exactly, but the treatment of AIDS is lifelong and without ongoing support, close follow up of all cases and future funding there will be a huge dropout rate. This would lead to widespread drug resistance to the first line drugs. It could be a medical catastrophe.'

How were you feeling after this briefing?
A little anxious at what I had taken on with such short notice. Sometimes, I wonder how missions are chosen and evolve. I was there because they could not find anyone else at that moment of time. It was sheer chance I was around and I felt like the dregs in the barrel.

At the beginning of any mission, there is always information overload. I was faced with an overwhelming amount of complex political background, treatment protocols and technical information to digest. It was daunting.

How did you manage this?
I had learnt to read as much as possible quickly and trust that I will absorb what I needed to begin the job and hope the rest will resurface as the mission unfolds. It has always panned out that way.

I was also beginning to implement the philosophy that *it will either work out... or it won't*. There is little point worrying either way. I created another little mantra:
If it happens... deal with it.
If it doesn't happen... deal with it.

Containing my expectations and only dealing with the present allowed events to unfold without trying to predict outcomes. I could maintain focus on the moment and create momentum. My experience in Nigeria had confirmed that.

PATONGO IDP CAMP, AGAGO DISTRICT, NORTHERN UGANDA
June 2006
Field Coordinator, Médecine Sans Frontière

'Welcome John.' Eric, an American logistician, early twenties, short haircut, clean-shaven, tanned, well-toned muscles from frequent workouts greeted me off the Beechcraft Baron aircraft with a cheesy grin. I had flown from Kampala to the newly constructed dirt airstrip beside Patongo. He grabbed my bag and threw it into the back of the Toyota 4WD. 'It used to be an eight-hour drive. Access by air is a great improvement,' he explained.

High from the air, Patongo had resembled a mosaic of black dots on a brown backcloth surrounded by a vast patchwork of green rectangular fields. As we descended, I could discern hundreds of round mud-walled, straw-roofed huts, blackened with soot from smoke fires within, set in no order or pattern but intertwined with a network of pathways. Wood smoke permeated the thatch of many roofs. A river gently meandered across the northern perimeter.

The tiny town was sited strategically on a crossroad of two dirt highways. Its population of hundreds had exploded to forty thousand with the influx of IDPs from the surrounding region. On one perimeter was an army outpost housing the soldiers who protected the camp from attacks by the LRA.

We drove through the town centre, passing several brick, corrugated-iron-roofed buildings, housing stores and warehouses and a small market selling charcoal and vegetables. A few hens clucked and pecked in the gutters, scurrying from the path of the car. We carefully drove around pigs that were wallowing on their backs and grunting in delight in numerous black muddy depressions in the road.

Eric pointed out the medical clinic that was set back from the main street. Two hundred metres past the clinic we turned into a compound contained by a fence of wooden poles.

'This is our accommodation and office. It is an unfinished motel that we've made habitable.'

He showed me around the facility. The reception area acted as an office. Two parallel wings of small rooms were allocated as bedrooms or had been converted into secure storerooms for our drug supply and medical equipment. At the far end of the compound were two wooden walled cubicles, one a pit toilet and the other for bathing with water provided by an adjacent black plastic water tank.

'The water is warmed by the sun's rays and is perfect to bath in the evening,' he advised.

A wide, roofed veranda dominated by a large wooden table and chairs created a cool and airy lounge and eating area. Beside the motel building was a small warehouse and ample courtyard to park the cars.

Whilst we sipped a cup of tea, Eric continued his briefing. 'The clinic has male, female, children's and infectious disease wards with a total of twenty beds but we can fit more in if necessary. An outpatient clinic contains three doctor's consultation rooms, dressing room and dispensary. The clinic is officially a government clinic and is run by Doctor Natango. He and Doctor Logi are government paid doctors who come and go as they wish. MSF hires and pays the rest of the staff.'

'Thanks Eric, I'll unpack then wander over to the clinic and meet the rest of the team.'

'This patient, Mr Mamboso, is suffering an atypical pneumonia and AIDS. I am treating his pneumonia but I suspect from his long history of cough and weight loss he also has TB. We need to confirm that diagnosis with a chest X-ray. His TB then needs to be treated and controlled before we can commence AIDS treatment.' Doctor Odongo briefly summarised the newly admitted patient's complex case. His face looked drawn and tired from a busy night's work.

It was the Monday morning ward round. Six of us stood at the end of the patient's bed in the infectious disease ward, each wearing a paper mask as protection from inhaling any TB germs that the patient might be exhaling. Doctor Odongo has been on call over the weekend. Doctor Mitoka, a Japanese doctor, Bruno, a national nurse from the MSF AIDS treatment program and Nancy and Wooli, local national nurses, made up the rest of our troupe.

Mr Mamboso was sitting on his bed, weakly leaning against a pillow propped against the wall. He was thin... very thin. His pale face was a mask of transparent skin draped over a skull with protruding eyes. His chest was a sheet of wrinkled skin covering meatless ribs. His limbs were wasted away to skin on sticks. Yet he smiled gratefully repeating 'Thank you, thank you', obviously thankful to be receiving treatment.

Everyone was becoming drenched in sweat. The two-bedded ward's corrugated rusty tin roof, beaten by the morning sun's rays was heating the mud-walled building like a bread oven. Even the rough concrete floor was baking hot. A fan whirled overhead, fanning the heat to roast us all evenly. I took a mouthful of tepid water from my bottle. At least I would not become dehydrated.

'There are many problems Doctor John,' Doctor Odonga continued.

'What might they be?' I encouraged.

Firstly, we have to drive him to the Doctor Ambrosali Mission Hospital in Kalongo for a chest X-ray. It is the only X-ray department in the district and a four-hour round journey through territory open to ambush by the LRA.

'Secondly, Doctor Atubo, in charge of the government's TB treatment program is short of TB drugs and cannot confirm a full six-month treatment.

'And thirdly, if and when he is ready for the new AIDS treatment, although the program provides sufficient first-line drugs, there are no monies or staff allocated for counselling, case tracing or adequate follow-up.'

Bruno interrupted. 'That is a big problem Doctor John. The patient must stay on the drugs for life and they often have many disturbing side effects. Continual psychological and social support and follow-up is essential otherwise treatment will be abandoned. In Arua, we have a dedicated team for psycho-social support.'

Thanks Doctor Odongo. Thanks Bruno. I think you've highlighted the dilemmas very well. The new government's AIDS treatment program sounds very worthwhile but it seems to be full of funding holes and lacks ongoing supervision. I also wonder at the wisdom of starting such a program during a crisis when the population is displaced. The long-established TB treatment program is already struggling to keep contact with its patients. But these decisions are political, way above our pay-grades! At least let us do what we can for this patient.

'I'll escort him to Kalongo Hospital tomorrow for the chest X-ray. It will allow me to inspect their facilities and meet the staff. We can treat his pneumonia and probable TB. It will give me time to assess the AIDS treatment program.'

You seem to have fitted in well again, John?
Yes, the staff was grateful to have a field coordinator who was a doctor and gave direction. They were very cooperative. I was especially grateful for Bruno's assistance. He was knowledgeable, enthusiastic and affable. Despite intensive reading, I was struggling to fully comprehend all the nuances of the AIDS treatment program. I was well out of my depth. He gave me good practical advice.

I was cynical that the government's program was going to be viable. However, I've learnt never to predict outcomes. In such volatile situations, too many factors change in short periods. It's better to allow them to unfold, stay flexible, be proactive and be ready to adapt. That was what made this work so enjoyable.

I could hear Billy laughing, 'You mean fake it till you make it, eh John!'

PATONGO IDP CAMP, AGAGO DISTRICT, NORTHERN UGANDA
June 2006
Field Coordinator, Médecine Sans Frontière

Oh no, not again, I inwardly sighed, my heart sinking, my shoulders sagging. The four-year-old boy lay across his mother's shawl on the cot in the side room of the children's ward as we watched him die. His name was Kojo and he had cerebral malaria, a treatable disease if diagnosed early, but the family had waited too long, attended by a local herbal doctor who had misdiagnosed the illness as... *I-don't-know-what, I-don't-really-care-what*, but *whatever-he-said-it-was*, it wasn't. It was cerebral malaria and the boy was dying because of the delay.

An intravenous infusion with anti-malarial drugs dripped into his veins but it obviously was not working as the boy's breathing was becoming irregular and gasping. We had no equipment, staff or training for ventilation of the lungs or intensive care. He was dying.

His mother knew. Her tired bony face was tear-drenched and strained.

His father knew. His lips were pursed and his shoulders tense as he tried to counter the heaviness-of-heart that consumed him. They looked at me pleading for a miracle. I impotently shrugged and slowly shook my head. I could not summon up any black humour to distract me. Some days it just doesn't work.

Gladys, a wiry, middle-aged national nurse came and stood next to me. Her dimpled face was set firm to maintain a matronly composure but I knew this was only a veneer for her huge heart. She mothered everyone, including me. 'You go, Doctor John. I'll look after them,' she urged, but I could not leave. I had promised myself during my days in Goma never to let a patient in my direct care die unattended.

It only took twenty minutes before his breathing finally stopped gasping and I could pronounce him dead. His mother wailed. There were no other family members to support her. His father spoke softly to Gladys.

'He thanks you for your care Doctor John and asks for a cardboard carton to make a coffin. They want to take the body to their village, twenty kilometres away.

130

They are willing to risk attack by the LRA to bury their son with dignity in their village. The body will be easier to carry on his bicycle if it is in a box. We have many in the pharmacy that would be large enough.'

'Of course. Let me go and have a look.'

I found a suitable drug carton, emptied it and with a sharp Stanley knife and a roll of MSF adhesive tape, took it back to the ward. Whilst Gladys wrapped Kojo's body in a blanket, his father and I fashioned a cardboard coffin. I lined it with absorbent bluey towels to prevent bodily fluids prematurely soaking through. It was the best I could spontaneously create.

Standing in the doorway of the ward I waved farewell as they began their twenty kilometres hike from the IDP camp to their abandoned village. The tiny coffin, reinforced with bands of wide white sticky tape emblazoned by the bright red MSF icon, was resting on the seat and tied across the handlebars. I could not imagine their feelings of grief but wondered how I would cope if one of my sons died and I could only honour him with a homemade cardboard coffin.

Did I hear Billy scoff, 'wrapping your failures now, eh John?'

How often did this scenario occur John?

A child would die of malaria two to three times a week. Malaria is a huge killer. Every day our community health workers were giving educational talks around the camp to increase awareness. We were handing out mosquito nets for protection against mosquito bites whilst sleeping but each small round mud hut, barely four metres in diameter, was cramped, housing up to ten people and a cooking area with an open fire. The congestion limited the use and safety of the nets. It was an uphill challenge.

And did you grieve each dead child John?

No. That would have burnt me out very quickly. But each child dying of a preventable, treatable disease eroded the euphoria of saving lives. It might be five lives saved for every death but it sometimes felt like five steps backwards for every step forward.

It was worse when I was tired and stressed, not uncommon on an emergency mission. I would often cry myself to sleep with frustration and feeling responsible for all the failed treatments.

What else did you do?

I practised my usual coping strategies; deep breathing exercises to slow my breathing and relax my muscles and repeating my well-worn 'what-is' mantra:

What is happening is happening, whether I know about it or not.
Life is not fair or just.
There is nothing I can immediately do to rectify injustice.
I do all I can do, however little that is.

I utilised two other novel activities.

I had acquired an ancient bicycle on which I pedalled around the camp, ringing the bell at everyone I passed. It made them smile and their smile made me smile. It was not as romantic as riding a horse in the Hindu Kush Mountains of Afghanistan but it was the best I could fashion. 'John of Uganda' just did not happen!

And finally, I cuddled Jimmy. He was a vervet monkey that one of the previous MSF expatriates had acquired and we inherited. He was tethered on a long rope attached to the warehouse next to our house where he lived in the roof. I would sit in a ragged armchair on the shaded warehouse veranda and he would climb down from the rafters and sit on my lap. A couple of peanuts made him a friend for life. He loved to be stroked. He would chatter away, scratch his armpits, shake his head and make me laugh. It was amazingly therapeutic. The physical touch was soothing and the unconditional attention relaxing.

I could hear Billy snigger 'Obviously a monkey is better than a psychologist for you John!
'

PATONGO, NORTHERN UGANDA
July 2006
Field Coordinator, Médecine Sans Frontière

'She has been in labour over twenty-four hours, Doctor John, with no progress. The cervix is not opening. She's obstructed. The baby has a transverse lie. I've tried everything to turn it but the baby is stuck. She needs a caesarean section... and quickly.' Dr Mitoka's voice was taut with anxiety, 'But Eric tells me the road to the hospital at Kalongo is closed. The heavy rain has flooded the river and the bridges are under water.'

I grimaced. 'There's nothing more to do but make her comfortable.'

'But it's urgent. She'll die with her baby.'

Our clinic was very basic with no surgical capability. Any patient requiring surgery was normally transferred to the mission hospital in Kalongo, two hours' drive along a narrow, dirt, corrugated track imaginatively labelled a highway on the map.

'Yes,' I admitted. 'But we cannot do the surgery here. We have no anaesthetic machine, no anaesthetic, no suitable surgical instruments or sutures, no trained staff. There's nothing more you and I can do. She may well die. If we were to attempt to operate it would be a disaster. The mother and baby would die and the local population would blame us for killing her. The clinic would be ever tarnished.

'I'll have the cars stand by and check the security situation. We'll go as soon as it is possible. I'll talk with the family.' I vocalised my concerns in full, not only for Doctor Mitoka's sake but also my own. It was a drastic decision and I needed to justify it to myself.

Doctor Mitoka stormed off in tears. I felt the same way. It was her first mission. The harsh reality of life in third world countries is heart-breaking. There are no retrieval teams, air evacuations or flying doctors. Life at times is brutal.

I immediately found Chico, the head of our community health workers (CHW). He was my eyes and ears in the camp. His twenty community health workers visited all sections of the camp every day, giving health advice and education, identifying the needy and vulnerable people and importantly listening to the gossip. I reckoned his information about the raiding LRA rebel patrols was more accurate than the formal security briefing given by the Office for the Coordination of Humanitarian Affairs (OCHA), the official body responsible for the whole region.

'If the rain settles how safe is it to go to Kalongo?' I asked.

He smiled. 'There's no need to worry. They've gone to ground Doctor John. Even terrorists don't like working in the rain.'

I was reassured.

The pregnant mother was lying in our emergency room rolling from side to side and groaning. Her husband sat beside her, face strained and downcast. He looked up hopefully as I entered but I shook my head.

'I'm sorry but the road is totally blocked. Our cars cannot get through. We will go as soon as is possible.'

He nodded. 'I know we have no time to wait. I have been thinking. My friend has a boat. We can carry her to the river and take the boat across. He also has a bicycle and we can push her to the hospital. There is a direct walking track that is much shorter than the highway.'

I knew from the map that the hospital was much nearer as the crow flies.

'My brother will help us on the other side,' he added optimistically.

I was stunned. I could not imagine such a journey was possible but this was Africa. His wife would surely die if she did not get to the hospital.

I nodded, 'If you think it possible then go. I will give her an injection to dull her pains but she will be groggy and need support at all times. Good luck.'

I found a stretcher and several volunteers to carry her to the river. Wearing plastic coats to keep dry they set off.

'You must be joking Doctor John. She is not fit to travel. Why did you let them take her? She will suffer and maybe bleed to death on the way,' Doctor Mitoka was furious.

'She is not fit to travel but she is fit to die here. The local people have a hardiness we westerners know nothing about,' I replied trying to justify my decision.

It was days before I heard the outcome. The phones were not working but the brother returned and visited me. The raging floodwaters had nearly swamped the boat but they managed to cross. The husband and brother had wheeled her halfway to the hospital on the bicycle before she collapsed. Too exhausted to continue, a local family sheltered them. Several of the local men rallied together, made a stretcher and carried her the rest of the way to the hospital where they immediately operated. Both mother and baby were well.

An amazing story John.

Indeed. Who would have thought a woman in obstructed labour could sit on a bicycle never mind be pushed along muddy paths in torrential rain. I was both impressed and humbled. It demonstrated how resilient the human body and spirit can be and how determination and tenacity can achieve near impossible feats of endurance.

I was also greatly relieved and thankful that both mother and baby survived. The pressure to undertake heroic surgery in these scenarios is immense, but if the mother had died in my hands, I would have been locally judged to have killed her, whilst her dying in childbirth would be been seen as a natural occurrence.

KITGUM, AGAGO DISTRICT, NORTHERN UGANDA
July 2006
Field Coordinator, Médecine Sans Frontière

'The FPA is not providing enough water in the camp.'

'If the RMD would stop complaining and use the water efficiently instead of wasting it washing their cars, it would be sufficient.'

'The flooding of the river has swamped all the latrines in our camp. We need a new contract with OCHA to build more.'

'If you had followed our initial guidelines to build the latrines, they would not have been near the river.'

'The grain supplied by WFP was delivered late for our food distribution. We need more tents to store a greater reserve.'

The whinging and whining interspersed with myriad meaningless acronyms continued...

I was attending the cluster meeting of NGOs under the umbrella of the UN's Office of Coordination of Humanitarian Affairs (OCHA). Eric, the logistician, was sitting beside me as bored, disillusioned and underwhelmed as I was.

'Why are we here John? This is just petty. So many NGOs are under-performing, over-competing and demanding more money for contracts with OCHA. It's all too restrictive. Thank God we are independently financed and not part of this cluster.'

'We're here because the coordination team in Kampala asked me to attend the cluster meetings, show some interest and keep tabs on what the other NGOs are up to. We don't want to duplicate anyone... but I agree with you, the agencies contracted to OCHA are all competing and have fixed outcomes. Stay awake. It will soon be over.'

It had taken us two hours to drive from Patongo to Kitgum in northern Uganda, the town where OCHA and most of the NGOs managed offices. I was embarrassed to even drive into the town. The main street was clogged with lines of parked white shiny polished four-wheel-drive cars emblazoned with logos and flags fluttering from aerials. Convoys of cars, escorted by trucks crammed with armed soldiers of the Ugandan Patriotic Forces (UPF) for protection, drove through the town en route for various camps. Small cafes and restaurants were dotted along the road to cater for the huge influx of western aid workers. The local cost of living had escalated beyond the means of the local population. Many IDPs sat on the roadside begging.

'It's you who needs to stay awake John.' Eric was prodding me with his elbow.

I tuned into the Chairman's report glorifying OCHA's programs... and tuned out again. Memories of the 'humanitarian circus' that enveloped Goma in 1994 flooded my mind. A proliferation of agencies and amateurs had swamped the region with western freebooters and 'humanotourists', duplicating services, providing unnecessary services, arriving without logistic support, all in an effort to gain praise and press. Missionaries, mercenaries and misfits were drawn to the disaster to follow their various agendas rather than help the beneficiaries. One small group had flown into Goma in a psychedelically painted plane bringing a few cartons of medicine but with no arrangement for unloading or storage. The medicines eventually found their way to our Red Cross warehouse. When I examined them, all information and instructions were written in Polish and they had to be destroyed... at great expense. Other groups wandered around preaching their gospel and handing out bibles. A German agency had flown doctors and nurses into Goma for two-week periods but had no clinics in which they could work. They ended up driving ambulances.

It was worse than a circus, it was a fiasco.

There had since been numerous international reviews of disaster management and a plethora of new recommendations... but it seems nothing had changed.

Now a new problem was emerging. Some agencies were signing contracts with OCHA to provide services in the camps but ran them remotely using national staff locally, but with all the supporting expatriate staff in distant offices in capital cities. It saved money and allowed them to tender lower prices.

The chairman of the meeting must have seen me daydreaming.

'Doctor John, it is good to see MSF attending. You should be part of our cluster. We are all on the same side you know.'

'Actually, Mr Chairman, that is incorrect. We are on no one's side. MSF is completely neutral and unattached to any other organisation. That is why we are not part of your cluster. But I am happy to be here and observe your good work.' There was a stunned silence whilst the other delegates digested what I had said.

The chairman coughed awkwardly and moved the meeting on to the next agenda item. At the end of the meeting, he attracted my eye and called me over. I was expecting some form of rebuke.

'Doctor John, the Japanese Ambassador is flying in tomorrow to inspect the region. The Japanese are a major donor to our funds and I would like to show him your clinic. It is one of the most efficient. Our convoy will arrive in the morning at about ten o'clock. Is that convenient?'

The question was academic.

'I'd be delighted to show him our work. I'll expect you at ten.' Eric and I departed for the two-hour return journey.

At ten o'clock I was waiting near the clinic gates wearing a freshly laundered but well-worn MSF T-shirt when six European men arrived wearing brand new red T-shirt flashed with a white logo.

'Hello Doctor John, we are the coordination team of MED. We sponsor Doctor Logi who works here three days a week. We are here to greet the Japanese ambassador.'

I was stunned. I had thought that Doctor Logi was a government doctor. I was to later learn that MED had offered the government some assistance and subsidised his wages.

It was not a problem... except that they were now about to swamp the about-to-arrive delegation of press photographers accompanying the Japanese ambassador and give the impression that they were running the medical centre.

I was bemused yet annoyed. How dare they front up and steal the show? I could not overtly complain. However, I had one trick left in my hand and it was a trump. I rushed back the two hundred metres to our accommodation.

'Doctor Mitoka, I need you at the clinic NOW to meet the ambassador. I know you don't want to come but this is urgent.'

Doctor Mitoka was a young shy Japanese doctor who was working with me. When I had told her, the previous evening, of the ambassador's visit she had elected not to meet him and I had not seen any reason to pressure her. But this was different. I explained the circumstances and she readily agreed.

I rushed back to the clinic as two cars followed by a truckload of soldiers pulled up at the gates. The ambassador alighted and was immediately flanked by the OCHA chairman and an army general carrying a machine gun. Several photographers followed in their wake tailed by several soldiers, all armed.

135

I met them at the gates and bowed a greeting. The six MED representatives stood beside me.

'Welcome to our clinic, Mr. Ambassador. Before we enter, may I ask the general to pass his machine gun to his men and request them to stay outside? This is a no weapon area.' I pointed to our *guns prohibited* sign beside the gate.

Everyone looked shocked. I heard the MED delegation beside me gasp in horror.

The general's face steeled. 'I am sorry Doctor John but for security, I must keep my gun. It is for the safety of the ambassador.'

'That might be so general but I cannot allow any arms inside. If it is too insecure for the ambassador, then maybe you must defer the visit. I am sure that your armed men surrounding the clinic can keep him safe.'

There was another gasp of horror besides me.

The ambassador interceded, his diplomacy shining. 'General, I am happy to enter the clinic without any arms. Would you mind?'

The general had nowhere to turn. 'Of course, Mr Ambassador. I was just considering your security.' He turned and handed his gun to his lieutenant but his facial expression was not as diplomatic.

The OCHA chairman introduced the six MED representatives but before they could enter into any discussion with the ambassador, I called out to Doctor Mitoka who was approaching the clinic. She was wearing a green patterned kimono with a stethoscope around her neck. Her dark hair, pinned above her head contrasted with her flawless pale skin. Walking slowly up to the ambassador, she bowed lowly and eyes downcast, welcomed him in Japanese. The press went crazy with a frenzied storm of flashes, angling their cameras for the best compositions. The ambassador was noticeably impressed and softly spoke with her. She agreed to show him around the clinic. It was hard for me to keep a straight face.

For the rest of the visit Doctor Mitoka led him through the wards, telling him of the work of MSF. I followed well behind as did the MED workers, cast aside into the shadows. The general kept at the ambassador's side and made sure that I could see the revolver on his hip. I pretended not to notice. It was not worth the fuss!

We toured through the outpatient and emergency rooms, the male and female wards full of AIDS patients and the paediatric ward that was brimming with sick and malnourished children. The ambassador was especially moved by these scenes of malnutrition but broke out laughing as a hen and her chicks were shooed through the ward by an embarrassed nurse. So much for our image of hygiene.

At the end of the visit, I pushed my way to stand beside Doctor Mitoka and thanked the ambassador for his visit. The general grabbed his machine gun, the OCHA chairman glared at me unhappily and the convoy sped off trailing a dust cloud. When I turned around the six MED representatives had disappeared... never to be seen again.

You were angry with them John?

I was. I was annoyed that the MED team would try to take the credit for the work that the MSF team was performing. I later discovered that four of them had flown from Kampala especially for the occasion. They were in cahoots with the OCHA chairman who had known about the ambassador's visit for a couple of weeks. He was probably irritated that MSF was not part of his cluster and was happy to see us humiliated.

I was incensed that organisations like MED sat in their offices every day, running programs from afar, giving national staff in the field little support and claiming payments and glory for shoddy work.

One reason I love working for MSF is because we stayed on the coalface of our medical work. We lived and worked in the IDP camp alongside the national staff. We became embedded within the community. At Patongo it was critical to our security for it was their eyes and ears that informed us of the daily conditions and dangers. Alongside our national staff we were able to adapt to changing circumstances without the encumbrances of external rigid contractual agreements.

For these charlatans to arrive and take centre stage was just too much. I admit that I took great pleasure in upstaging them and trumping them at their own game.

Billy advised, 'Always be sincere, John, even if you don't mean it.'

PATONGO, NORTHERN UGANDA
August 2006
Field Coordinator, Médecine Sans Frontière

'She... she... she was carrying the baby down to the river... to drown it,' stammered Brenda, visibly upset and shaking. 'It's got a cl... cleft lip and palate and the elder women of her village practically ordered her to do it. She's only seventeen and already has two young kids.'

Brenda continued, her voice beginning to calm. 'I met her as I was coming to work on the path to the river. She was crying and I asked what was wrong?'

Brenda was one of our senior national nurses. Her short frizzy hair was tied in tiny-ribboned plaits creating a mosaic of coloured tufts. She was an IDP and lived in the camp. Normally she was gregarious and ever laughing. This morning her face was strained with anxiety.

From the corridor, I could see the young mother sitting in the emergency room of the medical clinic holding a baby swaddled in a hospital sheet on her lap, but giving it no attention.

'I told her you could help the baby, Doctor John, and it was a sin to kill it.'

Inwardly, I cringed. The missionaries had been very effective in their indoctrinations. Outwardly I smiled, 'Let's not be too judgmental with the mum. Why don't you introduce me so I can examine the baby and talk with her,' I suggested.

I followed Brenda. The young mother looked up as I approached and seemed to shrink into her chair, her shoulders tightening and hunching up under her chin. I sat down beside her.

'This is Doctor John,' interpreted Brenda, 'Can he examine your baby?'

The mother pursed her lips, shrugged and placed the baby on the couch.

I smiled again, leant over and gently unwrapped the sheet to expose a newly born baby, the fresh but raggedly cut umbilical cord tied off with string. Opening a makeshift nappy of rag showed it to be a girl who looked healthy in every way except for a gaping hole replacing her nose that sank through the face to the back of the throat. This was a severe cleft palate birth defect that needed specialised surgery. But the most pressing problem was feeding the baby for, without an upper lip and soft palate she was unable to suck at the nipple.

Brenda asked, 'Shall I insert a nasogastric tube doctor?'

'Not yet,' I snapped and immediately felt guilty. Brenda was completely right to suggest putting a tube down the back of the mouth to the stomach through which milk could be passed, but I felt confused and uncertain and did not want to commit to any treatment yet. I needed to make some phone calls.

My mobile phone only connected if I attached it to an antenna mounted high on the office's roof. The antenna's wire was short and only reached inside the window in one corner of the room where I needed to stand. Even this connection only provided a patchy reception. Often the whole network was down. Today the atmosphere must have been stable and the network was operational for the call rang and was immediately answered. Hopefully, this was a good omen...

I had read somewhere in my briefing notes of a Dutch surgical team who visited the region every year to perform the surgery needed to repair the defect. Unable to find my notes I had phoned the OCHR offices in Kitgum, the UN agency that coordinated the IDP services across the region. I learnt that the program had been terminated two years previously for lack of funding and in fear of the increased violence of the region. No luck.

I next phoned the medical coordinator, Oscar, at the MSF coordination office in the capital Kampala. I explained the clinical situation and requested permission to send the mother and child to Kampala for specialist treatment.

'John, there's no funding available. If we send one child, it will lead to every birth deformity in the region being directed to us for treatment. It is not feasible.' No luck again.

A little bit of me, the realist fragment, suspected this would be the case and explained my initial reluctance to start active treatment... but another bit of me would not yet accept it.

'Can you escalate it to the desk in New York and see if they can fund it?' I persisted.

Oscar reluctantly agreed. The desk in New York had overall control of the missions in Uganda and might have other funding options. I asked him to do it now but the international time difference would cause delay.

The interval gave me pause to contemplate. This young mother had two infants at home, a one-year-old and a three-year-old. Her husband had moved to the south of the country to find work and send money home to the family. The grandmother was helping her with the babies but she had three other daughters, all with multiple children.

Her other two children demanded her full-time attention. They were already at high risk of malnutrition, especially the younger child. Food distribution in the camp only supplied sixty per cent of basic needs. The rest had to be found elsewhere. Her husband's money helped and her brothers grew some food in the fields beside the camp.

To nurse a deformed baby with little chance of survival to the detriment of her other two children was a poor investment. Life in the third world is grim. There is no advanced medical care, social service or welfare payment. Harsh conditions demand harsh decisions. Sometimes you have to cut off a finger to save the hand. It is not a sign of a hardened heart but that of a heart broken many times.

I received a phone call two hours later confirming that no money was available for any specialised treatment. I walked back to the ward and told the outcome to Brenda who burst into tears. I walked into the ward and with Brenda's sobbing interpretation told the young mother I could not help her and to take the baby home. She looked at me with contempt. The elder women, wise from the ages of reality, had known what had to be done. All I had achieved was to prolong the process and pain. I might as well have taken the baby to the river and drowned her myself.

How did you feel after this happened?
What do you think? I felt like shit. That night I wept the tears of frustration and failure. The next day the community health worker who visited that part of the camp told me the baby had died. I did not ask how. As I said before, I might as well have taken the baby down to the river and drowned her myself.

And how did you feel then?
I felt angry... so angry that anyone, any mother, especially a young mother would have to make such a decision in this day and age. Life might be unfair but this was such an extreme example of injustice.

I felt angry too that so many people in the wealthy countries would judge and condemn her to be a murderer, a heartless savage who would kill her new-born.

What gives the right for people with easy access to birth control, termination services, adoption agencies, advanced medical care, counselling services and social services to stand aloft and judge those without?

I read widely and learnt that infanticide has been practised by all cultures. Babies with a severe deformity or born in famine have been drowned or left in the cold to die. In medieval England, the monasteries and convents became common places for the poor to abandon their children rather than kill them. Even these facilities are lacking in the third world.

It did upset you immensely.
It did. It was not only the injustice and arrogant condemnations that irked me but also my own feelings of impotence at being unable to help. It was very humbling and gave me a tiny glimpse into how well-meaning aid can be harmful. It is easy to overlook and override evolutionary and cultural social processes that have smoothed the ragged edges of life for millennia. We may think we have the answers only to later realise our solutions are either not appropriate or premature. Rushing in with aid may disrupt delicate balances and can create false hopes and expectations that cannot be maintained, leaving the population even worse off than before.

PATONGO, NORTHERN UGANDA
August 2006
Field Coordinator, Médecine Sans Frontière

'Can you check them over physically, Doctor John? They have been in captivity for three years. One is fifteen and the other is thirteen. They only escaped from an LRA patrol three days ago. They recognised their home country and decided to risk running away. If they had been caught, they would have been tortured and killed.' I was asked by Faria, a psychologist from another NGO who help child soldiers reintegrate into their society.

She explained that over the previous fifteen years an estimated twenty-five thousand children had been kidnapped or coerced to be soldiers or slaves, often sex slaves for the LRA. Many children, orphaned by the AIDS epidemic had been

139

easy prey for this so-called army and, once intimidated into submission, the army provided a perverse family for them. Many had nowhere else to go.

'When you have finished, Doctor John, I will take them to a safe house.'

She explained how they were developing a strategy to support these children. Often their original village will not accept them back. It was proving a complex and prolonged process.

The two boys were both sullen, sitting on a bench outside my consulting room, their heads fallen, their bodies slouched, wearing a mixture of ragged camouflage jackets and T-shirts, torn shorts and thongs.

Marjorie, a national nurse, plump with close-cropped mousey hair and a smile of glistening teeth was acting as my interpreter. She originated from a village not far from where the boys had been kidnapped and had chatted with the boys before I arrived.

'Their names are Camo and Alok,' she confided. 'Their parents were murdered during the LRA raid on their village. Camo's sister was also kidnapped but he does not know where she is now. They were initially beaten and threatened. Camo was forced to shoot a 'traitor' or he be shot himself. They have been in a patrol for two years moving between Uganda and South Sudan, raiding villages on a whim. Both have carried rifles and killed.'

I could not imagine what these children had endured or what perspective of life they now bore. Thankfully all I had to do was check their physical health.

I smiled at them and asked Marjorie to tell them my intentions and ask their permission. It was given with a perfunctory nod. I asked if they had any complaints or injuries. Both shook their heads and stared at the floor.

Camo, the fifteen-year-old had a livid scar across his right cheek. An older soldier had slashed his face with a bayonet when he did not give him his food. He was anaemic, probably from a chronic hookworm infestation and a poor diet.

Alok's right lower arm was deformed from a fracture he endured from a beating. I had no ready access to X-rays but it was well healed and had near full function. An enlarged spleen in his abdomen reflected a probable recurrent malaria infection that a quick blood test confirmed. His skin was covered in a fungal infection. I feared their minds were far more scarred than their bodies.

I made up the medications to treat both of them for worms and Alok for malaria and his fungal infection. I added a bar of soap and a course of vitamins. I watched as Marjorie explained how to take all the treatments.

'The medicines will make you strong again,' I encouraged. They smiled fleetingly. I hoped that it was a sign for some recovery.

'Thanks, Doctor John. It's good to know they are reasonably physically healthy.' Faria was grateful. She was excited for she had arranged a meeting with the elders of the boys' village to assess their reaction.

'Even if they are accepted back, we cannot just leave them there. They have no social skills or normal boundaries of behaviour. They've been robbed of a childhood and it can never be replaced.'

A disturbing story John. Did it bother you?

My meeting with Cano and Alok was distressing. At this time I had two sons, both in their twenties. To imagine them experiencing such forced brutality, prolonged abuse and living such a perverted lifestyle in their teenage years, in any years, was unimaginable. How can they ever overcome the trauma and hope to have a normal family life?

It also humbled me. How can I complain of PTSD when the traumas I have suffered pale to near insignificance in comparison? Life can be brutal.

Sunshine Coast, Queensland, Australia
September 2006

How was it coming home from these missions John?
Compared to my tempestuous and troubled return from Afghanistan it was a breeze. I had a few problems but I had learnt many lessons from my earlier experiences. I was not going to fall into the same abyss of dislocation and despair.

What had you learned?
Firstly, I did not rush back home. I was single and had no commitments back in Australia. As promised my mission debrief was in New York and I enjoyed a week in the city, visiting the sights, museums and art galleries. I flew over to Europe and spent several more weeks touring and travelling, visiting family and friends in the UK, admiring the architecture in Barcelona and exploring the scenically stunning coastline of Italy. The novelty, sightseeing and reunions were exciting. My adrenaline levels were able to slowly subside avoiding the agitation of sudden withdrawal. I was distracted by nostalgia, history and beauty and I enjoyed many luxuries to recuperate my health and physical condition.

So, you were gentle with yourself?
You could say that.
Secondly, I had learnt not to expect anyone to be interested or knowledgeable in where I had been or what I had done. I did not mention my mission in conversations. If asked directly about my work, I would talk for a few minutes then change the subject back to the other person. If they asked me again, I would engage for another few minutes then change the subject again to a local topic.

Thirdly, when I was confronted by indifference or ignorance about the countries I had visited, I was disappointed but not triggered. My anger did not well up as before. I inwardly shrugged, smiled and accepted it as the 'what is'.

If anyone told me they thought I was brave I would thank them for their kindness, refrain from trying to convince them otherwise, then change the subject.

You had come a long way, John.
Yes, it was still an effort but I coped much better... but I was still triggered by the general lack of gratitude and appreciation for the western lifestyle and the amount of accumulated stuff that people hoarded.

I continued to be shocked by the expectations of people in first world countries; their lack of appreciation of their freedom, their judiciary, security, high standard of housing, easy access to education and medical care. Having just returned from a country ravaged by civil war and devastated by poverty it was difficult to bear.

The 'waste of the west' was especially challenging, particularly the discarded food. A friend's son, a six-year-old boy would not eat a tub of yoghurt because it had expired the previous day. He picked up all six cartons from the fridge and with a screwed-up face of disgust, as if they were all rotting and putrid, threw them in the bin. I had a flashback of a skeletal child lying in a cot, dying of malnutrition. I had to bite my tongue to stop screaming out, 'Eat it, you little spoilt shit. It's good food.' but I kept quiet. He knew no better.

141

How did you manage these triggers?

I journaled my feelings. I find it a potent therapy. I wrote everything going on in my head, filling page upon page with my ramblings.

I again came to realise that these were my issues, that my mission had changed my perspectives. I was overflowing with gratitude and appreciation for my life in Australia. I felt blessed and fortunate to be so lucky. I came to realise that other people's feelings and actions was not my concern or business. My challenge was to maintain my gratitude, not to become complacent and accepting. After several weeks I returned to Australia feeling more settled and stable and returned to my job in a local general practice. My patients were as therapeutic as ever reminding me that their needs were as relevant as those of patients in the third world. I still had vivid dreams but no nightmares and I suffered no flashbacks. My mood, energy levels and sleep were healthy. Everything seemed to be back to normal. I reunited with my partner and we eventually married. My troubles in returning from a humanitarian mission were over... or so I thought.

Despite falling back into domestic bliss there was still a background niggle, an itch, a calling... and then, two years later, a telephone call.

Sunshine Coast, Queensland, Australia
July 2008

'John, I know you haven't called us but we have a mission ongoing in Iraq which I think may interest you. We are running a major burn and trauma unit in the city of Sulaymaniyah, in the Kurdish region of Iraq and urgently need a Medical Coordinator. Might you be interested?'

I was sitting in a local bar on the Sunshine Coast in Australia with a group of male friends with whom I met each Thursday. We called ourselves the 'Echidna Club'. It was nothing nature-related or conservationist; just an 'aleing group of old pricks' who were full of bad jokes.

I moved away from the noisy conversations to a quieter spot. My heart was hammering in anticipation. The caller, Anton, was ringing from Paris. 'Tell me more.'

'Well, we've wanted to be present in Iraq for a while, especially to help treat the victims of the bombings. Baghdad is far too dangerous for an expatriate team. Instead, we have taken over a burn unit in Sulaymaniyah, which is further north, near Kirkuk and Mosul, two other violent hot spots. It is a university city of about a million people. We need an experienced medical coordinator, particularly someone to meet with the local doctors in surrounding hospitals and set up a referral network.'

'How dangerous is it?'

'It is a dangerous region but Sulaymaniyah is controlled by the Kurdish security agency who do not like the Arabs so insurgency is well controlled. There was one bomb blast in the city last month. There is also a small risk of kidnapping for ransom.'

'Do you pay ransoms?'

'We negotiate... yes...' He did not finish... as if worried that speaking it would bring it on.

'How long will this mission be for?'

'It will take at least three months to be effective.'

'Why call me?'

'You have the right experience, John and…'

'Yes… and…?'

'And there is no one else available at the moment.' He did not quite say that I was the last resort.

'I'll need to talk to my wife. I'll call you tomorrow.'

And what was her response?

My wife was amazingly supportive.

'If you want to go then you must go. We will cope back home.'

I did not need more encouragement.

What attracted you to go on this mission? It was very different from all your previous ones?

Firstly, the danger. I remember daring myself to go. Did I have the guts to go into an active war zone?

But what pushed it over the line was that it was a major burn and trauma unit. All my other missions had been in primary health care clinics in third world countries with very basic drugs and equipment. This was a secondary medical care unit in a developing country. I would be part of a large team of doctors. I would be living in a house in a city, not in a mud hut in a backwater. I just wanted the new experience: to deal with major injuries, not hookworm infestations, pneumonia or gastroenteritis.

So, what happened?

IRAQ
MÉDECINS SANS FRONTIÈRES
2008

Anthony, the logistics coordinator was showing me our accommodation. He was heavily built, his T-shirt bulging with well-toned muscles. His chubby face was framed with hair falling to his shoulders and a goatee beard.

We had driven from the airport through the city centre and into the suburbs, rows of modern brick flat-roofed houses all sprouting an array of satellite television dishes. We stopped outside one such nondescript house and beeped the horn. A guard opened the gate and we drove in. It was quickly shut behind us.

'This is the house for the coordination team which you share with me, Julien, the Head of Mission, and Anna, the Financial Controller.'

I looked around impressed with the décor.

'I feel odd, being on a mission and living in a modern unit with 24/7 electricity, comfortable beds, sofas and cushions, en-suites with hot showers, even a toilet that washes and dries your bum.'

Anthony smiled. 'You've obviously been to Africa too many times, John. Get over it. This is a major city in a developed country. It might be at war but it has not returned to the Stone Age. The work here is physically and emotionally arduous. Dealing with severely burned patients every day is incredibly demanding, especially for the medical staff. There is little respite or escape. We all need some comfort and relief to stay sane. This house is not excessive. You will earn it.'

I had just arrived in Sulaymaniyah, Iraq, after spending a day's briefing in the MSF mission in Amman, Jordan. I was tired. The flight from Amman was short but the airport security checks were exhaustive with roadblocks and car searches beginning a kilometre before the airport. A full and thorough luggage and body search occurred at the airport entry, at check-in, at the departure gate and even beside the aircraft before boarding. Bombs were a real threat. I was reassured by its thoroughness.

Anthony continued to brief me, 'There is a small but real risk of kidnap. For this reason, all travel outside the house and hospital is restricted. We only use unmarked, dedicated taxis, varying our departure times to break patterns.'

He paused to let its significance sink in. He explained how the insurgents used it to generate income for their operations. Any professional was at risk. Local doctors were worth about eighty thousand American dollars. An expatriate doctor was probably worth half a million. It felt a little unnerving.

He further reassured me. 'To keep under the radar the hospital has no MSF signage. We do not want to announce our presence. At the hospital entrance, everyone is frisked. Obviously, males and females have separate queues. The only people who are not frisked are the Iraqi doctors. They say they should not be publicly humiliated and are above suspicion. I cannot ban them so we turn a blind eye.'

'Fascinating.' I wondered what it would be like to work with these little 'princes'. I was soon to find out.

'I'll take you to the hospital now. It is only two kilometres. Julien is expecting you.'

'Welcome John. You are here at last. We have been expecting you for two weeks.' Julien, Head of Mission, greeted me warmly. He was a young thirty with a thin face sporting a day's old stubble holding a wry grin. I instantly liked him.

'But they only contacted me last week.'

'Head Office works in funny ways.' He finished without explanation. 'Since you left Australia, the situation has changed.'

I was not surprised. This seemed to happen to me every time I went on a mission.

'What's changed?' I asked.

'Doctor Dirk, the medical director of the burn unit is leaving early. I was hoping you could take over.'

'What about the medical coordinator's job? I'm supposed to set up a referral network with the local doctors and hospitals.'

'I was hoping you could do that too. I will give you a hand.'

'Is there anyone else who can do it?'

'No. You're it.'

My heart sank. This was going to be a hectic time.

Julien continued his briefing as if everything had been finalised.

'The hospital has ninety-two beds. There are twelve burn surgeons led by a specialist consultant, three orthopaedic surgeons led by a specialist, four anaesthetic nurses led by an expatriate anaesthesiologist, one hundred and fifty nursing staff with a national head nurse and a hundred paramedical staff. You'll be overseeing them all.'

I wanted to scream, STOP, it's all too much, but bit my lip.

'I'm tired and need a good night's sleep. Can we continue this tomorrow?'

'Of course.'

I was woken from a deep sleep with pounding on my door. My watch registered three o'clock.

'Doctor John, you are needed at the hospital. Some severe injuries have arrived.' Anthony apologised in his guttural French accent.

I dressed whilst half asleep, or was I half-awake, I'm still not sure, but later discovered my shirt was inside out, my socks were odd and my fly was undone. The hospital staff looked at me suspiciously as I arrived in the emergency department.

There had been a bomb explosion. Two severely injured men had been rushed in. One had both legs blown off and the second had severe burns to seventy per cent of his body. The floor was covered in bloody footprints.

'We are short of medical staff this weekend and cannot find many doctors. Thanks for your help.' Doctor Afan, the orthopaedic specialist, was overseeing the resuscitation of the legless patient. Two other doctors were dealing with the burned man. 'Can you scrub up for theatre?'

I changed into surgical scrubs, discovering my dress anomalies with embarrassment but too tired to care, and scrubbed my arms and hands.

We spent two hours operating on the amputee, cutting away all the damaged tissues and fashioning stumps. Doctor Afan was an experienced war surgeon, a legacy of the eight-year-long Iraqi/Iranian war between 1980 and 1988. He handled the complicated injuries with ease. I was able to show many of my surgical abilities and knew I had gained some credibility from the encounter. It was a good start.

Later that morning, I met with all the medical staff. I was thankful I had been able to shower and dress more appropriately for they were all immaculately attired in pressed suits, shirts and ties. I was viewed with suspicion... I could feel their mistrust... *another MSF coordinator who comes and goes, each with their own ideas.*

I introduced myself, keeping it short and sweet and concluding, 'You are working well and I do not want to change anything. I am here to help improve our services so please come to me with your suggestions'.

Your diplomacy seems to be improving?

It was again another good start to a mission allowing me to show medical competency and assert a passive authority. I was able to meet all the doctors individually, join ward rounds, watch and assist them work in the operating theatres. Unfortunately, personality clashes with my predecessors had caused friction and my 'softly, softly' approach worked well. I discovered they were not little princes as I had unjustly labelled them earlier but dedicated, competent, proud professionals who worked hard in a demanding environment. I was humbled.

I was also fascinated. They used unique methods for burn dressings unknown in Australia. Amniotic membrane from recent obstetric deliveries was isolated from the placenta, screened for infectious diseases and sterilised, to be used as a transparent burn dressing. It seemed to be highly effective. I had much to learn and understand.

MSF MAJOR BURN AND TRAUMA TREATMENT CENTRE, SULAYMANIYAH, IRAQ
July 2008
Medical Director of Hospital and Medical Coordinator,
Médecins Sans Frontières

'Doctor John, can I speak candidly with you?' Doctor Aly, the burn specialist, cornered me after our early morning ward round and we walked out into the garden. His face was impassive, a thin moustache outlining his upper lip, his closely shaven cheeks and chin glowing in the sunshine. His expensive blue suit and speckled red tie reinforced his slim figure. Although shorter than me he stood tall with authority.

'How can I help you Doctor Aly?' We strolled around the lush lawn.

'We are happy MSF is now running our hospital. We have more equipment, drugs and dressings than ever before. The expatriate specialists who visit are training us in the newer treatments. But I don't understand why MSF is not named on the hospital sign at the front gate?'

'I think we want to keep below the radar, Doctor Aly. We do not want to become a terrorist target,' I replied.

'But everyone knows you are here. I am positive the insurgent spies will have identified you. It is better if you are transparent, advertise your presence and show that you have nothing to hide. It will build up trust with the local and medical community. There is a growing suspicion of what MSF is doing in the hospital, that we are using new treatments and experimenting on patients. Being secretive only reinforces these rumours.'

He paused for reflection, then continued, 'I agree that MSF should enforce security measures; blocking cars from parking beside hospital walls to avoid a bomb blast; security screening all staff before employment; body searching everybody entering the hospital.

'But beware... it would be very easy to smuggle a gun or bomb into the hospital. The body searches are hurried and flimsy. A small bribe would turn a blind eye...'

He left the suggestion hanging.

'Thanks, Doctor Aly. I'll talk with the Head of Mission. I completely agree with you and I'll recommend we place an MSF logo at the front gate.'

It was only two hours later...

'Doctor John, come quick, a man has a gun in the garden.' Dahlia, one of the nurses had stuck her head through the doorway of my office. Her voice trembled as she outlined the crisis.

I ran down the stairs, along the covered walkway from the office to the garden. It was visiting time. Crowds of families were gathered around the windows of the adult intensive care ward. They were not allowed inside but could look through the locked windows to see their loved ones.

Inside the ward, each patient was allowed only one family member at the bedside to be a carer. They were dressed in surgical scrubs and were committed to stay inside the ward with the patient to avoid cross infection. All the other visitors were kept outside in the garden.

One man was standing beside a window waving a pistol above his head and shouting. He fired a shot into the air when he saw me approaching. Everyone froze, including me. Dahlia stood behind me.

'What's he been shouting?' I asked in as low a tone as I could muster.

'He wants to go into the ward to see his daughter. He is not happy.'

A bit of an understatement, I mused.

I stood as tall as I could stretch and walked slowly towards the man with my arms by my sides and palms facing forwards. He dropped his arms and the gun was pointing to the ground. Dahlia walked behind me.

'Hi, I'm Doctor John, the medical director. How can I help you?' Dahlia interpreted behind me.

'You have imprisoned my daughter. You are using her as a guinea pig. She needs her father. She is special. You will let her die,' he snarled.

My heart was pounding though my chest wall. I took some deep breaths...

'Your daughter is critically ill from the burn she suffered from the kerosene stove in your house. She may die. We are doing everything humanly possible to help her but if you go into the ward you will infect the burn and kill her. Is that what you want?' I spoke loudly so everyone could hear. Dahlia translated in an equally loud but wavering voice. I had no training in negotiation but I decided to put him on the spot and not allow his tantrum to continue.

It worked. He put his gun into his belt, slumped down on the ground and holding his face in his hands, openly wept. I went up to him, knelt beside him and put my hand on his shoulder. Another of his daughters sat beside him and hugged him, looked at me and smiled.

'Thank you, doctor, he is very upset. He would not have shot anyone.'

'Maybe, but I'd be happier if you would take his gun away from him.'

I returned to the offices.

'You've had a busy day John,' Julien smiled.

'It had its moments!'

Billy whispered in my ear, 'you know what they say about life in Iraq, John? ... Sunni one day, Shi'ite the next.'

MSF MAJOR BURN AND TRAUMA TREATMENT CENTRE, SULAYMANIYAH, IRAQ
July 2008
Medical Director of Hospital and Medical Coordinator,
Médecins Sans Frontières

'Doctor John, we admitted another ninety per cent burn last night,' Fatima, the nurse-in-charge briefed me as I walked into the nursing station of the burn intensive care ward. A burn is described by the percentage of the whole body it covers. A ninety per cent burn is a death sentence.

'She's sixteen. The family say she poured petrol over herself and set herself alight and that it was a suicide. She was due to marry a forty-year-old relative this weekend. She's in Room Three.'

Room Three was a six-bedded ward in which we nursed all major burns until they died. All our patients with burns greater than seventy per cent of their body surface died. In Iraq, we did not have the intensive care, surgical or nursing skills or medical equipment for the advanced treatments available in the west. We did not have ventilators to treat burns to the lungs. We did not have the artificial skin, advanced dressings and compression bandages to minimise scarring. Despite our restrictions, we had great success in treating many burns, but not horrifically large burns.

'Is she well analgised?' I asked. Burns are extremely painful. My main concern was to ensure the patient was prescribed sufficient pain killing drugs.

'She's on a morphine infusion and her pain is well controlled. Doctor Kafir performed several escharotomies to make her breathing easier.'

Badly burnt skin can form a charred, rigid crust that constricts the chest and prevents the expansion required to take a breath. It may squeeze the circumference of an arm or leg and cut off the blood supply. Both cause severe discomfort but are easily relieved by making a long cut through the full thickness of the dead, burnt skin, allowing it to split and expand. It sounds and looks terrible but is highly effective. The procedure is called an escharotomy.

'Her mother is with her. The family is saying very little. We have told them the prognosis.'

Fatima led me to Room Three. Before entering we both donned gowns over our surgical scrubs, fitted caps, masks and overshoes, all essential precautions to prevent cross-contamination between the rooms and between patients. A sign beside the door reminded us to disinfect our hands using the bottle of alcoholic hand wash beside the door.

Today there were only three patients in the six-bedded ward, each lying on their bed covered with a yellow sheet. I identified the new patient and introduced myself to her mother using Fatima as my interpreter. She said nothing. The patient was unrecognisable. Her face was completely charred, her hair frizzed to a thin mat, her eyebrows and eyelashes missing. The skin was blackened. Amazingly she was conscious and her eyes followed me. I smiled at her and said, 'Hello.'

She did not react.

'Is she comfortable?' I asked the mother. Fatima translated. The mother, eyes downcast, just nodded. I lifted the sheet and glanced over the rest of her burns. The whole body was black and charred. The superficial veins in her arms were black lines of cooked, congealed blood.

Ironically four electric fires glowed between the beds warming the room to help the patients maintain body heat and prevent hypothermia. They were a terrible fire risk but there was no other heating available during the colder months of the year. Although wire guards screened them, I lived in dread of them causing more tragedy.

Unfortunately, we were unable to take a history from the patient. She was heavily sedated and did not need any external stimulation or distress. Our task was to allow her to die painlessly and with maximum dignity.

You found working in the Burn Unit one of the most difficult missions. Why was that?

Burns are terrible injuries, one of the most devastating. The suffering of a burned patient goes on for years, probably for life. Multiple operations to clean and dress the burn are followed by multiple surgeries to graft skin, release contractures and reconstruct tendons and facial features. It is never ending. Simultaneously they must deal with their loss of function, ongoing pain and the social stigma of scarring. It's not only the patients. Their families suffer too. The nursing and medical staff also need constant support to deal with their own feelings and how they interact with the patients and their families. Day after day they are confronted with terrible cases.

But there was an even deeper issue that still haunts me. Some of the young girls who were burnt beyond hope of survival were probably not suicides. Some were family honour killings. They were murdered. And I had to stay silent.

That is a severe accusation. What evidence did you have?

Nothing provable. But the local staff all knew and told me.

Honour killing was not legal but the authorities, the culture and other families tolerated it. It was an age-old tradition of punishment for any young girl who threatened to dishonour the family by sexual misconduct or disobedience. Paradoxically, Sulaymaniyah was a progressive university where the girls wore western clothes with only a flimsy scarf around their heads. It was relatively liberal towards the rights of women. But in the surrounding countryside the villages were much more rigid and conservative and daughters had to follow the traditional family demands, maybe more severely enforced against the lax moral standards of the city. Most of our referrals came from the outlying villages.

Did you discuss your suspicions with the coordination team?

Of course, I did. They reacted like you. What proof did I have? What are the statistics?

I was also told that we were new to the area and had no credibility. We were outsiders tolerated for the excellent medical service we provided but no one had asked us to come. Who were we to arrive and start making serious accusations against their society? If we spoke out, we would soon be ostracised and our hard-won reputation would become defunct.

I knew they were right. It is important to choose your battles. We didn't openly condemn the Taliban for their policy on women wearing burqas. They would have thrown us out of the country and our clinics would have collapsed. But a bit of me was devastated. I had a twenty-five-year-old daughter and a twelve-year-old stepdaughter. I felt impotent, powerless... an enabler... now a part of the problem. It hurt me terribly.

MSF MAJOR BURN AND TRAUMA TREATMENT CENTRE, SULAYMANIYAH, IRAQ
July 2008
Medical Director of Hospital and Medical Coordinator,
Médecins Sans Frontières

'John, Anna and I need your help.' Julien, the Head of Mission had quietly entered my office looking unusually sheepish. Anna followed closely behind. She was the financial coordinator, a slim Croatian girl with short brown hair and sparkling green eyes wearing a faint perfume of vanilla. Her eyes too were downcast.

Anna continued. 'We have to reduce the staff's pay by twenty per cent.'

'Why for goodness sake? Who's demanding that?'

She explained. 'This mission was set up hurriedly, which is often the case in emergency missions. The team did not research local pay rates sufficiently and our present wages are set too high. They are undermining other local hospitals causing ill will. We are being accused of poaching medical staff and competing with the Iraq Department of Health. The desk in Paris demand we reduce the wages to local levels.'

'It will be hard to justify that to the staff,' I countered. 'We cannot take away benefits and not expect some outrage.'

'I know that,' Julien interceded. 'I've argued with the desk to keep our wages at present levels but they are adamant we must reduce them. We have no choice. That is why we need your help. I've called a meeting tomorrow afternoon with all the hospital staff to announce it and ask that you talk with the doctors in the morning during your team meeting. They may be more level headed and objective than the rest of the staff. If we have their support it may reduce the fallout.'

'Of course, I'm happy to talk with them but I don't guarantee any success.'
The following morning after discussing the handover of overnight medical problems and new admissions I broached the subject. Twelve doctors were present, all dressed in sharply pressed trousers, shirts and wearing ties. I felt I was fronting an official Board of Enquiry. They glared at me suspiciously. It seemed news of the pay cut had leaked out the previous day.

'I have some good news and bad news,' I declared.

'What is the bad news?' they demanded.

'The bad news is that we have been overpaying all the staff.'

'What is the good news?'

'The good news is that we are not asking anyone to repay the extra monies already paid to them.'

There was a confused silence. They all looked at each other wondering if I was serious or joking.

I seized the moment.

'I know no one is going to like this but the reduction in pay is going to happen. We have already tried to negotiate with the desk in Paris on your behalf but they will not back down. Our pay rates must reflect local values. You have two choices, accept the present offer or threaten to close down the hospital. Only the patients will suffer if we have to reduce our services. I'll leave you to discuss it in private and see you this afternoon at the general meeting.' I hastily gathered my papers and left.

That afternoon the meeting buzzed angrily like a disturbed hornet's nest. The assembled staff was seething with rage and discontent. Even before the meeting commenced, we could overhear the threats of strike, revolt and resignation. Julien bravely stood and explained the dilemma, describing the pay cuts as well as the benefits of working for MSF and its humanitarian focus, fielding questions on the amounts and justification of the pay reduction. There seemed little goodwill. One of the doctors stood and spoke, accepting the conditions and urging everyone else to be reasonable, but he was shouted down by a few vocal agitators as already being an overpaid doctor. So much for all my persuasion. Many stood and condemned MSF for being deceitful, disloyal and uncaring.

After the meeting Anna, Anthony, Julien and I debriefed in Julien's office. He was visibly shaken.

'That was terrible. I did not expect such a reaction. What are we going to do if half the staff resigns? This is a disaster.'

I had to interrupt. 'Hang on Julien. The staff is just upset as expected. A few hotheads are threatening resignation but I reckon most staff are happy working for us and will come to see reason. The effort of resigning and finding a new job, probably with a similar or lower pay rate, will be greater than the inertia of staying here. Let the hotheads resign. There are a few I would be happy see depart. In fact, tomorrow ask for any resignations. Call the bluff. We can make contingency plans to reduce our admissions and workload if we have staff shortages. We can refer to the other hospitals in town.'

'But I'm responsible for the hospital functioning. I cannot let it fail.' Julien was downcast.

'No, you are not responsible for what happens, only how we react to circumstances. The desk has caused the turmoil. The resignations will either happen or they won't. If they happen, we will deal with it. If they don't happen, we will deal with it. Let's wait and see.'

It was another week before the pay cuts became a reality. The tensions of revolt and resignation tempered with time and further explanation. Amazingly no one resigned and no strike action was ever planned. The critical payday passed as quietly as the millennium bug.

That night Julien arrived back at the house with two bottles of Jack Daniels whisky that he opened and threw away the tops. It was a celebratory party night.

So, you were happy?

I was happy to have been instrumental in containing the fear and countering some of the pessimism that threatened to snowball, lose all perspective and catastrophise events. I was unhappy with my hangover the following morning.

Are you always optimistic?

Mostly. I think it's something I learned from my father. In my childhood, he would wake my brother and I each morning with a cup of tea that he laid beside our beds before throwing open the curtains and, no matter the weather, would sing a chorus from the musical *Oklahoma*:

Oh, what a beautiful morning,
Oh, what a beautiful day,
I've got a wonderful feeling.
Everything's going my way.

I would curse and complain to be awoken in such a crass manner but, when I was studying medicine my anatomy tutor advised me, 'If you throw mud at a brick wall some will stick.' I learnt human anatomy after hours and hours of study and dissection of dead bodies. Maybe I became an optimist after mornings and mornings of my father's repetitive chorus.

Another mentor for my optimism was my Uncle Bob. In my boyhood I spent many summers on his dairy farm in Lincolnshire, England. He had been a general in the British army and taught me to shoot rifles, milk cows and stack bales of hay. His no-nonsense and go-do-it attitude to life instilled in me the belief that if something does go wrong, I could manage. He would advise, 'Face it, chunk it down and deal with it.'

So, do you just ignore negative possibilities?
It's not that I ignore negative possibilities. I certainly give no credence to the 'what-ifs', the 'maybes' or 'perchances' that are fed by fears, both rational and irrational. When given attention they are amplified by vivid imagination, malignant mistrust or a need to control. So much energy is wasted worrying about events that never happen.

A pessimist seems to have a problem for every solution, expecting everything to go wrong. An optimist does not expect everything to turn out well; they are OK no matter how things eventuate; they take life as it comes rather as they think it should unfold.

I don't expect a negative possibility to occur. It either will... or it won't, and it probably won't. But if it does, I will cope. Being free of anxiety for the future, my attention is focussed on the present, a reward that only strengthens my optimism.

I am also fortunate that when I have felt completely downhearted and downcast, and there have been many times following my missions when I was enveloped in desperation and despair, there's a smouldering fire deep within me, from where it comes I have no idea, that buffers me from plummeting into the bottomless pit of hopelessness, that softens my distress and melancholy with sparks of *let it be, this too shall pass, something good will come of this...* and... eventually... it always does... another beautiful morning.

MSF MAJOR BURN AND TRAUMA TREATMENT CENTRE, SULAYMANIYAH, IRAQ
August 2008
Medical Director of Hospital and Medical Coordinator,
Médecins Sans Frontières

'Hey John, we've got a problem.' Julien wandered into my office in the 'MSF Major Burn and Trauma Hospital'.

'Another one? What might that be?' I was curious. It was usually me going to him with problems.

'I've just had a call from the local military commander of the Kurdish Security forces. He has a severely burned prisoner that they want us to treat. The other hospitals have no beds. It's a thirty per cent, third-degree burn with shrapnel injuries caused when the bomb he was making prematurely exploded.'

'So, what's the problem?' I was confused. 'We have a bed and we'll treat anyone whatever side they're on.'

'Yes, I understand that,' countered Julien.

'Will he be under guard… not that he's in any shape to escape?' I questioned.

'Yes, there will be two guards 24/7.'

'Do the authorities understand that the guards cannot bring their guns into the hospital?'

'Yes. They are aware of our *No Gun Policy*.'

'And do they know that if guards want to be bedside, they will have to change into surgical scrubs?'

'Yes, I've made it very clear.' My interrogation was irritating Julien.

'So, what's the problem?'

'The problem is that the prisoner is suspected of making the bomb that exploded last week just outside the city and injured Ashrad.'

'Oh dear. That is a problem.' I was worried.

Ashrad, an eight-year-old-boy, was a patient in our hospital. He had picked up an object that looked like a play station but was actually a bomb. It had detonated and he had lost his right eye, right arm, lower right leg, suffered severe burns and shrapnel injuries to his face and torso. He was out of danger and moving about in a wheelchair but the family and local community were angry and would surely seek revenge.

'But the guards will protect him,' I added to mainly reassure myself.

'Yes, but they might not be too vigilant if put under pressure… and they'll have no guns.'

'We can put him in the end room of the adult intensive care ward. No one will have easy access.'

'Except for staff and other patient carers,' added Julien as a devil's advocate.

'Well, it's the best we can do.'

'I agree John, but we need to talk with the staff… all of them… to explain why we are accepting and treating this patient. I know we explained our principles of independence, impartiality and neutrality at our staff induction but the concepts are more confronting and threatening when actually faced with a scenario like this.'

He continued to express his fears that although everyone agreed to MSF's principles when they were employed, it was just another box to tick. How much credence did it have?

'We need to gently but firmly reinforce that MSF does not take sides and will treat anyone who needs medical attention, no matter what the circumstance. I'll talk with the non-medical staff. Will you cover the nurses and doctors?'

'Of course, I'll be happy to and I'll oversee all his treatment to ensure it is comprehensive. He'll probably eventually be tried and executed… but not here.'

And was he treated well?
Yes. He was guarded round the clock by the soldiers. They were not happy sitting without their guns and dressed in surgical scrubs.

Myriad rumours rumbled around the wards; that the boy's family would sneak in at night, overpower the guards and slit his throat; that he would be given a fatal overdose of a drug; that his wounds would be deliberately infected and he would die of septicaemia, but nothing untoward happened. His wounds were debrided and grafted. He was given blood transfusions and antibiotics. After ten days he was thankfully transferred to a government hospital. I've no idea of his final outcome.

It was a tense test of MSF's principles of impartiality and neutrality. MSF treats anyone no matter his or her belief, nationality, race or lifestyle. MSF staff honours these principles dearly. It is one reason I work for them. On emergency missions, when MSF hires national staff, they are educated and inducted on these principles. Their acceptance is a condition of work. But in this instance, we employed the hospital staff en masse when MSF took control from the Iraqi Department of Health. Our national staff did not individually choose to work for us. We had commandeered them. They had been educated about the principles but no commitment was ever individually made.

When I spoke with the medical staff, there was some disbelief that we would offer our full medical services to a bomber, a murderer, a terrorist. Eventually, after being reminded of our mandate and realising that the bomber would face justice after discharge, they were more understanding. They probably understood better than me what type of justice that may involve.

As one staff member commented, 'He will get his just deserts, Doctor John, just not yet eh?'

Billy might have reassured, 'Don't fret John, these situations get blown up out of all proportions!'

MSF Major Burn and Trauma Treatment Centre, Sulaymaniyah, Iraq
September 2008
Medical Director of Hospital and Medical Coordinator,
Médecins Sans Frontières

'John, we have a plastic surgeon arriving in two weeks. She's only here for two weeks to perform any reconstructive surgery you consider to be helpful. Can you read the portfolio of files of possible cases and make a selection?'

'Bloody hell Julien, how can I choose cases from files? I need to examine the patients first.'

'John, that's not possible. Some of these people live far away. There's not enough time.'

'Why can't you send the files to the surgeon and let her choose. She is far more qualified.'

'She's too busy. We're lucky she is even coming out here. This has all been arranged hurriedly. Hopefully, if it works out the next visit may be better managed.'

'And I'm not too busy?' I snapped.

'Just give it your best shot, John I'm sure there are many worthwhile cases.' Julien replied Ignoring my snipe.

I spent the next two days perusing patient files, reading of the horrendous burns and seeing pictures of their scarring, deformities and contractures aggravated by lack of physiotherapy, compression bandages, reconstructive surgery and psychological support. I could not imagine how the patients coped both physically and mentally in such an impoverished medical system. It highlighted how the treatment of burns is life long, physically and psychologically.

I made a short list of the cases where a short plastic surgical intervention would have the best functional improvement and ignored the cosmetic benefits. Most cases were contractions of the limbs and neck, common complications of burns limiting movement and function.

And that is how I met Madelin, an eighteen-month-old baby who a year previously had fallen into a fire... face first. Her facial burn had healed into a thick mask of featureless scar tissue except for two slits through which her eyes peered, two holes for nostrils and a thin lipless mouth. Her immediate problem was contractions of her eyelids that were preventing complete closure of her eyes causing dryness and possible scarring to the corneas. A plastic surgeon could release the contractures and skin graft the lids to ensure they closed fully.

My first sight of her face broke my heart. How could this happen? She giggled in her mother's arms and my heart melted. Behind this devil's mask was a heavenly soul; an innocent, vulnerable being that had a lifetime of unimaginable challenges ahead. I took her from her mother's arm and sat her on my knee to examine her eyes more closely. She snuggled close and I began to shake and have flashbacks of the Kibumba refugee camp... the nameless girl with the crushed foot... Nancy, the orphan girl with the burnt hands. Their vulnerability and suffering were so great. The intensity and suddenness of the recollections shocked me and I struggled to keep control of myself and not burst into tears.

Madeline stared at me with a trust and acceptance that astounded and embarrassed me. I took slow deep breaths to calm myself and was captivated and disarmed within seconds. Guilt and confusion overwhelmed me. All we could do was to protect her vision. She needed a total face reconstruction, ongoing physiotherapy and psychological support. This would never happen. I fell back to my self-preservation mantra, *Do what you can, ignore the rest...* but it seemed completely hypocritical... for I knew what was coming.

'Julien, most of the burns we are receiving are domestic, most related to kerosene fires, children's scalds, self-inflicted petrol burns or suicides-cum-honour killings. Very few result from bombings or terrorist violence, the reason we are here.'
I hated telling the Head of Mission the raw truth... that we were too far from the violence to be effective. When a bombing occurred in Kirkuk or Mosul the area was immediately shut down by the military to prevent the insurgents escaping. Although the doctors in local hospitals would like to refer their burn patients to us, no one was allowed to leave the region, even in ambulances, often for weeks.
I hated thinking what would happen to cases like Madelin without MSF's support.

'I know John. I have read your report and forwarded it on to the desk in Paris. We are presently locked into a memorandum of understanding with the local medical authority for the rest of the year and it is up to the desk what happens then. The hospital is very costly to run and I'm sure the donors did not give their money to subsidise the Iraqi medical services. It's very probable we will pull out. All we can do now is continue as is, as best we can.'

'OK, but my report also highlighted our lack of compression garments to minimise scarring. Are they going to provide them until they decide what to do?'

'I've no idea, but if we are going to abort this mission, I doubt they will be expanding the equipment. We are already spending a fortune to upgrade the open wards into isolation rooms. It all seems to be pointless now.'

156

This was a watershed for you John?
Yes. I was totally deflated. I was pulling the plug but wanted the bathwater to stay. I knew the mission would be aborted but I only had a month of my mission to complete and nothing would be decided in that time span.

I had become attached to many of the patients. I knew after we left their treatments would decline. At least we could probably save Madelin's sight but what of her long-term treatment?

I had also become attached to many of the national staff. I hated to think of their working conditions after our leaving. I was sure MSF would initially leave abundant medical supplies but when they ran out, what would happen? The standard of care in the hospital for pain relief, infection control, surgical treatment and physiotherapy had vastly improved but could it be sustained once MSF left. I doubted it. Had we done more harm than benefit by our intervention? Had we given hope for it to be dashed? Had we made promises and then not followed through? I knew the staff would feel abandoned. I would if I was in their shoes.

You say you had become attached to some of the national staff. That was not like you in past missions?
I had been close to numerous national staff in past missions but this was different. Whilst working alongside the Iraqi doctors I had fallen into a role of mentorship with many, helping them in both their studies and personal lives. Every day we had a morning medical meeting. I introduced weekly case reports and tutored many of the junior doctors with their presentation. I facilitated clinical discussions and encouraged the junior doctors to participate. I assisted them in the operating theatres with their surgical techniques and anaesthetics. I was learning from them too. It was a great joy to watch them grow and I realised I was having an influence.

Your style of leadership seems to be evolving?
Well it couldn't have got much worse but yes… from being coercive and dictatorial I was now coaching and democratic… and you know what… it felt great.

SUNSHINE COAST, QUEENSLAND, AUSTRALIA
September 2008

How were you after this mission John? You seem to have coped well after Uganda.
Yes. I managed my homecoming with little drama.

I was warmly welcomed home by a loving wife and stepchildren. I rested for a couple of weeks to acclimatise and recuperate. After living in comfort in a city in Iraq, the culture shock of returning home was minimal, the contrast between mission and home less dramatic. I happily resumed my former job in general practice and enjoyed treating patients that were not critically injured.

I was still aware of the many factors that used to disturb me. I completely avoided talking about my mission. It was not difficult since most people found the severity of the burns and injuries too horrific and repugnant to discuss. I could understand and accept this reaction and at times was grateful for their silence. I now accepted that other people were only vaguely and transiently interested in other cultures and countries.

I was able to observe the general lack of gratitude, the seemingly excessive high expectations of life and the general accumulation and waste of 'stuff' by

157

others with distaste, but without being triggered. I kept a quiet life avoiding social gatherings.

I still felt a lingering angst at the enablement and injustice of the honour killing that I had witnessed. I suffered recurrent nightmares of patients bursting into flames, running and screaming into the hospital and into my arms when I would wake drenched in sweat.

How did you manage?
I again journaled my feelings: the injustice, the cruelty and the inhumanity. My writing allowed them to be quietly expressed, vented and dissipated. I continued relaxing with deep breathing exercises and mindful meditations.

Did you seek professional help?
No. Psychologists were still taboo. I knew by now that I was suffering from PTSD. It was now widely advertised and discussed in lay and medical press and I recognised the classic symptoms that I suffered. But my symptoms were much less severe than after Zaire and Afghanistan and I was convinced this was only a temporary relapse aggravated by recent events.

Over the weeks I began to sleep more soundly and my nightmares receded. My energy improved. I socialised more widely. I was convinced that my PTSD had been cured... that is... until the fire.

What fire would that be?

SUNSHINE COAST, QUEENSLAND, AUSTRALIA
July 2010

The family was away visiting friends. The dogs, Sandy and Socks, woke me with their barking. I smelt smoke, put on my dressing gown and wandered into the lounge. The dogs ran to me shaking with fear. Picking them up I walked out the back door to see what was happening. An acrid grey smoke was gushing and swirling from the garage beneath the house.

I turned to re-enter the house but the smoke within had become so dense it was impossible to enter. A deep rumbling growled menacingly under the floor. I walked around the house to its frontage to explore. Flames were now bursting from the garage door and with a frightening roar and *Whoompf*, exploded out through the windows above, shards of glass showering the ground. Within two minutes the whole house was totally engulfed by fire, the tin roof glowed red before collapsing and the flames hurling themselves skywards. If the dogs had not awoken me, I would have been roasting inside.

I banged on my neighbours' doors and we hosed their roofs to stop them catching fire. My house was all consumed. The rural fire brigade arrived after fifteen minutes. Nothing was salvageable. We lost everything.

Were you devastated?
Funnily enough, no. No one had been injured. Fria, the cat, was missing and we were worried she had died but to our great relief, she returned after a couple of days. All we had lost was 'stuff'. In fact, to me it was a relief to lose that burden! My wife was philosophical and accepting of the circumstance. We had moved house a couple of times already in our relationship and we had no strong emotional

attachment to this house. Even my three stepchildren were stoic and patient. Our neighbours, friends and the insurance company were very supportive and we soon had alternate accommodation. A couple of personal items could not be replaced but nothing memories could not replace.

It was the dreams that upset me. That night I began having nightmares about many of the burn patients I had treated in Sulaymaniyah. They walked out of my burning house with their faces charred, distorted in agony, their clothes and hair aflame, their blackened arms outstretched… I would wake in terror, my sheets saturated with sweat, my heart thrashing my chest. It was terrifying. I would get up to make a cup of tea, reluctant to go back to sleep in case they recurred.

Why do you think they occurred?
I'm not sure. I was hoping you could tell me. I journaled, racking my brain for reasons.

And what came up?
I wondered if I was guilty that I had abandoned them… again.

What do you mean… again?
In all of my missions, except in Nigeria, the missions were eventually destroyed or disbanded.

In Goma, the RPF raided the Kibumba refugee camp two years after my departure and destroyed the surgical hospital and camp. A hundred thousand refugees were herded back into Rwanda. Another fifty thousand escaped into the Congo and suffered terribly in the ensuing war.

In Afghanistan, all our clinics were looted and destroyed during the invasion following the September 11th attack, four months after my departure.

In Uganda, MSF withdrew from the Patongo medical clinic three months after my departure. They realised the government's AIDS treatment plan was not sustainable and handed the clinic over to another NGO who wished to continue our work.

In Iraq, MSF handed the burns unit back to the Department of Health and moved their operations closer to the violence.

Was I guilty of desertion of duty? Was all the work I had achieved of no consequence? Did I care?

…and then I realised… that I did care, that I had always wanted to help others. I realised that behind my early bravado of adventure and thrill-seeking a bit of me, maybe only a tiny bit of me, but a bit of me nonetheless, had been driven to make a difference… and with this realisation came the question and the doubt as to whether I had. Had any of the work I had undertaken made the slightest difference in these disasters? How ironic and bittersweet. Was this poetic justice?

Was this revelation a surprise?
Not really. It humbled me. Maybe I was always aware of this motivation but subconsciously squashed it as being too enlightened and sophisticated.

I fell into dark times. I felt somewhat ridiculous in myself to only now come to this late recognition. There were moments when I questioned my worth and worthiness. I even imagined, fleetingly, that the fire was a divine intervention to bring me to my senses.

Fortunately, I again found that time does temper troubles. After the fire my nightmares slowly settled, my fears faded and I fell back into routine and regularity. My interest in mental health in my general practice was rekindled. I found solace in helping patients suffering from depression, psychosis and ironically, PTSD. It only reinforced the truth in the saying, *you can see everyone else's problems but you never see your own.*

But that niggle, that rumble in the gut, that itch persisted and I knew I wanted to go on another mission... I began to accept that I might even make a difference?

Sunshine Coast, Australia
April 2012

'John, we have a mission that might be of interest to you. Theodora in the Australian MSF office told us you were available. It is an unusual mission. She said you liked that sort of thing.' Marie was phoning from the MSF-Swiss headquarters in Geneva.

'Go on,' I encouraged.

'We are sending a small team into the Nuba Mountains of North Sudan to set up a primary health service and we are looking for a doctor. Although situated in North Sudan, the region is home to many indigenous tribes who are predominantly Christian and are not aligned culturally with the Arabic north who follow Sharia Law and speak Arabic.'

Marie continued this mini briefing to say that, like the tribes in Darfur, they had long been discriminated against and had rebelled against the Khartoum government. A rebel army called the Sudanese Peoples Liberation Army (SPLA) defended the region, which was sporadically attacked by the Sudan People's Armed Forces (SPAF) both by land and from the air. Their air force had been indiscriminately dropping bombs on civilian targets. Locals were fearful of even tending their crops. Now the region was drought-ridden, food was becoming scarce, the local economy had collapsed and medical services were few. All NGOs had evacuated the region a couple of years prior. Refugees were now beginning to abandon the region and head to camps in South Sudan.

'If possible, we want to prevent that happening. If we go in now with aid, we may encourage the people to stay and other agencies to follow.'

'Two medical teams are planned; gamma team is to be based in Faradella, in the south of the mountains and Yankee team, your team, will venture deeper north into the region.'

'Has anyone from MSF been there?' I questioned.

'An exploratory team visited the region a couple of months ago. They only stayed for forty-eight hours but they reported their impressions and made several contacts,' Marie clarified.

'What are the "unusual" features you mentioned?'

'The North Sudanese government refuse to give us permission to access the region so this mission will be unannounced. We want to keep it under the radar so our recognised missions in North Sudan will not be compromised. You will not be working under the MSF banner.'

'It sounds very covert?'

'You could label it that.'

'Will we be spies?'

160

'Of course not.' Marie was startled by the suggestion. 'You will be totally independent and unaligned to any party or army although the SPLA will be fully aware of your presence. We have their permission for you to enter their territory... but the North Sudanese may not see it that way.'

'If it's in North Sudan how do we get there without their permission?'

'There is a twenty-kilometre-long supply "corridor" or umbilicus from South Sudan which is not protected by the North Sudanese and allows access.

'There is also one more aspect you should consider.'

'Apart from getting bombed or caught as spies?' I queried.

'Yes. The corridor crosses desolate, unpopulated land of no political or commercial import. It is a dust hole in the dry season but transforms into a swamp in the wet and is often impassable. Several rivers in the mountains also swell with the rains and cut the road. During these times there is no sure method of evacuation. Aerial retrieval is too dangerous. The North Sudanese have made it a "no-fly-zone". The only planes in the air are North Sudanese Sukhoi fighters and Antonov bombers.'

My mind was racing, my heart pounding. 'We'd be cut off?'

'Yes. We are planning to send in tractors that can tow the four-wheel drive cars through swampy regions but it is no guarantee of passage.'

'When is this happening?'

'Now. The rest of Yankee team is already in Juba in South Sudan finalising preparations. They are just waiting for a doctor to join them.'

I expected her to say, 'This message will self-destruct in five seconds.'

'Phone me back in an hour. I need to talk with my wife.'

What happened?

My wife again readily agreed for me to leave. Fortunately, all my vaccinations were up to date and the medical practice where I worked were again happy to release me for a mission. Twenty hours later I was on a plane to Geneva for a briefing.

Were you scared?

No, not scared, more excited and alive. I realised I loved working with so many unknowns.

SUDAN
MÉDECINS SANS FRONTIÈRES
2012

'Hi John, welcome to the Yankee team.' Yves, the field coordinator for the mission, a quietly spoken Swiss man, short hair, trim physique and firm handshake, warmly greeted me. 'Come and meet the rest of the team.' He introduced Katie, a muscular American midwife, Melanie, a very slim French nurse and Damien, a stocky Australian logistician. All grinned and nodded happily.

'Damien's been here five weeks organising the logistics. Melanie, Katie and I arrived two weeks ago. The nurses have been checking the medical equipment. I've been making contacts, following the security situation in the region and organising our communications. We are ready to leave and have been waiting for you. Now we will fly to Yida in the wilds of Unity State very near the South/North Sudanese border where a refugee camp is rapidly growing. MSF are running its medical clinic. It will act as our logistical base from where we will cross the border into the corridor. The other team, gamma team, entered the mountains a week ago and are presently setting up their clinic in Faradella, near the end of the corridor.'

'So, what's the plan? Do we have one?'

'Of course, John.' Yves continued not reacting to my teasing. 'At Yida we collect some basic equipment and two four-wheel-drive cars. Once we have security clearance from Geneva, we will cross the South/North Sudanese border and enter the mountains via the corridor.'

He continued to outline that after spending a night at Faradella to meet the gamma team we would drive north another two hundred kilometres across the region to establish a base incorporating a small inpatient facility and several outreach clinics. The exploratory team had already identified two or three possible sites for medical clinics but their reports were sketchy at the best.

The main bulk of the equipment would follow in trucks. Unfortunately, Damien had discovered that the only trucks available in this insecure area were ancient, poorly maintained and unreliable. There was a distinct possibility of breakdowns and banditry.

'What happens if our equipment is lost?'

'We'll manage as best as we can. Doctor Sylvester, a doctor originally from the Nuba region, is accompanying us for the first week. He will help us identify local nursing staff and ask the SPLA to watch out for our supplies.'

'That sounds great. When do we leave?' It is sometimes better not to ask too many details, especially when they do not exist.

'We fly to Yida tomorrow.'

How did you feel at this stage?
It was a relief to set off. The previous week had been a blur of activity. Now we had a journey into the unknown. I had little idea what to expect. I was as excited as a kid in a fairground.

THE CORRIDOR, NUBA MOUNTAINS, SOUTH KORDOFAN, NORTH SUDAN
May 2012
Doctor, Médecins Sans Frontières

'John, for God's sake put the camera away. We've crossed the border and are now in the corridor. Who knows who's watching us? Taking photos, especially video could be interpreted as spying.' Yves, the field coordinator, admonished me for what I already knew but I had been filming from inside the car hoping it was not obvious. I dropped my camera into my backpack.

Our two Toyota Land Cruisers, entirely encrusted with red mud in an attempt at camouflage, sped along the twisting, pot-holed track, winding through copses of scrubby, stunted trees. A plume of dust billowed high into the air behind each car, like the wake of a boat churning the water. I stared out of the window scanning the sky, attentive for any plane that would easily see our cloudy track. The only planes in the air were North Sudanese fighters and bombers searching for targets just like us.

Damien, the logistician, had already briefed us on our response to an aircraft attack. 'The drivers will immediately pull over, if possible, under a tree. Everyone should immediately jump out and scatter, lie down, if possible, with cover, at least fifty metres distant so if the car is strafed or bombed you will be less exposed.' It sounded routine but I doubted it would be so calm and orderly.

The sky remained empty. A few refugees, walking in the opposite direction reminded us of the unfolding humanitarian crisis into which we headed. Their faces and clothes were laden with dust and grime. Their few possessions were balanced in bundles on weary heads or carried under sagging arms. Young children dragged tired heels, some in tears as they trudged behind their parents.

A fraying weathered rope draped across the track marked the end of the corridor and the border-crossing into the Nuba Mountains. We felt a surge of relief that we had successfully run the twenty-kilometre gauntlet. It seemed a good omen that the first hurdle had passed with no incident.

Sitting outside a squat, iron-roofed, mud-walled shed was a motley group of soldiers clad in a variety of tattered battledress, torn jeans, faded T-shirts, battered caps and dusty black boots. Beside them a collection of ancient rifles leant against a tree. They were enjoying the warmth of the morning sun. Our permits were carefully scrutinised. I suspected we were the first and probably only vehicle for the day. It seemed we were expected. We had obviously been spied and reported leaving our base in Yida in South Sudan.

'Welcome to Nuba Mountains. We hope your visit is happy,' announced the sentry handing us back our permits and sporting a grin any dentist would have begged for on his advertisement. I giggled to myself. It was funny for I felt a fraud, like a tourist, not someone undertaking a covert mission to establish medical services in a war–ravaged region.

We kept scanning the sky. It remained empty, even of clouds. After several hours, boredom set in. I rationalised that the fighter planes would patrol the flat unoccupied land of the corridor where vehicles were more obvious and vulnerable. Amid the mountains there would be a greater danger from concealed, camouflaged anti-aircraft guns. Or was this security creep starting? We were tired and battered from bouncing around the bumpy, pitted tracks. Our faces were plastered with the fine red dust that permeated every crevice, highlighting my many wrinkles. Our mouths were parched despite constantly sipping water and our eyes were reddened, dry and irritated. But my excitement continued unabated. This was my type of travel. This was going *beyond-the-lonely-planet*. How many people would ever come to this part of the world?

Billy whispered, 'Yes, but how many idiots would want to come to this part of the world?

Is this an attraction for you on these missions John?

Very much so. To be in such a remote, hostile environment with only a vague plan to implement accompanied by a group of like-minded, equally driven people is exhilarating and challenging. It's an environment in which I thrive. In some ways, however, it was an anti-climax. Everything had all gone to plan. There had been no hitches. It seemed too easy. But then, it was still early days

Tujor, Nuba Mountains, South Kordofan, North Sudan
May 2012
Doctor, Médecins Sans Frontières

'Antonov overhead.' I heard the warning shouted out by one of our national staff but could not hear the plane myself. I looked up and saw it glinting in the sunshine high above, a spark of danger. Standing in the doorway of our clinic's ward, I watched how the national staff reacted. If they ran… I ran.

'They fly high to avoid the rebel army's anti-aircraft guns,' explained Anton, the national head nurse, who emerged from the ward to stand beside me. He scratched his curly hair as he surveyed the sky, twisting his head and squinting his eyes to focus. 'They drop barrels of aviation fuel loaded with shrapnel as bombs. To do so they must open their back doors and lift their noses to allow the barrels to roll out. Luckily this decreases their bombing accuracy. If you listen carefully, the change in engine note gives a clue to an imminent attack. That's when you run.'

Several foxholes, two metres deep, had been dug around the clinic into which we could jump and squat for shelter. It gave protection from shrapnel flying through the air but none from a direct hit. The lowest metre of the inpatient ward's walls had been reinforced to allow patients to climb under their beds and have some protection too.

No one ran. I remained in the doorway, watching.

'Do you think muddying our white tents and camouflaging the building roofs with branches gives us any protection Anton?'

'Doctor John, I am sure the North Sudanese have plenty of spies here and know exactly where we are and what we are doing but maybe it stops the pilots from easily pinpointing us from their height. But our greatest danger is thievery from the local population, as they are getting hungrier and hungrier. It is good that Damien has nearly finished organising the outer fence.'

I looked out from the doorway and watched the hive of activity. Men were digging holes, erecting poles and fixing intertwined brushes of branches between, to close the gaps. A line of women, massive bundles of dried reeds balanced on their heads, marched in single file like a line of ducklings, across the grounds to our accommodation area where several *tougals*, round mud-walled huts with thatched roofs, were under construction. I would soon be able to move out of my tiny tent.

Another line of young women, twenty-litre containers of water balanced on their heads were gracefully gliding in another single file across the compound to the water tank where they gratefully poured their load into the storage tank. They had already walked the one kilometre from the nearest well with their heavy burden three times that morning but they did not look weary.

'It is good the women have employment with you, Doctor John. It will give them extra money for their family.' I did not point out to him that the women were carrying the water because the men would not do 'women's work'.

'And here comes more of the supplies, Doctor John.'

A flat-bedded lorry, loaded high with boxes of equipment, mattresses bulging through restraining ropes, drove through the entry gate, blasting its horn to announce its arrival.

Was it only a week earlier that the five of us with our drivers, interpreter and Doctor Sylvester had arrived, tired, grimy and gritty, battered and bruised after a three-day, dusty drive? The dirt track had crossed open valleys sparsely studded with stunted trees then twisted through the rocky hills fringed by massive rounded rocks piled at their base and crowned with boulders precariously balanced and perched like prehistoric monuments on their ridge tops.

On arrival we first inspected an abandoned *Save the Children* clinic in Tujor, set snugly in an amphitheatre of rock-strewn hills. Intuitively we had all known this would become our base but had spent several more hours inspecting two alternate sites before committing. The existing brick buildings were ramshackle but salvageable, able to be converted into an inpatient ward, an emergency room, a consulting room and storage rooms. Tents would be erected for a pharmacy and outpatient clinic. With Doctor Sylvster's assistance we had quickly identified and selected our local national staff of nurses and logisticians and provided them with two days of basic training.

'The clinic is nearly complete. It's amazing it has all been achieved in under a week. Shall we start to see patients tomorrow, Doctor John?' pondered Anton.

'I don't think so. Here's one now.' I pointed to a rickety, wooden cart, pulled by a geriatric donkey with an elderly man prostate on its tray that was following the supply truck into the compound.

'Over here,' shouted Anton waving to the driver. The cart pulled up in front of our newly scrubbed emergency room. Several nurses attracted by the shouting eagerly carried the patient inside. He writhed and rolled side-to-side groaning in pain, clutching his abdomen.

A younger man, presumably his son, who had led the donkey and cart, was nervously watching.

'How long has he been in pain?' I asked. Anton interpreted.

'Two days. We have walked for over one day after we heard you were here. He cannot piss.'

The patient was a weather-beaten, wizened man, a hundred and fifty years old by looks but only sixty by birth. I gently examined his abdomen and noted his bladder distended to his umbilicus. Further examination revealed a huge hard prostate blocking his bladder. No wonder he was in pain.

'He needs to have a urinary catheter passed into his bladder.' I outlined the process to the nurses. 'Let's get him ready and find a catheter from the stores,' I directed. Not all the supplies had yet been unpacked.

After an hour I was able to perform the procedure but no matter how hard I tried, the catheter would not pass through the penis into the bladder. The blockage was complete.

'He needs a supra-pubic catheter; one that is inserted through the abdominal wall,' I explained. 'Let's search the supplies again.'

Another hour later we were ready again and I inserted a large bore needle through his abdominal wall directly into the bladder. A catheter was fed through

166

the needle that could then be withdrawn and discarded. As the bladder drained the old man sighed a smile of joy from the immediate relief. The catheter was secured with a stitch to the skin, the wound covered with a dressing and a drainage bag attached. Although a simple technique everyone was impressed, especially the national staff who had never seen the procedure.

Barely had we finished when a young mother arrived at the door clutching her screaming six-month-old son. The old man walked to our medical ward proudly clutching his new urine bag like a newly won sports trophy.

The baby boy was laid down on the couch. Earlier that morning he had rolled off a table a metre high on to a concrete floor. His right thigh was swollen and tender. Without X-ray, I assumed it to be greenstick fracture of the femur. Luckily treatment was simply to hang the child by the legs to keep the buttocks off the bed using sticking plaster adherent to the skin of his legs. This gave adequate traction and immobility for the femur to heal. It would take four weeks. His mother carried him to the ward and a frame was quickly constructed over a bed for the traction. As we were finishing the final touches, I heard the shout, 'Antonov overhead.' I waited and watched the staff. They started to run. I ran too.

Fortunately, it was a false alarm. No bombs fell and we all returned to the ward.

Another good start to a mission, John?
Yes, I was lucky our first patients were dramatic yet straightforward with easy conditions to diagnose and treat. It helped create credibility and give confidence to the national staff that the clinic could be effective.

Tujor, Nuba Mountains, North Sudan
June 2012
Doctor, Médecins Sans Frontières

'We have to get out of the mountains... and quickly... there's a strong possibility of an attack on Kauda by the North Sudanese army and we could get cut off. We'll leave at first light.' Yves, the Swiss field coordinator, urgently briefed the four of us. He had been following the e-mailed security updates all day and had just talked to the 'desk', the coordination team in Geneva, on the satellite phone. 'If we're cut off there's no way out, maybe for months.'

We all looked at each other and paused, absorbing the information and all its implications. We had only arrived two weeks before and I already had twelve patients in our small hospital, two of them critically ill children with malnutrition and sepsis. There was much to organise. Our local staff of forty needed to be briefed and directed until our return... if we returned? Nothing was certain.

We had all known this could happen. The possibility of urgent evacuation had previously been fully discussed but we were all still devastated at having to abandon our mission so abruptly. Would the staff continue to work in our absence? Would the patients survive? Would the hospital get looted? Its storeroom was crammed with medications, electrical and communications equipment and fuel, all precious commodities in an area under siege.

Yves started briefing the local administrative staff and arranging ongoing wages. Damien, the logistician, briefed the national logisticians on their rosters and duties. Melanie, Katie and myself discussed the ongoing care for our patients with the nurses and midwives.

We decided to evacuate the two critically sick children and their mothers with us in our two cars and transfer them to a mission hospital en route back to South Sudan. Luckily it was still the dry season and the roads were still passable. Even so we estimated the two-hundred-kilometre journey would take us over fourteen hours.

As the rising sun broke over the horizon the five of us with our drivers, interpreters and patients drove out. We had crammed computers and other critical items into the cars. Melanie and I nursed the two sick children on our laps. They curled up and wriggled until their tiny fragile bodies were entwined with ours, intravenous infusions, hanging from the car's roof, continued to drip life-giving fluids and medication into their skinny arms. Their mothers sat anxiously beside us, confused and disorientated by this sudden turn of affairs. Sitting on the bench seat in the back of the car I jammed myself against the opposite seat to minimise the shuddering and shaking, the rocking and rolling as we sped along the rugged tracks, a dust trail billowing high into the sky behind our track.

Did this incident upset you?

At the time I was very upset to leave my patients behind. A small boy had only just arrived with third-degree burns to his arms. We had no room in the car to evacuate him and his mother. He was at great risk of getting an infection and dying.

It was a mixture of failing in a doctor's duty of care towards my patients and a recurrence of the deeper core fear of abandonment, a running out on a problem, something that I seemed to be good at in my personal life. I felt a failure professionally and personally.

I was also cognisant of being stranded in Tujor, or even worse, of being captured by the North Sudanese army. We had been forewarned that we would be treated as spies for they had specifically refused us permission to enter the Nuba Mountains. I was sure, if captured, we would not be treated well.

That must have been a worry. How did you cope this time?

As always, in the heat of the moment when there is so much happening, I was focused on getting through the day, tending to the sick children and, after dropping them off at the hospital, ensuring the rest of the team were well hydrated, fed and humoured. After a very long fourteen hours of travel we arrived at Yida physically and emotionally exhausted. I slept a long deep sleep despite all my angst. Luckily, rather than return to the coordination team's base in Juba, Damien and I were able to remain at the Yida refugee camp to wait for further developments. I filled my time working in the camp's medical centre and hospital, supporting and teaching the national doctors and assisting in a measles vaccination campaign. Damien and I both enjoyed playing the card game, cribbage, which filled many waiting hours.

Happily, after three weeks we were given security clearance to return to Tujor and continue the clinics. Happily, our facilities were found intact, our stores secure, our staff working and our resident patients all still alive. Unhappily we learnt that the two small children we had transported to the mission hospital had both died. I am sure the journey killed them.

But the staff and patients gave us a warm welcome and I was soon fully immersed in the mission at hand.

Oh Shit! The snake uncoiled and slithered away from my feet, its three-foot-long body undulating with gentle wave-like motions, a series of V-shapes painted in various shades of brown along its back. The movement highlighted its presence but amongst the rocks, coiled and still, it had been well camouflaged to my sleepy, bleary vision. It was early morning and whilst returning from the latrine to my tougal I had stepped on its tail. Its head had snapped sideways to sink its fangs into the top of my left foot before slinking away.

My expletive was stimulated first by surprise, then by a burning pain, as if I had dropped a charcoal ember from a smouldering fire on to my foot. I looked down at the two bloody puncture wounds and silently swore again.

The early morning sun was surprisingly warm, stretching long shadows of trees across the path. Not wanting to wake anyone I quietly limped the two hundred metres to the medical clinic to get a bandage.

'What's wrong John?' Pierre, the French nurse, was tidying the dressing cupboard. He flicked his shoulder-length hair off his face and peered at me.

'You're up early. Not sleeping well?' I countered.

'You don't look well. Are you sick?' he persisted.

'I need a bandage. I've just been bitten by a snake.' I pointed to my foot.

'John, lie down. You're an idiot. Why did you not call out? Walking is the worst thing you can do. You know that.' Pierre shook his head in exasperation and disbelief.

'Yes, but I did not want to wake you.' It sounded so stupid, even to me.

'Never mind. Lie down and I'll bandage it,' Pierre insisted. 'What type of snake was it?'

'A puff adder I think.' I had treated several patients with snakebites since arriving in Tujor and had researched the local species.

My mind went into overdrive... the first aid of snake bite was compression bandage, immobilization and observation... the complications of snakebites included severe swelling and necrosis of the tissues, anticoagulation (or thinning) of the blood and neurotoxicity, which paralysed the breathing muscles... the treatment was supportive, antivenene to counter the toxin and respiratory ventilation if needed.

That was the theory. I had fewer options. The two ampoules of snake venom antivenene transported with us from South Sudan had been improperly packed and had become frozen, deactivating their efficacy. At the time, I was just grateful that our other precious children's vaccines had been perfectly packed in the cold box and were fully active. Now I was not so circumspect. There was certainly no possibility of my lungs being ventilated. Evacuation was impossible. No aircraft could enter North Sudan airspace without getting shot down and the road to South Sudan was now flooded and swamp-bound. I was on my own... it only took seconds to compute. I was a little reassured that of all the snake and scorpion bites I had so far treated, only one had died.

Pierre had been following the same thought line.

'We'll carry you back to the lounge area and you can rest there with your leg elevated.'

'I'll walk Pierre. There's no need to trouble anyone.'

'John, you're a pain. We'll carry you. Keep your leg still. Is that clear.'

It seemed like overkill but I knew he was right. Being the patient, dependant and passive, was terrible. The national nurses had great fun carrying me back, creating a fuss and making fun.

'Why did you not catch the snake, Doctor John? They are good to eat.'

'The toxin can make all your hair fall out Doctor John... and teeth too.'

'Make sure you brush your teeth well, Doctor John, in case we have to give you mouth to mouth resuscitation.'

I did not know whether to be amused or scared.

Even as I was being carried, I began to feel nauseated and lightheaded. My foot was on fire.

'Hey Pierre, get some morphine and metoclopramide. I need a fix.'

Several minutes later he returned. 'Hey John, Yves and I have contacted Geneva and they are giving us directions for your treatment. Lie back and let me do my job, OK? I have some morphine for you and I will take some blood to check your clotting time.' He rolled up my sleeve and injected me.

'Thanks, Pierre.'

The next twenty-four hours are blurred, distant and confused. Whether it was the injections of morphine or the venom I do not know or care. Halfway through the morning, a bomber appeared in the overhead sky. A warning was shouted out and all staff and waiting patients scurried to the bomb shelters and foxholes. The patients in the ward climbed under their beds. I was neither capable nor caring and was left alone on the sofa in my delirium. A bit of me wanted a bomb to fall and put me out my misery. Out-of-focus bodies came and went, taking my pulse, giving injections, extracting more blood, wiping my face. My leg swelled to double its size. I was nauseous and wretched. *Was I dribbling out the side of my mouth? Were my eyelids getting heavy or just tired? Was I developing a paralysis? Was I dying?*

You obviously survived John? How were you feeling about being so isolated?
Before I became delirious, I was philosophical. I had known the dangers and risks before I left. I knew evacuation for any reason was not an option. Knowing and accepting that risk negated any right to feel regret or blame.

I knew there was now little to do except avoid aggravating the spread of the toxin. I accepted there was a chance of dying. Fortunately, my inherent optimism... or was it my capacity for denial... pushed doubt to one side. I would live... or I wouldn't... but probably would. And did.

Were you scared of dying?
Not at all. But the threat of dying does enhance the joy of living; at least it does if you survive. There is an infusion of determination and direction, exhilaration and excitement that enriches every moment.

The following morning, as my mind lifted from the mist of morphine, it was clear I would survive. My leg was still like a watermelon but my nausea and confusion had resolved. I could walk back to my tougal and rest in private. It was all an anti-climax and I felt wonderful.

I could hear Billy sniggering, 'You forgot to mention that the snake died of food poisoning.'

'Doctor John, I need some tablets for my high blood pressure and my diabetes. Since all the NGOs left two years ago, I have not been able to easily get the medications. I have been having them sent from South Sudan but sometimes they never arrive and now I am about to run out.' Rashid was a man in his forties, a village leader and a successful local businessman. He was the only overweight person I had met since arriving in the Nuba Mountains seven weeks earlier. His English was fluent.

We sat in my small consulting room with its peeling paint and bare concrete floor, the only light from a small grimy window beside the door. On my desk lay all my diagnostic equipment: stethoscope, otoscope, sphygmomanometer (blood pressure machine), a blood glucose monitor, torch, thermometer and tendon hammer. Outside a queue of patients sat patiently waiting their turn.

'Sit back and take some deep breaths, Rashid, while I examine you.' As expected, his blood pressure was high and his blood sugar was elevated. His fingers were heavily nicotine-stained. His eyes showed early signs of damage from diabetes.

'I'm sorry Rashid but I don't have any suitable tablets to give you. Our present medical supplies are for acutely ill patients. We are waiting for other medications to arrive but they are long overdue and may never arrive. We can only wait. But I can help you.'

'Thank you, Doctor John. What can you do?'

'There are three things, Rashid, that you can do to treat yourself. I see you have a motorbike. It is one of the few private vehicles I have seen since arriving here.'

'Yes, it is a BSA Bantam. It cannot go very fast as the roads are so rough but I can go to and fro between home and work quickly.'

'Well, firstly, Rashid I want you to leave it at home and walk to your warehouses and stores like the rest of the population. Use the motorbike only for your long-distance journeys to Kauda but locally, I want you to walk.

'Secondly, I want you to stop eating or drinking anything with sugar, especially soft drinks. I promise you your weight will fall, as will your blood pressure and blood sugar.

'And thirdly, Rashid, your smoking plus your high blood pressure puts you at high risk of a heart attack. Giving up smoking will add years to your life.'

'It cannot be that simple Doctor John?'

'It is that simple Rashid. Maybe it is not that easy as old habits are hard to change. If you follow my advice you will live long and watch your children grow. If you don't, you are likely to die before they are married. Give it a try and come and see me in a month.'

He looked at me with a mixture of amusement and uncertainty, wondering whether I was serious or joking.

'I'm not joking Rashid. It's your choice. Good luck.'

'Next please!'

That was very direct John?
Yes, direct, to the point and graphic. Not that I had anything else to offer.

One factor in Rashid's favour was that processed and fast foods were not readily available and particularly Coca-Cola was not sold in the region. It is the only part of the world where I had not seen the gaudy red Coca-Cola's signs blotted over roadside stalls or village shops. Maybe its absence should be a marker of global remoteness.

You see that as a benefit?
Very much so. Coca-Cola is the master of designer brainwashing and galloping greed. Its global advertising power has seduced the world to view drinking Coke as cool and trendy, even sophisticated, instead of the act of swallowing a huge dump of sugar for a huge profit.

Coke is not only to blame but is symbolic of the food industry whose push to provide long shelf life, quick preparation, perfect presentation, sweet, even addictive taste and of course highly profitable products has undermined healthy nutrition. Foods now have too many calories and too few nutrients and fibre. Generations of misinformation have distorted expectations and experience so who knows what is healthy anymore? It is only when you visit remote areas with few of the myriad tempting choices of processed and fast food that you find an entire population with flat, not fat bellies.

Maybe western medicine might be more effective for many conditions if lifestyle choices could not be so easily dismissed and medication not so easily prescribed?

TUJOR, NUBA MOUNTAIN REGION, NORTH SUDAN,
September 2012
Doctor, Médecins Sans Frontières

'Doctor John, lie her down on her mother's lap. Let her die.' Estel whispered in my ear. Her tightly plaited light brown hair crowned a long, thin face that framed ebony eyes that pierced my wavering gaze. She was practically pleading and obviously frustrated with my determined but futile efforts to save the little girl who she was holding to sit upright on the bed. Her dark red jilbab contrasted with the dingy blue dress of the patient.

'The treatment did not save the boy yesterday. It will not work on her today,' she persisted.

The little boy had arrived in the ward early the previous morning with a high fever. The nurses, not wanting to wake me for I had been working most of the night with a head injury patient, had admitted him thinking it was malaria and had commenced treatment.

When I arrived for the morning ward round and heard his harsh stridor and inspiratory wheeze I was gripped with terror. Even before I examined him, I cried, 'Quickly, get that child into the emergency room.'

Anton, the head nurse, picked him up, ran out of the ward and across the muddy courtyard. The label, 'emergency room', is misleadingly grand; a single rusting couch covered in plastic sheeting lies central in the small room with water-stained plaster and a sagging flaking ceiling. Resuscitation equipment includes a pedal-operated sucker, a bag and mask, an oxygen concentrator, an oximeter and intravenous fluids. The boy, limp in Anton's arms had saliva drooling out of his mouth, his skin tinged blue and his chest heaving. Anton lay him down.

'No Anton,' I instructed. 'Sit him up… straight up.'

I gently sucked the saliva from his throat, fitted an oxygen mask to his face and connected the oximeter to his finger that confirmed he was starved of oxygen. The boy's father had followed us. Anton showed him how to support his son so that his head was maintained vertical. Slowly the oxygen reading rose.

'He's suffering epiglottitis, a swelling of the valve between the gullet and the windpipe. It's choking him,' I explained to Anton. 'It's caused by an infection.'

'What's his name?' I asked. I hate treating nameless patients.

Anton replied, 'Abdo. He's three years old. He became ill last night.'

'I'll get an intravenous infusion going so we can give antibiotics. Can you help the father keep him vertical?'

Over the ensuing hours, we watched Abdo slowly lose the battle to maintain an airway. I did not have the equipment to perform a cricothyroidotomy, inserting a tube into his trachea to bypass the obstruction. The antibiotics and steroids dripping into his veins had no immediate effect.

The blood's oxygen saturation kept falling.

'Doctor John, we cannot save this boy. Let him lie in his father's arms,' Anton advised.

Eventually, I conceded. It was agonising to watch. His father nursed Abdo lovingly in his arms whilst he struggled unsuccessfully to breathe.

At last all breathing ceased. A calm momentarily fell over our small group, happy the suffering was over before coming to an abrupt end as his father broke down and collapsed on the floor. We placed him on the ER couch, gently disentangling his dead son's body from his arms, and gave him some oxygen as he recovered from his faint.

I held back my tears till later that night. *Had I prolonged the agony unnecessarily?*

The little girl had arrived during the next day's ward round. Again, I heard the stridor long before I saw her. We rushed her into the emergency room and followed the previous day's process only this time it was the mother holding the child.

Her name was Teresa and she was four.

I persisted for four hours before it was obvious even to me that I was prolonging the agony. I stood and watched her die in her mother's arms.

This time the tears filled my eyes. I could not hold them back. I dropped my head and stormed out of the emergency room. The nurses were able to help the parents wrap the body and send them on their way.

You were very upset John, more so than before?
This was the straw that broke the camel's back; another child dying of a preventable, treatable disease. It was just so cruel. I felt hypocritical, useless and ashamed, all rolled up into a misery and monsoon of tears. I cried again that night which gave some solace but a little bit of me died that day, a little bit of my optimism and faith in humanity. Two children dying, dragged out over several hours on two consecutive days at the end of my four-month mission was just too much. Maybe I was just over-tired and over-wrought but I had had enough. Luckily my replacement arrived a few days later and after a short handover I left.

'How much further to go?' I asked.

'Another fifteen kilometres,' replied Anton, our driver. 'This swamp is ten kilometres wide and we're about halfway. The border to South Sudan is five kilometres past the swamp and the Yida refugee camp another five kilometres. Then we are safe.'

The muddy waters splashed over the Toyota cruiser's bonnet and windscreen. The car slipped and swayed side to side, bounced and bumped as we were dragged through the stagnant swamp, towed behind a Massey Ferguson tractor that ploughed through the mud and metre deep mire like a destroyer through a rough sea, its huge rear tyres throwing a trail of brown sludge high into the air.

Pierre, Albert and I were shaken, rattled and battered, like clothes swirling in a washing machine. Anton frantically clung on to the steering wheel, keeping himself steady and desperately trying to keep a direct line between tractor and car to prevent the front end being jerked and yanked sidewards as we skewed off course. We had already broken two towropes.

For three days we had driven across the Nuba Mountains to exit North Sudan. Despite only being two hundred kilometres in distance, the rains had transformed the dusty roads to muddy, slippery tracks, the idling rivers to raging torrents and the low plains into sodden swamps. It was slow progress. Without the tractor the route was impassable. We were towed across creeks, out of ditches and through swamps.

I had finished my four-month mission and felt tired and emotionally depleted. The last drama I needed was a breakdown or to become bogged in the middle of a noxious, odious, mosquito-infested swamp. The end was so close.

As the track inclined upwards over a small grassy knoll that had become an island amid the rising marshy waters, we came to a grinding halt. Ahead I could see a soldier standing in the middle of the track pointing his rifle straight at Bernard, the tractor driver. Bernard looked back at the car, his face a mask of anxiety and silently shrugged, 'What do I do?'

I leaned out the window. 'Stay where you are Bernard.'

I turned to Albert, our interpreter. 'Find out what the soldier wants Albert. Pierre and I will stay in the car. We do not want to inflame the situation. Whatever it is, don't annoy him. Come back here if you are threatened.'

It didn't take long. Albert returned to the car panic-stricken.

'The soldier says his car has broken down a hundred metres up the road and demands our tractor tow him back to the mountains... or he will shoot us and take the tractor himself.'

My heart sank. So near safety and yet so far...

'I'll come and talk to him. Just interpret what I say. Do not join the conversation,' I instructed.

'It's probably better if you stay in the car, Pierre. Two Europeans might freak him out.'

The soldier was agitated. His pupils were pinpoint, his speech slurred and his hands trembled. My mind wandered back to my encounter with the psychotic armed soldier in Zaire and my heart missed another beat. My mind questioned... *not again? Why me? Do I attract this danger?*

I took some deep breaths. It did little to calm me for the air was fetid and rank. I patiently listened to the soldier's rambling, slurred diatribe without interrupting.

'What did he say, Albert?'

'He is a soldier with the SPLA-N. He says he is a patriot saving his country. He is on important business. His car is bogged. He cannot re-join his regiment and it is our fault so we must help him.'

'Tell him we are unable to help him but we can send a message to his commander to inform him of his delay.'

'It won't help Doctor John, he is crazy.'

'Just tell him, talk slowly with an even voice.' I tried to keep my voice even and not show my agitation.

Albert spoke. The soldier listened then looked at me with cold eyes, but I sensed a tinge of doubt.

'Tell him I have just been talking to the commanders at their headquarters. Ask him the name of his commander.'

The soldier gave us the commander's name.

'Tell him. I can get a message to him once we arrive at Yida. He will send someone to help him.'

I thought my bravado and bluff had worked for he became quiet and thoughtful... but I was wrong.

He started to shout and jab his gun at me. I raised my hands high to show I was unarmed and hopefully act as a submissive, calming gesture. It did not. His shouting increased and the gun's barrel swung across my chest and abdomen. He pressed it into my sternum.

Albert fell back and sheltered behind me.

'What's he saying, Albert?' I whispered.

'He says you are all bullshit and bollocks, a "whitey" that has it all and thinks he is super-shit. He wants the tractor and he wants it now... or he will shoot you.' I thought Albert was very eloquent in his translation but the humour quickly dissipated as I watched the gun barrel waver over my chest.

'OK, OK,' I submitted. I needed no more convincing. I was about to tell Bernard to uncouple the tractor and tow his car out of the swamp when a second soldier, AK-47 slung over his back, walked out of the tall grass and spied us. I kept my hands high in the air. I did not want any misunderstanding.

He approached, took a long dispassionate glance at me and had a long conversation with the first soldier who became quieter and thankfully slung his gun over his shoulder, its barrel pointing to the sky and more importantly, not at me.

The second soldier turned to me and speaking in stilted English apologised, 'Hello. I am sorry my friend that he is troubling you. He is very worried for his car. But it is OK. I will look after it. We are in the same regiment. You can go.'

I did not need any more encouragement.

'Thank you very much.' I practically sighed with relief. 'Thank you for looking after him, he is not well.'

Bernard and Anton already had the engines revving and Albert was back in the car by the time I returned. We sped away, out of range of any rifle.

After three days travel, mud-splattered, sweat-saturated, dehydrated, ravenously hungry and physically and mentally exhausted, we welcomed the sight of the refugee camp at Yida, our logistical base.

'You did well John to refuse the soldier,' Sven, the Swedish Head of Mission at the Yida camp complimented. 'We'll be attempting to cross the corridor a couple of times every month during the wet season to help resupply and re-staff the two clinics. If word is out, we will tow and rescue vehicles, it would be a huge impediment.'

It was small consolation. I was just glad I would not be going back.

This was another terrifying experience for you John?
It certainly upset me. I was already feeling emotionally and physically fragile after my four-month mission with no respite and many difficult, heart-breaking cases. As I left Tujor I thought it was all over and I was safe. This unforeseen incident was a deadly blow that struck me after I had subconsciously lowered my guard. I suddenly felt vulnerable, exposed and insecure.

My journey back to Australia via debriefs in Juba and Geneva is a blurred memory of meetings, long haul flights and hotel rooms. I became super-hyper-vigilant, always checking my surrounds, ensuring doors were locked, double-triple-checking fire escape routes, avoiding crowded places, restaurants and shopping centres.

My nightmares flared again. It seemed the floodgates of past traumas had fully opened. I was nightly tormented by horrendously sick and injured patients; malnourished children dying in my arms and parents screaming abuse at me; adults with horrendous bullet injuries, blood pulsating, bones protruding, intestines dangling, all groaning at me; severely burned patients, charred and blistered flesh hanging from their limbs, silently staring at me, accusingly. I was often too afraid to go back to sleep. Even during the day, I would momentarily be paralysed with flashbacks. I was a mess and started drinking alcohol again to dull the dreams and numb the memories.

What happened when you returned home?
My life disintegrated from bad to worse... to worser.

The injustices of want versus waste, of poverty versus plenty, of flat bellies versus fat bellies confronted me every moment. I was surprised, shocked and even scared by the intensity of my anger and disgust. I thought I had contained these triggers after previous missions but now they exploded and enraged me.

The galloping consumerism and wanton waste horrified me. The high expectations of people who demanded rights that overrode moral duties and responsibilities screamed hypocrisy. The vast number of morbidly obese people waddling the streets scared me.

The children who died from malnutrition and epiglottitis haunted me. Their preventable premature deaths, so easily treated in any western hospital, had been obviously caused by the excesses and apathy that surrounded me.

To take things from worser to worsest, my marriage was disintegrating and I seemed incapable of reacting or repairing. I was overwhelmed, withdrawn, distracted and unsupportive.

To take things to the worsest-of-all-the-worst, I returned to work.

'Your diabetes is out of control because you don't keep to your diet, you feed your face on fast food, you don't exercise and hardly get off your couch whilst watching mindless TV all day. You don't even test your own blood sugar levels.'

I was sitting at my desk in my surgery, stethoscope around my neck. The overweight diabetic patient was perched on the seat beside.

'There's a new pill out, Doc. They say that it will control my blood sugar. I saw it on the news on TV yesterday.'

I grabbed the front of his shirt and pulled his face towards mine.

'Don't you get it? You don't need another pill. You need some focus to eat healthy food, get off your bum and begin gentle exercise and take some responsibility for your health and stop looking for quick fix solutions. You've consulted dieticians, exercise physiologists and diabetic educators. Go and put their advice into practice.'

He looked blank. No one was home. Nothing I was saying was being received. I wanted to throttle him with my stethoscope. I was angry, sweating and shaking with rage.

I woke up sweating and shaking. Relief flooded through me that it was only a dream... but I knew it was a dire warning.

Where was my empathy? Where was my professional demeanour? Where was my humanity? I was being critical, intolerant and unkind. Who was I to judge, denigrate and condemn?

Do you really think you might have become that inappropriate?
No, I would never be so disrespectful but I was too scared and upset to even risk it. I knew I had to take a break from medicine before I actually became inappropriate. I needed to take time off and deal with my distorted perceptions, my anger and frustrations, my hypervigilance and irritability... my PTSD.

What did you do?
I left my job in general practice, bought a small caravan, left home and started travelling. I went 'walkabout'!

I've heard the same story from you before John. Are you running away again?
I know. It seems similar to my escaping my first marriage by running off to Afghanistan and years later heading out to Nigeria after the breakup of my subsequent relationship. At least I am consistent. Behaviour always repeats itself until the lesson is learnt. But I believed I had learnt the lesson. This time it was different. I was not running off to lose myself in another mission. I was moving forward to find myself.

Why did you become so suddenly insightful and aggressive? What was the catalyst that channelled your determination?
I was scared. Shit scared! I had lost all confidence in myself, my perception of other people and the world in general. I had lost sight of who I was, if ever I knew?

My head was full of terrible images and fears that were consuming me. I knew I had to follow my Uncle Bob's advice: *Face it, chunk it down and deal with it.* It was a choice: climb out of it or slide a downward spiral of despair and depression and die.

How did you achieve that?

The first major hurdle was to acknowledge and fully accept that I was suffering PTSD, that it was a major problem in my life and needed my complete attention. In the past I had always minimised, temporised and trivialised the diagnosis. Now I knew it was real, permanent and dangerous. I did consult with a psychiatrist to confirm the diagnosis but all he did was to tell me to take the break and offered anti-depressant medication. I refused. I wanted resolution, not suppression. I was determined to find peace without pills.

Secondly, I grasped that I had to be proactive and give my health and sanity my full-time attention. Part-time treatment would not work for me, it had to be 24/7 with no pause to lose momentum or be distracted. I was at war with myself. I knew I had to delve deep into my psyche to find a place of peace. Fortunately, I could afford to take time off work and go 'walkabout'.

Thirdly, I began to identify the emotional blocks that were holding me back, the stigma of PTSD, the excessive alcohol that I was drinking and an underlying conviction that I did not deserve treatment.

I decided to view PTSD as a psychological injury where there is no blame or judgement. It negated the old labels of lacking *the right stuff*, being *soft in the head, weak-willed, over-emotional*, a *sissy* or a *failure*. It helped me to normalise the condition and overcome the immense shame and inadequacies I felt.

I finally admitted to myself that my excessive intake of alcohol was only avoidance, temporarily deadening symptoms whilst the PTSD continued to moulder, like numbing the gums over a festering tooth abscess that would eventually erupt. I accepted that only complete abstinence would be effective.

I had always struggled to accept that I had any right to complain of PTSD. I could easily understand that those who 'innocently acquired' PTSD, those exposed to abuse, violence, severe injury or illness were deserving of treatment. But those who 'wilfully acquired' it by voluntarily venturing into hazardous regions and situations, the military, first responders and humanitarian workers, were somehow culpable and undeserving... *if you can't take the heat, don't step into the fire.*

Moreover I had met so many people on all my missions who had been exposed to terrors and tragedies far greater that I had ever experienced; Doctor Nukunda in the Nyariragamwe refugee camp in Zaire whose wife was murdered and his three children lost; the father in Kibumba who carried his son's body into the forest to bury; the parents who pushed their son's body twenty kilometres in my cardboard coffin at Patongo; the boy soldiers who were abducted and tortured by the LRA; the innumerable patients with their life-threatening and life-changing injuries and burns in Iraq. The list was endless. Who was I to complain?

After much deliberation I came to accept a wisdom that over the years I had pontificated to patients but never applied to myself, that 'life is not a competition in suffering'. Just because others suffer more does not negate one's personal suffering and I was as deserving as anyone else to be treated.

With renewed vigour I continued to read avidly and widely but found there was no *Dummies Guide to Treating PTSD*. I still vehemently refused to see a psychologist, a block I seemed incapable of overcoming.

So, what did you do?
I created my own strategy, a two-pronged treatment using a computer analogy: reboot, then reprogram.

And did it work?
It gave me a skeleton on which I could hang my ideas.

My reboot regime was basic. I have learnt that most faulty machines will work again if they are switched off, allowed to cool down and switched back on. Hopefully, my mind would too... not that I could switch it off but hopefully I could simplify my basic functions.

What did you do?
I used the strategies that had helped me after Afghanistan, Africa and Iraq and added a few more. Now I would practice them daily and intensely. I created a headspace for a personal retreat:

I imposed a discipline that when I arose each morning, I immediately made my bed. It was one thing accomplished and no matter what happened during the day there was always a comfortable bed to fall into.

I exercised at least twice daily; walking, swimming, star-jumps, push-ups, planks.

I ate healthily; plentiful porridge, muesli, yoghurt, fruits, vegetables, salads, lentils, fish.

I stopped frequently and took ten deep breaths letting any tension drain out of my body. These 'still moments' as I called them relaxed both my body and mind.

I listened to moving music, visiting the *Dark Side of the Moon* with Pink Floyd, floating with *Air on the G String* with Bach and unravelling with *Bolero*! Music is how emotions sound and when listening, my frustrations, anger and confusion were more readily exposed and expressed giving understanding and acceptance.

I danced my jigs and drummed my saucepans encouraging my natural bodily rhythms to rebalance.

At times, when feeling overloaded and overwhelmed, I allowed myself to gently cry, remembering my first releasing cry in Goma, drowning and washing away my fears in tears.

I watched comedy movies, read humorous books, anything that would give me a belly laugh. As crying helped to release my emotions, laughing helped them dissolve.

I practised gratefulness. Each evening I listed all the day's wonderful happenings: walking a forest trail, watching a butterfly flutter on the breeze, sipping an Americano coffee, savouring a Turkish Delight. I carried a gratefulness-pebble, a small smooth pebble that I had picked up from a riverbed, in my pocket with my loose change. Whenever I felt its rounded surface, I was reminded to think of something positive that was near to me at that moment.

I performed 'mindful meditations' to bring myself into the present, enhancing my senses as I strolled the beach, or swam a billabong, or cooked a tagine, or twirled a dance, or lit a campfire. I caressed the sand between my toes and hugged the bark of trees, inhaled the scent of wattle flowers and wood smoke on the breeze, listened to the morning song of the birds and the pounding of the surf, savoured the flavours in my stews and tasted the sea salt in the air, watched the sunrise flame from the horizon then later melt into the sea.

I self-talked and repeated my mantras.

Were they the same mantras that you had after Iraq?
Mostly, with some refinements:

What is happening in the world is happening whether I know about it or not, whether I am there or not, whether I care about it or not.

Life is not fair or just... and at times it really sucks.

I cannot carry the injustices of the world on my shoulders. It is not my business.

I did all I could do to help, however little that was.

They guided me to rationalise, accept and let go of the past.

Where did you go?
I immersed myself in nature, camping for weeks in beautiful national parks, walking their paths, climbing their peaks, bathing in the surf, learning to be still and reflective. I lay on my back on moonless nights far from artificial illumination, star-struck, in awe of the Milky Way, feeling humbled and minuscule. I sat on logs and watched ants carrying enormous loads of leaves along twigs of trees, feeling colossal and clumsy.

Did it all help?
Very much so. Following these constant practices and rituals locked my focus on my goal of overcoming the PTSD.

Being sober was paramount. I carried no alcohol to my remote locations and surprisingly found it easy not to drink. Fortunately, I had no withdrawal symptoms. Being solo reduced temptation. I was happy to be alone with my thoughts where no one would witness me weeping on my bed, dancing around my campfire to the Beatles, U2 and ABBA, or drumming the beat with a wooden spoon on an old tin can. I might otherwise have been committed.

And how did you tackle your reprogramming?
It was a combination of journaling, meditation and visualisation.

Every day I journaled to expose what was festering in my psyche, a frank self-confession of feelings. I wrote whatever came into my head, at length, with no attempt to edit or censor. At times it was brutal, even murderous, attacking everyone and everything. At times it became self-pitying and pathetic. On other occasions, it was reflective and mellow. I set a daily minimum of writing three foolscap pages. It often extended to ten. Amid this disorganised litany of lunacy, islands of clarity and insight would emerge, small whirls of wisdom dropped in from heaven-knows-where? I always destroyed these missives. I would be so embarrassed for anyone else to read these uncensored diatribes.

When fears or anxieties welled into my consciousness, I learnt to immediately record them whilst still fresh in my mind. Over the weeks they amassed: fears of failure, fears of being abandoned, fears of not being good enough, fears of not being brave, fears of rejection, fears of being unlovable, fears of trusting. Some were intense, others mild. Just noting them, exposing and confronting them seemed to diminish their ferocity. I was embarrassed to realise how many fears I harboured deep within. I discovered a few unorthodox, scientifically-unproven techniques to help release them further. Emotional Freedom Therapy (EFT) proved the most effective with, at times, palpable relief. Eye Movement Desensitisation and Reprocessing (EMDR) also helped.

I practised what I called 'mindless meditation'. I had read of transcendental meditation and its claim of inner peace and wellness but had been suspicious that eastern philosophy was usually lost in translation. But now I had time to experiment and, with practice, sitting comfortably with a silent meaningless mantra, fortified by the sounds of silence, I allowed myself to fall into a void. It took much practice to achieve. I would commonly sit on a camp chair in a quiet, secluded spot. My favourite was on a deserted beach with my feet awash in the ebbing waves. Initially I would drift away from my intrusive thoughts for only a minute or two but with practise my time extended to five, to ten, to twenty minutes. Clearing my cluttered mind felt like cleaning the leaves from a gutter to allow rainwater to escape. I knew that when my mind was empty it was more liable to catch any falling insight or inspiration.

And did you catch any?

Yes, many. There were moments when an unexpected insight, a snippet of wisdom, a sudden inspiration dropped out of nowhere and startled me by its abruptness and clarity:

Just be somebody... not somebody else
No matter how hard the past... you can always begin again
The secret of life is letting go
Trust your gut instincts

Was any particular strategy the most helpful?

There was no special, magical ingredient or technique. As with a recipe each ingredient added to the flavour, aroma and texture of the final dish. I disciplined myself to follow a daily routine but felt free to chop and change following intuitive needs as they arose.

I often sat and visualised how this continual input of positive and peaceful thought was rewiring my brain, laying down new circuits for joy and peace, converting my inertia to inspiration, my years of stagnation to solution, my self-pity to self-respect.

In this solitude, I had ample time to read widely – Echart Tolle, Wayne Dwyer, Katie Byron, David Hawkins, and Caroline Myss. Their ideas reinforced my determination to heal and helped to weld together my homemade therapies.
I reread *Winnie the Pooh*, a favourite book full of ancient wisdom:

'What day is it?' asks Pooh.
'It's today,' squealed Piglet.
'My favourite day,' says Pooh.

Over time I began to find and accept myself... and most importantly, I began to forgive and love myself.

What did you forgive?

I forgave my earlier ego, my arrogance, my selfishness, my abandonments and my mistrust. I came more into the present and left my past behind. I came to accept that I am who I am, scars, sins, failings, foibles and all. I had done the best I could, even if it hadn't seemed very good at the time... and most importantly, that is was over. I was happy to *Let it be.*

With self-forgiveness came a calm, a new spiritual awareness, a new meaning for my life no longer ego driven but one of acceptance and allowance, to let life flow and leave a heartprint rather than a footprint on the world.

How did all this therapy conclude, John?

I used an ancient and powerful tool that has been popularised in recent New Age philosophy and the film, *The Secret.* It is based on the 'Universal Law of Attraction': *that we manifest what we give our attention to.* It infers that we can create our own reality by deciding and focussing on how we want it to be.

Now it might be true, or it might be a load of rubbish, but it strongly resonated with me. I imagined my life to be a blank canvas on which I would paint the picture I wanted.

I wrote down my intentions for my future. There was nothing specific or detailed. I included the ways I wanted to be; of abundance and generosity; a continuation of close and loving family and friends; new meaningful friendships and relationships; optimal health and mobility; frequent fun and laughter; challenging and rewarding medical work in unusual and interesting places.

It is an organic, ongoing process that I often revisit, reaffirm and adjust. Importantly it concluded 'or something better' otherwise I might just get what I ask for and miss out on opportunities beyond my imagination.

As I travelled and followed my daily therapy, I began to feel more confident and started to visit friends from long ago with whom I had lost contact. To my great delight I discovered deep ongoing friendships, forged by time, were rekindled and fortified.

What happened when you returned home?

It was obvious my marriage was over. I was sad but accepting and we parted amicably. The caravan was securely stowed at a friend's farm. Everything else I owned fitted in the back of my car. Since the house fire I had accumulated very little. I stayed with close friends and began locum medical work at various locations. I no longer feared being professionally inappropriate. My empathy, tolerance and compassion had returned. I could listen and observe patients without feeling any judgement or anger.

Then I saw an advert for a job in Africa.

CANBERRA, AUSTRALIA,
November 2014
Doctor, Aspen Medical

'Ebola is a most infectious and deadly disease. The epidemic in West Africa is spreading. Already it has killed over six thousand people. If not controlled, it may spread globally. We are joining an international effort to stem its advance.'

Bruce, the CEO of Aspen Medical gave the pep talk to inspire us to action. Aspen Medical had been contracted by the Australian Government to set up and run an Ebola Treatment Centre (ETC) in Freetown, Sierra Leone. I was one of a team of medical staff and environmental officers who had hastily been recruited. An email offering me a position had only arrived the previous Sunday asking I be in Canberra the following Wednesday morning. Two days had been set aside for briefings before twelve of us departed for Africa via Brussels on Friday.

'At the moment, the British government are building six new treatment centres in Sierra Leone. We will be responsible for running the Hastings Airfield ETC. It is your task to become proficient at treating Ebola patients, fit out our Ebola Treatment Centre, train the national staff we have hired and treat new patients. We want to open in three weeks.'

'Not too much to ask for as none of us have ever seen a case of Ebola,' I whispered to Lisa, a nurse who was sitting opposite me. She mouthed me to shut up and kicked me under the table, but the speaker must have heard.

'We have arranged with Médecins Sans Frontières to train you in one of their ETCs in Sierra Leone. They are the world's experts and will cover the treatment and protocols in personal protective equipment or PPE. We have organised some initial training here in Canberra over the next two days. You'll be trained to don and doff, or put on and take off the extensive PPE essential for your safety. Obviously, this is a hazardous mission. We have taken advice from the infectious disease specialists. Thermometers are being issued to you all and we insist you take your body temperatures twice daily and immediately report to the programme manager if it is elevated. Also, we ask that there is no bodily contact between anyone for the duration of the epidemic... no hugging or even shaking hands.

We'll be supporting you all the time. Good luck.

How were you feeling?
I was excited. I love the challenge of heading into a void, making it up as we go along. I was reminded of setting off on the mission to the Nuba Mountains with little idea of what was to come; the excitement, the anticipation, the adrenaline flooding the brain, energising every cell, sharpening the thinking. I was on a high. This was a similar opportunity... but even better... we had huge resources at our disposal, of equipment, of staff, of logistics.

What about your PTSD? Were you having any symptoms?
No, all my symptoms had settled. I was confident I would manage the mission. Since leaving my home I had worked again as a locum doctor in several general practices and refugee detention centres. I had enjoyed practising medicine again. In between locums I had stayed with various friends, helping out on their properties and farms and enjoying life.

Even more importantly I continued to abstain from alcohol and continued to journal, meditate and exercise. My nightmares had settled and although I had occasional vivid dreams, these were not invasive or disturbing. I considered them a safety pressure valve, allowing any rogue thoughts to escape.

In this mission my responsibilities were small and well defined. The team was enormous, composed not only of medical, administration and logistical staff but also environmental officers to organise the sterilisation and incineration of the contaminated materials and areas where we would be working. Moreover, our team was just part of a huge international program coordinated by the World Health Organisation to control the epidemic. I was to be just a tiny cog in a massive machine.

I also knew in advance that on this mission half our patients would die. I was comfortable that they were dying of an untreatable disease and that we would be giving them their best chance. It did not trigger or disturb me. It was a very different scenario from the Nuba Mountains where children died of malnutrition and preventable infections due to the neglect and apathy of the world.

Finally, our living conditions in Sierra Leone would be very comfortable and the team was skilled and supportive. Overall this promised to be an easier ride compared to previous missions. It would be a perfect trial to test if I had contained my PTSD.

Nevertheless, did you think that wise? Why put yourself through another mission? What if you did not cope and you reactivated all your symptoms as happened after the Nuba Mountains?
Maybe you're right and it was stupid. But then I would never know... and I needed to know... as well as have another adventure... and help others in the process. This was a unique epidemic, an extraordinary opportunity. I was well qualified to join this effort to contain Ebola. If I hadn't gone, I would have been wondering and regretting for the rest of my life.

So, you didn't consider working in an Ebola Treatment Centre as risky as your previous missions?
Yes and no. I knew Ebola was deadly and there was risk. I knew that that working with Ebola patients required wearing the extensive personal protective equipment or PPE, which could be challenging but there were no guns, no overhead bombers, no kidnappers, no drunken soldiers or terrorists. Living conditions would be comfortable and working with a team of Australians and New Zealanders would be fun.

And were you right?

184

SIERRA LEONE
ASPEN MEDICAL
2014–2015

We stood and looked at the array of tents enclosed in a wire fence. 'This is it, the Hastings Airfield ETC, one of six that has been built by the British Army Royal Engineers in only six weeks, the ETC that the Australian Government has commissioned us to run.' We had driven out to the decommissioned airfield with Jay, the medical director for the project, to view the facility and plan our preparation. Jay had preceded us to Sierra Leone and had been overseeing the construction. Straggly beard, receding hairline, dark glasses, he looked tired. Twelve of us, doctors, nurses and environmental officers had arrived at Freetown, the capital, a week earlier from Canberra and had spent three days in an intense training course run by MSF in Bo, a three-hour drive from the city. Even driving to Bo was a lesson in how Ebola was affecting the country. Every twenty minutes our cars were stopped at roadblocks where everyone had their skin temperatures recorded. 'It is one method to stop sick people from leaving their neighbourhood and spreading the disease,' Jay clarified.

'This ETC is constructed with numerous tents that are divided in to three zones, White, Green and Red.' He continued to explain that the White Zone, surrounded by a high wire fence with a single entrance guarded by security, contained administration, kitchen, dining, the psycho-social team, logistics and warehouses. In one corner sat the water and chlorine plant where water from a bore was collected and two strengths of chlorine solutions were mixed and stored in huge tanks, to be piped into the Red Zone.

To enter the Green Zone required all staff to change into scrubs. Here were the medical and nursing offices, laundry and pharmacy.

The Red Zone, isolated by a double fence, accommodated the patient wards, mortuary and incinerators. It had two outer gates, one for patients arriving in ambulances, the other for dead bodies to be collected. One part of the outer fence had been lowered with seats either side where patients, once recovering, would be able to safely see their families. A dressing tent bridged the fences between Green and Red Zones where all staff entering the Red Zone had to don full PPE. Further along the boundary was the doffing tent where all staff exiting the Red Zone was carefully supervised to safely remove and dispose of their contaminated PPE.

Jay concluded. 'We have hired a hundred and fifty local personnel including nurses, pharmacists, hygienists, laundry, kitchen and security workers to staff the ETC. All the equipment has arrived. Our priority is to unpack and organise the equipment, induct and train the staff and write the protocols and procedures. We would like to open in two weeks.'

We all stared at each other.

'I know it's a big ask but if in two weeks you do not think it is safe to begin operations it will be delayed. But let's not waste any more time.' He smiled and led us through the security checkpoint at the gate.

'Stay still Doctor John. I still need to tie your hood. Bend your knees so I can reach. You are too tall,' commanded Fanny, one of the dressers.

I was in the dressing tent donning my PPE, looking like a transmutation of Michelin Man, a penguin and a nun. Yellow overalls zipped to the neck with an adhesive flap over-seal, leggings over white Wellington boots, white hood over head and shoulders tied firmly around the back of the head, blue apron from neck to knees, orange mask over mouth and nose, goggles over eyes, two pairs of gloves. No skin or mucous membrane was exposed. I was completely cocooned.

I stood in front of the full-length mirror and checked the mask on my face. Even with Fanny's assistance, the PPE had taken ten minutes to don. The routine had become a mantra of my persona, a ritual for survival. The PPE had to be perfect. I had gleaned many subtleties to improve its efficiency. To demist the goggles, they needed to be rinsed with a solution of baby shampoo, but not wiped. To prevent the second pair of gloves sliding down the wrist they needed to be circumferentially taped to the overalls.

'Are you OK Doctor John?' Alfred the 'timer', a staff member dedicated to recording entry and exit times into the Red Zone, wrote my name in bold letters on my hood, over the goggles, and on my upper back. In the yellow suits and white hoods, everyone looked the same. Except for height, it was impossible to identify personal features. A.K.A., one of the hygienists, measuring six foot eight inches and Martha at five feet no inches were the only staff easily distinguishable. An 'M' for medic was written on my left shoulder and 'A24', my entry number, on my right. Finally, the time, 10:05, was marked on my inner left arm, well within the field of vision of my goggles, allowing me to calculate the duration of my PPE exposure.

The day's heat rose to forty degrees Centigrade and the risk of heat exhaustion was high. Forty to sixty minutes was our usual limit, keeping in mind it may take over take over ten minutes to doff the PPE.

The process was complete. I was sealed like a roast in a vacupack being put in the oven. I could already feel the heat building up in my body. One colleague called it her personal sauna. A bead of sweat formed on my top lip.

I likened my PPE to a space suit. It protected me from the harsh external alien environment I was about to enter. I wished it could have been more sophisticated as seen in movies like *Contagion*, with a built-in electrical cooling system and the hood incorporated into the overalls allowing a full-face mask. But the cost for such a state-of-the-art PPE was prohibitive.

Nonetheless, I treated my PPE with similar respect for I was about to enter the Red Zone of the Ebola Treatment Centre, a Petrie dish of Ebola virus, one of the deadliest viruses in the world. Any exposure of the virus to the eyes, mucous membranes of the nose or mouth or any tiny abrasion of the skin could result in an infection that carried a fifty per cent death rate. Not great odds. This was not an area to enter casually. I would be handling critically sick patients and be exposed to their vomit, diarrhoea and blood. I would be inserting cannulas into their veins. I would be lifting dead bodies into body bags, probably the most infectious and dangerous manoeuvre of them all.

My long history of scuba diving fared well for me; the habit of checking my companions, or buddies, before and throughout the dive had become second nature. The narrowed field of vision limited by the goggles felt comfortable. My training in surgical sterility also reinforced my safety. I always knew where my gloved hands were positioned, never to touch my face even for an itchy nose or bead of sweat on the brow.

I rechecked my PPE in the full-length mirrors of the dressing area, double-checked the seal around the outer glove and triple-checked around the eyes, the commonest site for a breach. I nodded at Silvia, the nurse to accompany me on this ward round, and Michael, the hygienist, and we all checked each other. Michael carried a pressurised spray pack of chlorine solution on his back with a spray head on a wand in his hand. He would follow us throughout our entry to spray our hands and anything we touched, limiting the spread of the virus. We paused before crossing the bold green/red boundary line painted across the entry into the Red Zone.

I paused and briefed the team. 'We are entering the Red Zone. It is a dangerous environment but we are well protected and prepared. Be mindful of every action. Go slowly and deliberately. Watch for each other and we will all be safe. Let's go.'

I gave this little talk before every entry, mainly to remind myself. I was very aware of 'security creep' and cognisant that taking any shortcuts in safety could easily be fatal. Ebola is less forgiving than minefields.

That night I had an 'awakening'. Whilst lying in bed drifting off to sleep, reflecting and self-congratulating my thoroughness at caring for my PPE, I was struck by the realisation that I had never so thoroughly checked or cared for my 'earth suit', my own body, the one I could not discard, the suit that I wore every day.

What triggered this sudden insight do you think, John?
I've no idea. It was one of those 'AHA' moments. The clarity and suddenness of the revelation amazed me. Maybe it was that the deliberate, meticulous and repetitive donning of the PPE sharply contrasted with the casual, chaotic and careless attitude that I had to my own body's well-being. Maybe the intense and near-obsessive focus that the whole team gave to donning and doffing the PPE sensitised my awareness of self-survival.

How ironic it was that my PPE had only to be perfect for the forty to sixty minutes of the Red Zone entry after which it was carefully removed, discarded and destroyed but my body, my earth suit, was a fixture for life. How ironic it was that it had taken me most of my life to come to such an obvious conclusion.

Why did you dwell on this analysis so much?
The moment was powerful for I was not only acutely aware of the irony but also that all was not lost. The healthy habits I had acquired during my walkabout therapy had been declining but could be revitalised. I could renew my daily habits and checks and maintain focus. Maybe my earth suit, physical and mental, could be salvaged for a few more years to come. We do not only live once; we live every day and I could start anew today. We only die once.

It was only a handprint but it lifted all our hearts. Her right palm and fingers had been brushed with yellow paint then pressed firmly against a large white board. It was only a small girl's handprint but it was a massive symbol of success, of hope, of joy in being alive. We cheered, clapped and cried with excitement.

She was our first Ebola survivor, Amina, aged only eleven-years-old. We had nursed her through hell; calmed her crying and callings for her father with repetitive reassurances, guided her back to bed as she randomly roamed the walkways and even jumped the inner fence. We had hugged her, anonymous in our white hoods, goggles, blue aprons and yellow overalls, aware she was highly infectious with a deadly disease but knowing human contact was her best medicine. Her mother and aunt were dead. Her grandmother had been admitted alongside her and she had watched her slowly weaken, die and be carried out in a white body bag. She had lain lethargic, depressed, drained by diarrhoea as we fretted for her life. We fed her fluids, sip by sip, to rehydrate her; fed her food, spoonful by spoonful, to nourish her; crushed her medications, pill by pill, to syringe gently into her mouth. Her slight, slim body, seeming so frail and vulnerable had refused to die and she slowly recovered, gained strength and again roamed the walkways, wanting her father.

She was the first ray of hope that our Ebola Treatment Centre was making a difference. Three patients had died over the past two days. She was the spark we needed to reignite our enthusiasm and swing our focus back to our purpose of saving lives. Five days after being symptom-free, a blood test had been taken to check for Ebola... and came back negative. She was cured. She was our first survivor.

Between the Red and Green Zones, there is a tiny, anonymous building, two metres square, with a door on either side. Inside is a shower. It had never been used. As Amina walked from the Red Zone escorted by a nurse wearing full PPE, into the tiny room we all waited excitedly on the other side. The national staff led us in local songs and we all danced. The atmosphere was exhilarating. In the room Amina stripped, showered, changed into fresh clothes leaving behind all her possessions to be incinerated, before walking out of the opposite door... into the Green Zone.

As Amina emerged the waiting crowd of staff all cheered, clapped hands and laughed with joy. She was hugged and hugged again. Her face changed from bewilderment to delight realising she too was free... free of disease, free of fear of dying, free to go home.

Ben, the head nurse, painted her hand yellow and slowly pressed it on to a large white board specially built for the occasion. All survivors would have their coloured hand imprinted.

Although the white board only had the one small handprint... it was more... one hand clapping, one hand high-fiving, and one hand waving, waiting for more to join it. We called it our 'Wall of Hope'.

Had you had anything like this before on your missions John?

Never. Previous missions were too fragmented, too widespread, too disorganised to create such a focal point of success and accomplishment. We were dealing with multiple diseases and injuries and working several locations with ever changing conditions. In this instance, we were treating just one disease, in one location and in an organised and contained environment. It was a perfect outlet to celebrate our successes.

It taught me the power of symbolism. In any tragedy where heartbreak is overwhelming, a simple symbol can be a powerful focus for grief and resolve. It concentrates the positive where negativity flourishes. It heightens hope where despair reigns. It draws out our humanity when we want to withdraw in fear. A candle in the wind with Diana, ground zero in New York, Charlie in Paris are examples of its global and viral effect. Our Wall of Hope was our symbol.

We celebrated every survivor in a similar fashion, dancing and singing, clapping and laughing and painting their handprint on the Wall of Hope. I'm delighted to say that, over the months, my dancing and singing improved.

HASTINGS AIRFIELD EBOLA TREATMENT CENTRE,
FREETOWN, SIERRA LEONE
December 2014
Doctor, Aspen Medical

'Doctor John, Mariatu is deteriorating. She is delirious, her eyes are rolling around her head and her arms are flexed and externally rotated. I think she is brain damaged and will die.'

Sebeyeh stood in the entry of the medical coordination tent. Her scrubs were saturated and her hair was matted with sweat. She had just doffed all her PPE after leaving the Red Zone and had not yet changed from her sodden clothing. As she spoke, she greedily drank from a bag of cold water to help quench her thirst and cool her core. She knew I was especially interested in Mariatu and wanted to immediately update me on her condition.

'Thanks, Sebeyeh, I'm booked to enter the Red Zone in thirty minutes for a ward round so I'll examine her then.' All entries into the Red Zone had to be prior planned and logged on the entry board to help maintain a constant presence as well as avoid congestion at the doffing station where we carefully removed our PPE.

Mariatu was a seventeen-year-old girl who had been admitted a week earlier. She had nursed her father when he became sick at home and later died. A week after his death her mother, aunt and herself had all become ill and were diagnosed with Ebola. Her mother and aunt had died two days before. Mariatu was struggling. She reminded me of my stepdaughter and I was determined to make sure she lived... not that I had anything special to give her... except a commitment however shallow it seemed. Twice a day, I would hold her and help her drink a couple of cupfuls of rehydration fluid and eat a little food. She was so weak she could barely swallow but I insisted. I sometimes extended my ward-round to ensure she drank a sufficient volume of fluid.

An hour later I was horrified. Arriving in the medical ward in the Red Zone I had immediately sought out Mariatu. She was barely conscious and seemed to be lost in another world. I called it 'Ebola-land'. I had seen many patients become zombified early in their illness, eyes staring nowhere, uncoordinated, uncommunicative, unresponsive, the mind wandering. Many died whilst in this trance-like state but when it passed recovery would commonly start. I thought it similar to the 'crisis' of a fever, which, once broken, signalled the beginning of the body's recovery. Mariatu was deep in Ebola-land, but even more worrying were the signs of possible brain damage. If she lived, would she be disabled?

I cradled her in my arms, protecting myself from her thrashing arms that threatened to knock off my goggles, and trickled fluid between her cracked lips.

'Don't you die on me Mariatu... I'll kill you if you do,' I muttered in frustration.

She stared through me but I kept on with my diatribe. 'You're going to get well. Just keep swallowing and I'll keep on pouring it in.' I rambled on until she drank the fluid, and then laid her gently down on her mattress on the ground. Back in the medical tent in the Green Zone I wrote in her medical notes asking all staff to keep pushing her oral fluids. Despite knowing her prognosis was terrible, for some reason, I was convinced she could be saved.

Why did you adopt her so, John?
She became a reflection of my wellness. If I could make her well, then I would stay well too.

That was quite a gamble, knowing the prognosis.
This was not a logical or rational choice. It was intuitive. I had a sense of knowing I should do it. Was it a challenge to the universe that sheer willpower will succeed or a doubt lingering within me that I was still vulnerable? I do not know. I cannot explain any more clearly.

Why should it occur now?
I was cruising along in this mission without any feelings of trauma. Many of my colleagues were anxious and stressed by the daily dangers, dramas and deaths. I was counselling and supporting many of them to deal with their emotional overload. Although I did not feel any of the anger, guilt or impotence I had experienced in previous missions I still had a deep-seated, nagging worry that my PTSD was lingering and would suddenly unravel. Mariatu became a symbol to me. If she could beat the odds, then I could too. I had no exit strategy or plan B. It was a test, a toss-up, win or lose.

What happened to Mariatu?
My intuition triumphed. She made an amazing recovery. After ten days in 'Ebola-land', she became responsive, communicative and began to drink of her own accord. Her diarrhoea and vomiting resolved. Her neurological symptoms rapidly subsided and two weeks later she was walking about helping to nurse the sicker patients.

When her Ebola blood test turned negative, I was the first at the door of the decontamination shower to welcome her back into the world and guide her painted hand to press a print on the Wall of Hope. It was a beautiful day in a beautiful world. I now felt confident that my PTSD had fully settled.

'Family funerals are a massive cause of the epidemic spreading.' Brian, an epidemiologist from the World Health Organisation (WHO) was visiting the ETC to update the new medical staff that had recently arrived from Australia and New Zealand. 'The corpse of a person who has died from Ebola is highly infectious. It is customary for the family to wash and dress the body. Culturally it is an important ritual of purification. They will often caress and kiss the deceased person before burial. Anyone touching the body will probably become infected with Ebola. It's common for six or seven family members to become sick following a funeral and this spreads the disease widely. An essential strategy to prevent the spread of Ebola is to stop the ritual of family funerals.'

He continued to explain how the Red Cross and Crescent Society had taken responsibility for safe body disposal. They had several teams who, whilst wearing full PPE will collect any dead body from any home or ETC and transfer it to a safe burial site. He detailed how teams of WHO epidemiologists were investigating every death in the country, quarantining contacts and educating the families about the disease and its spread.

'Many people still do not believe Ebola is dangerous. Others believe it has been introduced by the west. Many family members do not want to be quarantined for twenty-one days and run away. It is a slow painstaking process. The government is even shutting down the whole city of Freetown for two-day periods, prohibiting all movement and traffic in the city except emergency services to allow the teams to gain access to the families.'

Fabrina, the leader of our 'psycho-social team' who supported all the patients and their families in our ETC from admission to discharge or death, continued the briefing.

'After many trials we have made the transfer of any deceased patient from our ETC to the burial ground as dignified and safe as possible.

'We stand with the family and a religious minister outside the outer fence beside the mortuary. As the body is being wheeled from the mortuary to the exit gate for collection, we ask you to stop and expose the deceased person's face by unzipping one end of the body bags and allow the family to identify them. I know this exposes you to extra risk of infection but it is important for families see and identify their loved one. They then say a final prayer and farewell.

'Once this is complete, continue to the exit gate where the Red Cross team will be ready to accept the body and transport it to the graveyard. The family will have no direct contact with the deceased. We follow with the family and observe from a distance. Having told the families of why contact is so dangerous they happily have accepted this procedure.'

Were you involved in this process John?

Yes. The expatriate doctors and nurses all took their turns to transfer the dead bodies from the ward to the mortuary and later from the mortuary to the exit gate for collection. Although not a medical procedure we wanted to show the national staff that we were prepared to do the unpleasant and risky tasks too. It was a stark contrast to the celebration of discharging a survivor... but as important.

The entire body was sprayed with chlorine, wrapped in their bed sheets and enclosed in two body bags for safety. I found the process heart breaking. I had admitted and treated many of them, observed the terror in their eyes, unable to reassure or console, just note their decline to death.

It was tragic to observe the other patients watch us collect the body. I could imagine them thinking *who's next* or *that could be me tomorrow*. How they coped with all this dread and sorrow was incomprehensible.

As part of the body-transfer team we were able to reinforce the strict protocols required for safety and ensure no short cut was taken. My earlier experiences of 'risk creep' on missions were still prominent in my memory. Any laxity or lapse of our protocols could easily be lethal.

HASTINGS AIRFIELD EBOLA TREATMENT CENTRE,
FREETOWN, SIERRA LEONE
January 2015
Doctor, Aspen Medical

'Doctor John, someone's collapsed in the doffing tent.' Binta, one of the doffing supervisors, the person who oversees and directs the doffing procedure, had run into the medical tent flustered and frightened. I did not wait for any details but jumped up and ran the thirty metres to the tent that bridges the boundary between the Red and Green Zones where everyone leaving the Red Zone must doff their PPE. The tent spans three lanes allowing three people to doff simultaneously. Each lane has a red / green boundary line drawn across the middle. No one in the Green Zone must cross the boundary into the contaminated Red Zone. No one in the Red Zone can cross back into the Green Zone until they have fully decontaminated and disposed of their PPE. There are no exceptions.

A body in full PPE was sprawled on a plastic chair at the red end of one of the lanes. The name on her forehead identified her as Meg, one of the expatriate nurses. The green end of the tent was full of curious bystanders who had wandered in from the nearby laundry.

Raymond, a doffing supervisor, saw me enter.

'Doctor John, it is Meg. She started to doff but felt faint and was going to fall. I passed my plastic chair to Zaria who was supporting her and she managed to guide her to sit before falling. But she is still not moving. What do I do?'

'Well done Raymond. You have done well.'

Zaria, a national nurse usually easily identified by her frizzy hair with a mini ponytail tied in a bright ribbon, was standing in her full PPE behind the chair. It was frustrating having Meg so near yet unable to reach over and help.

I turned around and asked everyone not necessary to doffing to leave the tent.

'Zaria, can you lean Meg forwards so her head falls to her knees... but don't let her fall off the chair.' It was impossible to do any medical assessment of Meg, as I could not see any skin or even check if she was still breathing. The PPE was too enclosing. I assumed she was suffering heat stroke and dehydration and had fainted with a low blood pressure.

Zaria managed to lean Meg forward and I heard a few groans emerge. At least she was breathing.

"Meg, it's John. Don't move. Just stay as you are.' I was worried she would be disorientated and confused and try to pull off her mask and contaminate her face. 'Zaria, keep a constant pressure on her neck to keep her forward.'

Suzel, the charge nurse, ran in behind me. 'I heard what's happening and I've sent two nurses to the dressing tent to don up and be a backup. It will take them about ten minutes.'

'Thanks, Suzel. Hopefully they won't be needed.'

Meg was beginning to stir. 'Can you hear me Meg?'

'I feel terrible. I want to be sick,' she moaned.

'Stay still.' I shouted. 'Raymond, spray her head and upper body with the chlorine. I want to get her mask and hood off as quickly as possible.' He leant forward and without crossing the line used the chlorine spray wand to extend the spray all over Meg's upper body and head.

'Zaria, pull her mask off over the front of her face… now wash your hands under the chlorine tap… now snap the ties of her hood.' Zaria followed the commands.

'… now wash your hands again and lift her hood over the top of her head.' The hood came off. '… now wash your hands, untie her mask and let it drop.' It was essential for her to wash her hands in chlorine between each action to prevent cross contamination. Zaria was shaking with nerves but kept in control and the mask came off.

Meg suddenly vomited all over the floor. I sighed with relief that it wasn't in her mask and mouth. Slowly, with Zaria's help, the rest of her PPE was sprayed and cut off with a pair of scissors without contaminating her body or scrubs. Raymond and I were able to then lean forward, grab her bare hands, pull her out of the chair and catch her as she fell forwards into our arms and on to a stretcher to be carried to the medical tent where Doctor Scott would check her over.

Was this common John? Did many workers collapse like this?

No. It only happened three times during the four months we ran the ETC involving over ten thousand entries into the Red Zone. The helplessness and frustration of being so near, yet so far across the Red/Green Zone boundary, stirred a few memories of previous occasions of professional impotency. It was, however, a stark reminder to strictly maintain our safeguards to prevent anyone over-staying in the Red Zone, especially in the heat of the day. Every entry was timed and a warning siren sounded when exit times were overdue.

Other than heat stroke the other hazard that caused even more concern was accidental contamination with skin breakage.

HASTINGS AIRFIELD EBOLA TREATMENT CENTRE,
FREETOWN, SIERRA LEONE
February 2015
Doctor, Aspen Medical

'Doctor John, Doctor Karen's in the doffing tent with a needle stick injury.' I didn't even see who had shouted the warning but ran to the doffing tent where Doctor Karen was sitting in the Red Zone with her gloved hand in a bowl of chlorine solution. She looked scared, her head turning and her eyes darting around the room.

'I was inserting a cannula into a patient but slipped and the needle penetrated my gloves into the back of my hand.' The regular PPE involves wearing two pairs of gloves in case one is torn. Both gloves had been breached. 'My gloves were highly contaminated from blood and vomit.'

'Let the doffing supervisor help you doff your PPE as per protocol then we can talk back in the medical tent.' She nodded.

There is little reassurance that can be given in such circumstances. I remembered the anxiety that gripped me after my needle stick injury in Goma when the principle danger was contracting HIV. This was far more serious. We were all aware that the few studies on previous cases of Ebola-contaminated needle stick injury showed a very high death rate. It was the injury that all the medical staff feared. We could not even give Karen a comforting hug as any physical contact between staff was forbidden.

I phoned the medical director of the mission who would confer with the program manager and the British Army medical team who ran a special ETC especially for local and expatriate medical staff at Kerry Town, forty kilometres out of Freetown. They would organise ongoing treatment. Luckily Aspen Medical had an arrangement with the British government that any incident involving their expatriate medical team would be evacuated back to the UK for treatment.

Ironically Karen could have flown to London on a commercial flight over the next two days. There was safe window of forty-eight hours before symptoms and contagion began. But this had become politically unpalatable. The previous month a Scottish nurse, who had acquired Ebola in Sierra Leone had inadvertently flown on a commercial flight after she became feverish and contagious. There had been a media frenzy and scare mongering and the British Government was not taking any chance of more bad press. We were amazed when a dedicated aircraft with a full medical retrieval team was flown from the UK to repatriate her. We were also very reassured that such facilities were available to us.

Karen was given high doses of antiviral medication and observed in London for the twenty-one-day quarantine period and, to everyone's great relief, she suffered no illness.

What were your feelings about this John?

I was impressed and reassured that we had such a level of support. Compared to my snakebite experience in the Nuba Mountains when air evacuation was impossible, this was luxury. But I also felt guilty that if one of our national staff had become infected, although there was a special unit for them in Kerry Town, they would not have been evacuated to the UK with access to all the possible sophisticated and experimental therapies. It felt unjust.

HASTINGS AIRFIELD EBOLA TREATMENT CENTRE,
FREETOWN, SIERRA LEONE
March 2015
Doctor, Aspen Medical

'Doctor John, the paraplegic patient who refused to stay in the ETC has collapsed outside the main gate and is having a convulsion. What should we do?' Sara, a national nurse and Ousman, one of the security guards, had run in to the medical tent. I was on afternoon shift. The second doctor, Doctor Scott, and two nurses were in the Red Zone for a ward round. Lisa, the nurse in charge sat at her desk. I looked at her and shrugged. 'Don't say it "I told you so".'

The paraplegic patient was Maliki, a thirty-year-old man admitted that morning into the triage ward where patients with symptoms of Ebola were isolated and had a blood test taken to check the diagnosis. If negative they were discharged. If positive they were admitted into the 'confirmed' ward. He had had fever, headache, muscle pains and vomiting for five days, possible symptoms of Ebola.

Maliki had been paraplegic since a car accident ten years previously. His body was thin and his legs were wasted. He sported a short scruffy beard. His wheelchair was wasted too. Many of the wheel spokes were broken and the wheels wobbled. The material of the seat was frayed and split. The armrests had disintegrated.

He initially agreed to be admitted but later changed his mind and started to wheel his chair up and down the triage ward, approaching other patients and even threatening to enter the confirmed ward. He was afraid, rebellious and unreasonable. I had sat with him and tried to explain the danger of becoming contaminated and the possibility of him contaminating others. He was not interested and insisted on being discharged.

In the medical tent the medical staff on duty had held a mini conference. I discussed the possibility of chemically restraining him but we did not have staff to continually supervise him. It was too dangerous. Ousman the guard came up with the solution. 'Let him go Doctor John. He will soon be back. The local population will not let him roam far. They will drive him back. I'll make sure no one harms him.'

Lisa chimed in, 'It's a risk but the least risky option. He cannot stay running riot in the wards. He may infect other patients waiting in triage. We cannot safely heavily sedate him. But anything could happen to him out there.'

I had agreed.

He had left the ETC though the entry gate and wheeled off in his rickety wheelchair towards the road. I was later told he met a barricade of locals who had been forewarned and refused to let him pass, holding him at bay with long poles. He was ordered to return, prodded by the poles. With little choice he reluctantly rolled back to the ETC but when nearing the gates, he began to convulse and fell out of his chair on to the ground. No one went near.

I dashed out of the ETC and found him lying unconscious beside his toppled wheelchair. A wheel had been terminally bent. Luckily, he was on his side and breathing. The guards waved from their post beside the main gate. A few locals peered from afar but no one came to help. Ebola is a strong deterrent.

Lisa had gone to the dressing tent and organised a team of nurses and hygienists to don PPE and leave the Red Zone to where he lay with a stretcher to carry him back to the triage ward. I ordered a dose of diazepam to prevent further fitting and took blood for his Ebola test. When he awoke the following morning, he was a different man, thankful, compliant and friendly. The Ebola test result was not yet available and he was happy to stay in bed. I talked with the logistics department who sourced a second hand wheelchair from the city. Compared to his original chair it was a supersonic Rolls Royce.

His test returned negative later that day and he was discharged. Carried to the decontamination room, he showered, dressed in new clothing and, leaving behind all his possessions for incineration, was carried out into the Green Zone. On these occasions there was no celebration with singing and dancing or hand printing. He was not a survivor of Ebola, only a negative case. But when he spied his new wheelchair he was stunned and speechless, eyes sparkling and a grin that split his face. All his Christmases had come together. He began to cry, maybe with relief of not having Ebola, maybe in joy of an unexpected gift, maybe both. I broke the no-contact rule, gave him a hug and lifted him into his wheelchair where other staff patted his back and congratulated him. We pushed him to the main gate from where he happily wheeled himself back to the road.

Why tell this story John?

It was near the end of my mission and it gave me immense satisfaction that from such a threatening and devastating experience that had nearly driven him to self-destruction, we had given him a simple gift that would enhance his life. He had moved from despair to hope. It was exhilarating to watch, and hopefully symbolic of the waning of the epidemic and a sign of Sierra Leone's changing fortunes.

'I'm sorry to trouble you but I've just arrived from Brussels. Before that, I was working in Sierra Leone in an Ebola Treatment Centre. I've been running a fever for the last few hours and now it has risen to over 38 degrees. We were told we must report any fever when we arrive,' I confessed to the immigration officer as I emerged from the automatic passport control booth at Sydney airport. His podgy face exploded with surprise. His eyebrows shot up, his mouth gasped and his eyes nearly popped from their sockets.

'Can you repeat that sir?'

I did, slowly, as if he were a bit deaf. He stepped back.

'Just wait over there please sir,' he snapped, pointing to a spot well away from the crowd streaming from the flight. 'Don't move.' Immediately he widened the gap between us and talked into his radio. He didn't even ask my name or examine my passport. Within a minute a second immigration officer arrived huffing in haste.

'Follow me please,' he commanded from afar, hurrying ahead, ushering me through a coded doorway, along a corridor and into a small, windowless room. Traumatic memories of a previous encounter at Sydney airport flooded my mind but I was reassured that this room was medically orientated. A thermometer, stethoscope and sphygmomanometer lay on a desk against a wall. Public health posters were plastered on the wall. *Are you up to date with your vaccines? Use Condoms for Safe Sex.*

He took my personal details but was not interested in handling my passport. 'Please wait here. The nurse has been summoned. She'll be half an hour.' He rapidly backed out the room and shut the door.

I waited. It was forty-five minutes.

A middle-aged lady entered wearing a paper gown, hat, mask and blue rubber gloves. 'Sorry for the delay but none of the medical staff work overnight. I was called in.' Her eyes were warm and friendly. She did not offer a handshake. 'They tell me you have come from Sierra Leone. What were you doing there?'

I told her of my work at the Ebola Treatment Centre. 'All the staff were issued with their own thermometers and we routinely took our temperature twice daily. Before returning to Australia, we were briefed to declare any fever on our arrival.'

She nodded in encouragement.

'I started feeling hot with a headache, body aches and a runny nose at Dubai airport. I took my temperature and it was 37.2 Centigrade so I boarded my flight. I just wanted to get home and I was confident I was just getting a cold. On the flight I began to feel much worse. When I took my temperature before we landed it was 38.2. I took some more paracetamol but I still feel terrible.'

She filled out a medical history form with all my details before tentatively examining my throat and taking my temperature. She took it again.

'John, thanks for declaring your fever. As you know, it is essential we are informed but now your fever is only 37.4 degrees Centigrade, not high enough to fit the criteria for any further action. You can go to your hotel, but if it persists and rises above 38 degrees then phone me immediately.'

She handed me her business card and escorted me back into the luggage area, still wearing her gown and mask. It was deserted. My bag sat all alone beside the

197

conveyor belt. I picked it up and walked through customs. All the customs officers stood well back. They had seen the nurse fully gowned. No one was going to search my bags.

My fever flared at three o'clock that morning. I awoke lathered in sweat, my head pounding and my heart racing. I took my temperature with trepidation. It was 38.8 degrees Centigrade. My mind went berserk.

Could this be Ebola? Was it more than a cold? I had not had any serious breach of my PPE in the Red Zone before I left Sierra Leone. On one occasion whilst examining a patient my mask had slipped exposing facial skin, eyes and nose but I had left the Red Zone immediately without touching my face. How could I have contracted Ebola? I felt confident it had to be something else... but the doubt lingered. I phoned the nurse.

'John, do not leave your room. I need to make some calls and will phone you back.'

Four hours later the phone rang.

'John, there's been a teleconference and we want to admit you to the intensive care in the infectious disease unit at Westmead Hospital for a blood test. An ambulance will arrive to transport you. I'm heading to the hotel now to help with the arrangements. Do not leave your room. Do you understand?' I understood very well. The hotel was now in quarantine.

'Can you get me a coffee while I wait?'

'No problem.'

Ten minutes later there was a knock at my door. I opened the door and looked up and down the corridor. There was no one in sight. A sealed paper cup of coffee sat on the carpeted floor at the base of my door. I felt like a leper.

Two hours later there was another knock. Two aliens peered at me fully clad in white suits, hoods, boots, plastic apron, gloves and goggles. 'Hi John, we're the ambulance officers to transport you. Can you climb on the stretcher and we'll wheel you down to the ambulance?'

'I'm quite capable of walking thanks.'

'John, it's usual to use the stretcher.'

'Sorry but I'd rather walk.' I put my bag on the stretcher and walked down the corridor to the lifts. What could they do but follow? One officer accompanied me in the lift, keeping as much space between us as possible. The other took the second lift with the trolley. I began to appreciate the intensity of the cloud of fear that surrounded me. I was worse than a leper.

The hotel foyer was empty, the reception desk deserted. The front window was crammed with staring faces pressed against the glass, all safely on the other side. I was ushered through the back door where a solitary ambulance waited, blue light flashing its warning.

Inside the ambulance I lay down on the stretcher and was quickly strapped in... tightly... to stop any further disobedience. The ambulance set off, lights flashing, siren howling.

Despite the drama I had to stop myself giggling. The ambulance attendant sitting beside me was scratching his chin through a huge gap between his body suit and hood. So much for PPE protocol. I hoped I did not have Ebola... for his sake, as much as mine.

My musings were shattered on arrival at the hospital. Cameras flashed and TV cameras whirled as the ambulance doors were opened and I was rolled out to a celebrity's arrival.

'How did the press know about this?' I asked. The ambulance attendant just shrugged. 'They have their sources.'

The hospital lobby was deserted. Several heads peered around doors but pulled back as I passed. The infectious disease intensive care room was spacious with one central bed. At its head numerous mechanical arms, protected in transparent, condom-like sheaths, projected from the ceiling to hold monitors, infusions and ventilators. Eight medical staff, all fully cocooned in their PPE stood around whilst I jumped on to the couch. I felt like the freak. They looked it. I began to appreciate how my patients in the Ebola Treatment Centre had felt surrounded by these faceless anonymous beings encapsulated in plastic. They did not even have their names written on their foreheads.

The infectious disease specialist carefully documented my history and with great caution drained blood from my arm and swabbed my throat and nose.

I glanced around the room and identified three of the staff breaking PPE protocol. One scratched her nose around her visor, another adjusted her visor with both hands, a third scratched under his chin, all breaches a recipe for passing infection from contaminated gloves to skin, nose and eyes. Having just spent four months in and out of the Red Zone housing highly infectious patients, I began to appreciate how highly skilled and competent we had become with our training and daily practice. This might be the best infectious disease unit in Australia but I realised that they were just amateurs. Again, I hoped I did not have Ebola... for their sakes as well as mine. When I mentioned to a nursing sister the breaks of procedure in PPE that I had observed I was given a look that could have turned me to stone. 'Thank you, doctor. I'll let them know.' Her voice growled with indignity.

After six hours I knew I was clear. The consultant walked into the room without wearing any PPE. 'It's just an upper respiratory viral infection, John. You can head off when you wish. But keep on taking your temperature until your three-week quarantine period ends and if it rises again contact the public health nurse. They will be phoning you every day to check up on you. Good luck.'

So, your mission ended on a dramatic but amusing anecdote. Were you scared of having Ebola?

I have to confess I was scared. Although confident it was a false alarm, an underlying niggle of doubt kept surfacing; *could it be Ebola?* If so, how ironic. Had I had survived all my missions relatively unscathed and reached home safely... only to be caught out in the final moment? I had a flashback of the armed soldier threatening me in the swamp in the Sudan... the feeling of safety being shattered so close to home. Was this to be my fate?

Even more ironic was that the fear of my PTSD recurring was even stronger. Getting Ebola momentarily seemed preferable to a recurrence of PTSD.

Lying alone in the intensive care room waiting for my test result gave me time to ponder and reflect. How are the survivors of Ebola coping after their horrific experience? Not only do they have to come to terms with the fear, stigma and debilitation caused by the illness whilst grieving the deaths of many of their family members but also the possibility that the Ebola virus may live on in their bodies, in the fluids of the eye, in the central nervous system and in sperm. One woman had become infected after unprotected sex with an Ebola survivor. Male patients were being advised to use condoms for at least six months post recovery. Was their ordeal actually over? Would it flare again or cause post-infective symptoms and complications? Little research had been completed.

I speculated how the Sierra Leone would recover after the epidemic. The economy had been slowly recovering following the devastating ten-year civil war that ended in 2002 but was again paralysed during this Ebola epidemic; businesses shut down, restriction of people movement, obliteration of tourism combined with low commodity prices had brought the economy to a standstill. How would the economy revive?

My fleeting concerns about my PTSD seemed pathetic.

But did your PTSD recur?
Happily, no. Despite being homeless and jobless, I felt quite at ease. I was able to spend my three-week quarantine period with friends near Coffs Harbour where I relaxed in luxury, soaked in a mineral bath with mountain views, perused art galleries and strolled the beaches.

I found a great sense of peace and satisfaction at what we had achieved in Sierra Leone, at the lives we had saved, even for the people who had died, for we had cared for them and allowed them to die in dignity and comfort. Most importantly, we were able to quickly quarantine those infected with Ebola and stop the infection from spreading to their families, their friends, their city and the world. The epidemic had been quickly contained. We had done ourselves out of a job.

During the final week of my quarantine period, the offer of a job in Antarctica arrived which I grabbed. It was very synchronistic. I had set my intentions and they were manifesting. My life seemed to be blessed and blossoming, not cursed and corrosive as had previously occurred post mission.

So why did you really come and see me, John? You seem to have overcome your PTSD. Are you gloating, showing how you did it on your own, that your first impression of psychologists was right?
No, I am not gloating. I know I have come a long way but I still had that lingering doubt... has the PTSD really gone? I was confident I had it beaten after returning home from Uganda and again after Iraq but I became completely unravelled after returning from Sudan.

Even after all my self-therapy and successful mission with Ebola I still had the fear of my PTSD rebounding. That is why I came to you. I wanted to confess everything to an objective, detached professional and allow what I had forgotten, what I had hidden and what I had repressed to emerge. I wanted a safe place to dredge up any demons from the sump of my psyche, and hopefully get some reassurance this is not just a lull in the storm but a long-term peaceful haven. It was a final test of provoking my PTSD. What do you think?

John, there is no guarantee that nothing will ever emerge that might upset or unsettle you. Your dreams may continue forever. But your awareness, insight and emotional intelligence have developed, not since your traumatic experiences but because of your traumatic experiences. You are more accepting and at peace with yourself than ever before.

However, you have done it the hard way. Your early experience with psychologists was unfortunate. Had you sought earlier professional help you might not have had such a rocky road. Recognition and treatment of PTSD has come a long way since the 1990s. It is more focused and intense than ever before. You were fortunate you had the resources and finances to stop work and go walkabout. You were fortunate to have some medical and life

experience to guide you. You were fortunate to have some resilience; your optimism, your humour, your ability to cry, all helped protect you from more serious adverse consequences, depression and suicide.

Others are not so fortunate, so I hope you do not recommend your independent action as a model for others. Yes, everyone needs to be proactive and explore their feelings and your methods are indeed practical and effective, but with professional supervision and support, they would be even more so.

Where to from now John?

Recounting and reliving my stories to you has been cathartic. I have shed many tears, relived many moments and savoured many joys. I believe my PTSD is now resolved. I have only now come to realise how much I have learnt from my missions; how much I have grown emotionally and spiritually and how much I have changed because of them. The miseries and marvels, the trials and triumphs, the people and populations that I've encountered have been remarkable. I feel truly humbled and grateful.

I now fully appreciate that traumas not only cause stress but are also unique opportunities to learn and mature. As Christopher Robin advised his teddy bear, Winnie the Pooh, *You are braver than you believe, stronger than you seem, and smarter than you think*. Only when exposed to adversity do we discover our true capabilities.

I feel sheepish that my self-treatment was not the best way. I'm embarrassed by my blinkered and bolshie prejudices against psychologists and thankful I was fortunate to have blundered my way forward alone.
I encourage anyone with any symptoms of PTSD to seek professional help early.

I believe anyone in the military, emergency services, police, first responders and humanitarian work is at risk. In fact, I would think that everyone working in these areas should expect to suffer the symptoms. It is a normal response to seeing and dealing repeatedly with the dangers, tragedies and heartbreaks commonly encountered. All these services should provide a regular support mechanism, easily accessible, free and anonymous to promote early and simple intervention without fear of being stigmatised. If symptoms do become problematic ongoing professional treatment should readily be available.

Despite all my past troubles I would still encourage anyone to undertake humanitarian missions in whatever capacity they are qualified. The experience, the adventure, the satisfaction will change them forever.

Those not inclined to go on a mission may be interested to learn more of humanitarian work by actively participating in organisations such as the Red Cross and MSF or even joining a refugee support programme, helping newly arrived refugees to settle and integrate in their country. In doing so they will learn and gain more from the refugees than they teach and give.

For those who do not want active involvement in humanitarian work I only hope that they will become more aware of world poverty and urge them to respect and have compassion for those living in poverty, who daily struggle for survival and are continually vulnerable to small changes in their circumstance, economic, climatic or political. They may even generously donate money.

I ask everyone to have gratitude for their own good fortune of having wealth, access to clean water, ample food, efficient sanitation, health care, education, employment and living in a secure country with law and order, to allow enough to be enough, to possess less and stop the wanton waste of excessive consumption.

With this peace of mind, we may more contentedly accept our past... *let it be*... allow our future to happily unfold... *it will happen, or it won't*... to live, love and laugh in our present, to achieve our full potential and, hopefully, to leave a legacy.

I am now confident I can safely accept more humanitarian missions and have set my intentions for them to appear and unfold. As I age the catch-cry *Adventure before Dementia* rings loud.

Finally, I am grateful for this late realisation that although my primary motivations were adventure, personal and professional challenge, my missions have made a difference. It is satisfying to reminisce that I may not have changed the world but I may have changed the world for a few people, including me... and that is a wondrous feeling.

Goma and surroundings maps

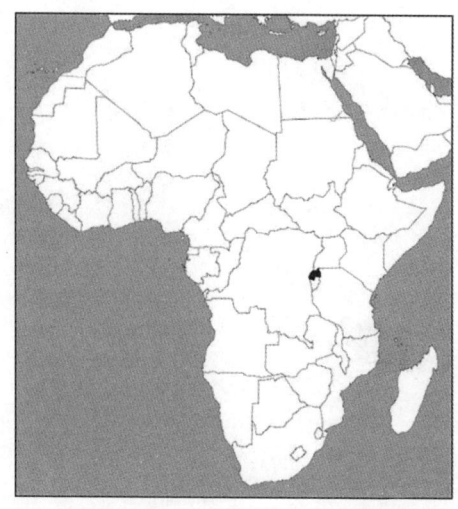

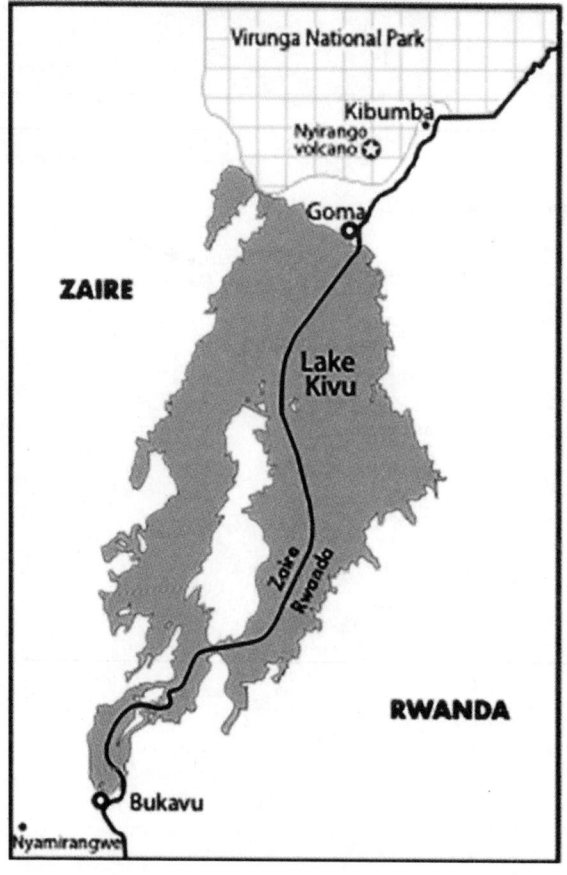

Afghanistan maps

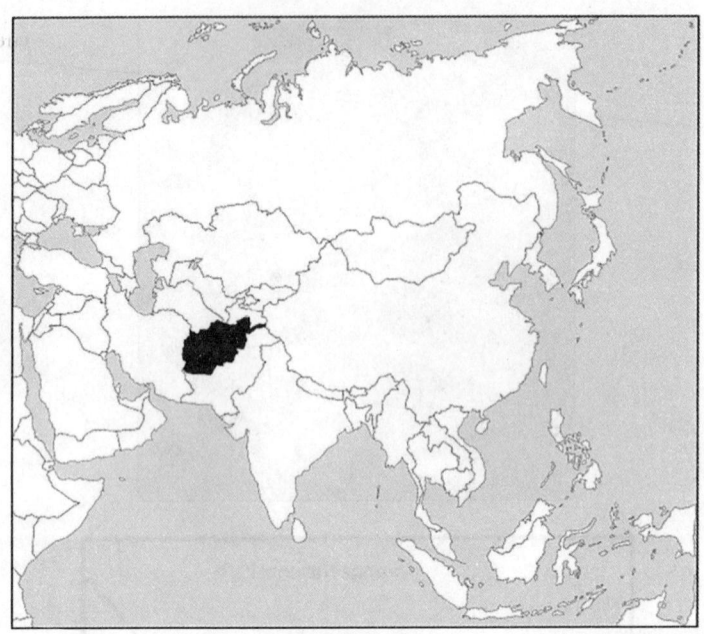

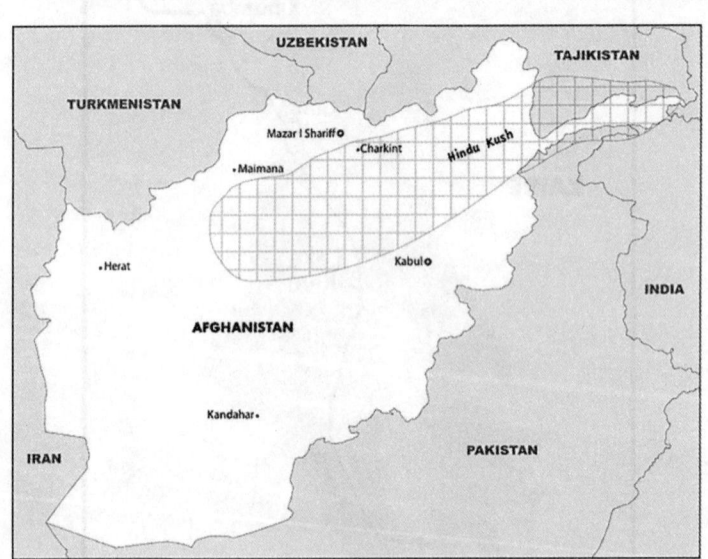

Nigeria maps

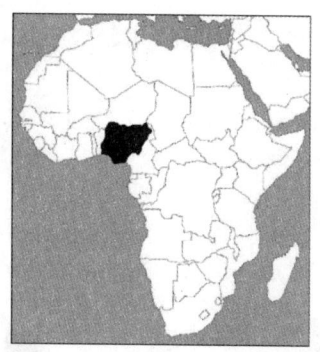

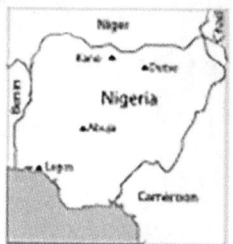

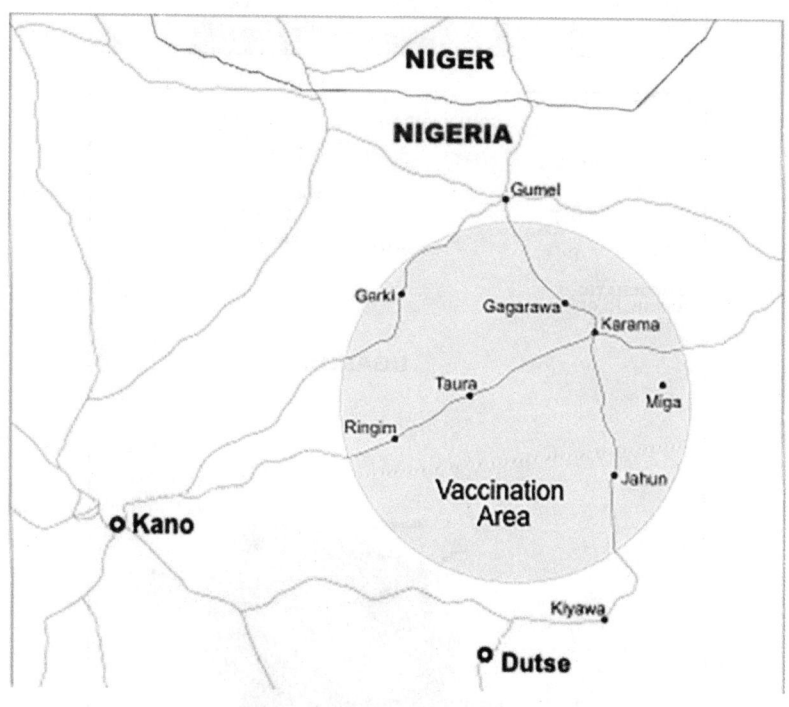

Uganda maps

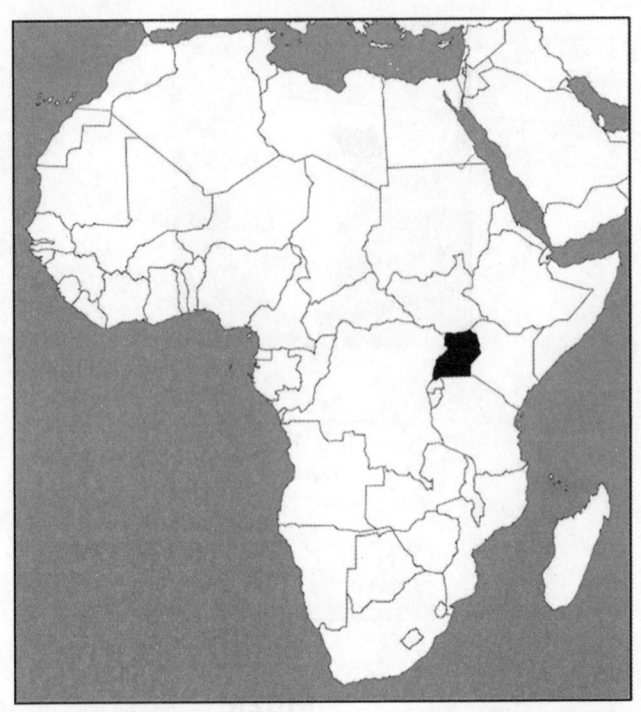

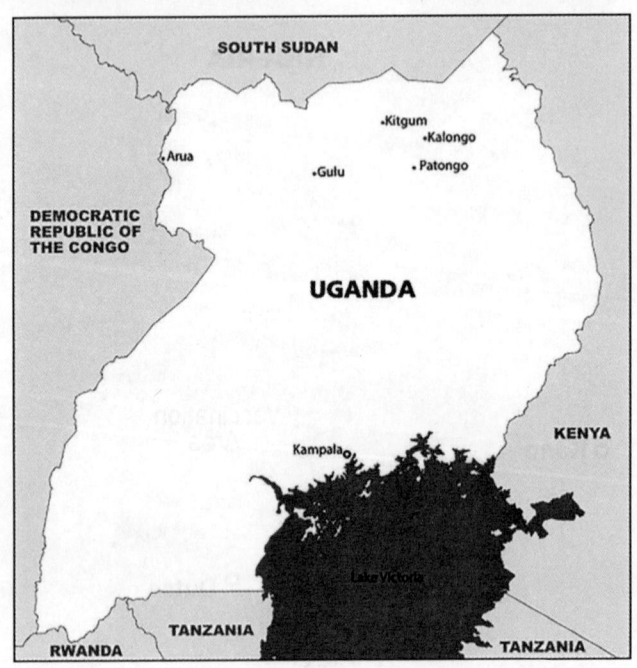

Iraq maps

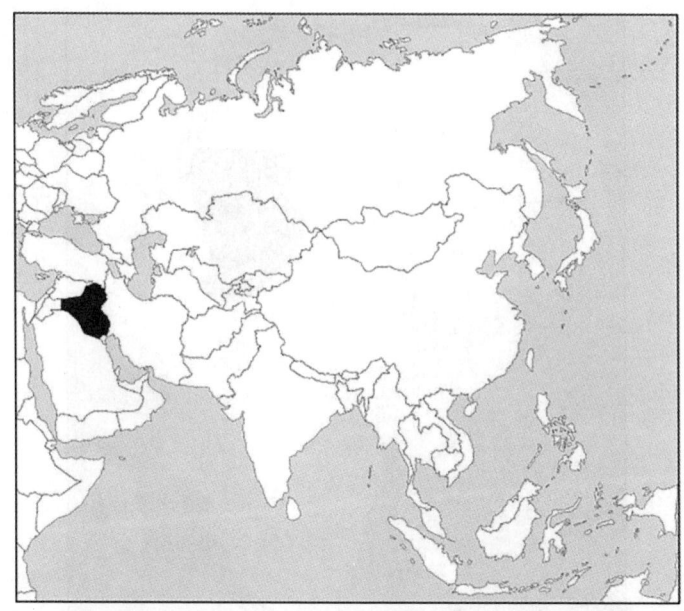

Sudan maps

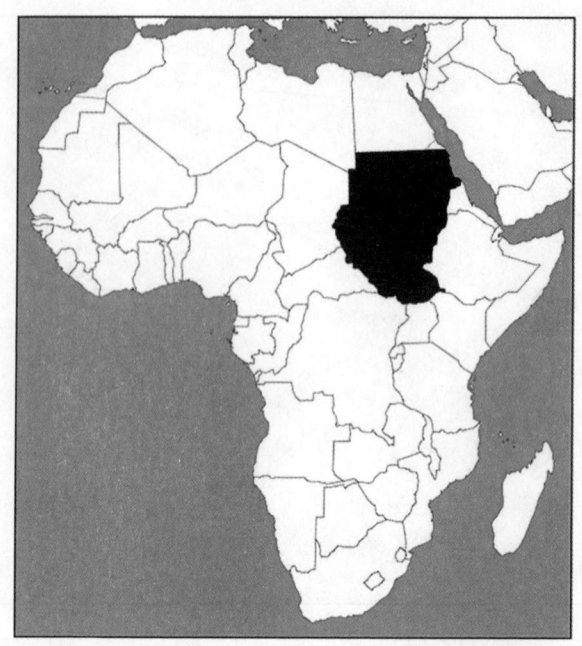

Sierra Leone maps

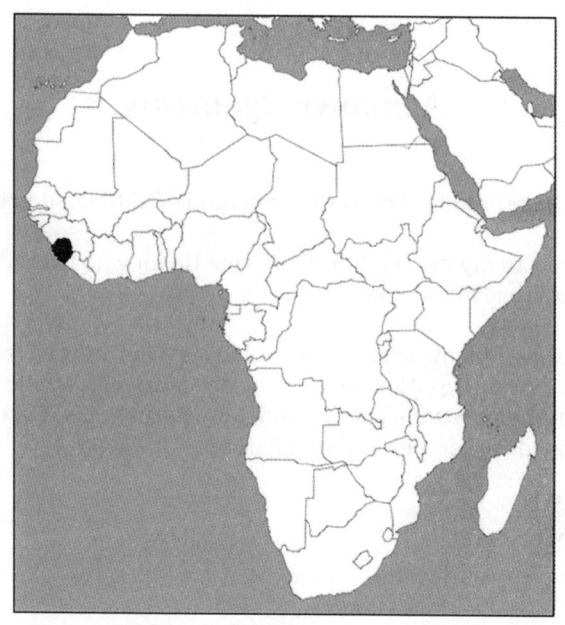

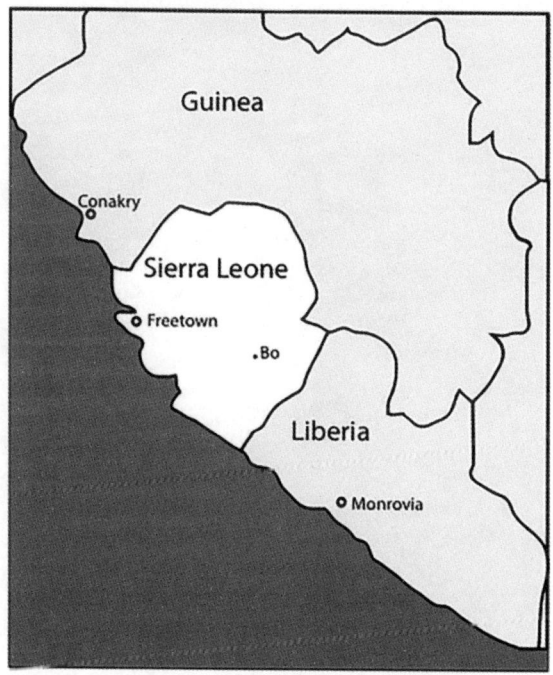

Acknowledgements

Lyrics to *Carry Me* reproduced by kind permission of BMG London Ltd.

My sincere thanks to my proof editor Catherine Heath who hacked and honed my manuscript into a readable format.

Many thanks to my many friends and relatives who offered suggestions and encouragement including Alex Hofer, Jackie Maxwell, Geoffrey Ward, Lisa Vermelen, Alison Hempenstall, Jane Wilson, Judy Barnett, Gail Baker, Ricky Lynch, Lyn O'Meara, David Parker, Ben and Jake Parker.

Dr John Parker was born and bred in Liverpool, UK and medically trained at Edinburgh University. He came to Australia to scuba dive the Great Barrier Reef and never returned. He commenced a medical practice in Airlie Beach in Queensland to follow a passion in diving medicine and later worked at Golden Beach in Caloundra on the Sunshine Coast. Intermittently he has ventured with the Red Cross and MSF on humanitarian medical missions including 3 war zones, 2 epidemics and several refugee camps. More recently he has worked as SMO in the refugee detention centres on Nauru, Manus Island and Christmas Island, medical officer in an Ebola Treatment Centre in Sierra Leone and spent a year as an expedition medical officer on Davis Station in Antarctica. He is presently working on Thursday Island in the Torres Straits. He has written 'The Sports Diving Medical" and "Poetic Prescriptions for Feeling Good".